Righting Native Places

Adventures in Northwest Geography

Edited by

Jay Miller, PhD

Table of Contents

Appendices

Righting Native Places
Adventures in Northwest Geography

Introduction

Place names relate us to our lands, confirming a sense of intense belonging. Throughout the Americans, native names have been instituted by primordial beings, rarely overtly by humans, to refer to inherent characteristics of that place and steeped in thousands of years of traditional uses and experiences. Then another layer of names, often honoring a known person, such as a politician, was added by Newcomers to a land. These shifts are aspects of a dynamic world in which languages themselves change, preserving evidence of their pasts in place names such as Chelan, an ancient Salish word for lake since replaced by modern words. In the Northwest such shifts were due to leading families tabooing words that sounded like the name of their deceased loved one, and replacing it with a substitute that became the accepted word in use. Similarly, some Northwest languages shifted from nasals to orals so M > B and N > D such as in the B of native place name *Takoba*, where the English Takoma ~ Tacoma[1] shows the original M. Huge amount of time and money were spent by Seattle vs Tacoma to claim its native spelling and meaning, generically any mountain always capped with snow, instead of the Rainier name assigned by 1792 Captain Vancouver for a fellow British admiral.

Indeed, the righting of such writing is the aim of this book. Comparing five lists over a century, with a good start, good ending, and murky middle, is instructive. These complex factors are often unknown to would be geographers, who often began by covering a vast area. While we are very grateful for their efforts, often termed "salvage", this wide variety of people of very mixed abilities recording purported native names of the Northwest, produced works fraught with mistakes and miscues because English is a pitiful means for reporting the many complex sounds of Northwest native languages. Many of these indigenous tongues belong to the Salish family along the international border, with Wakashan and Sahaptian families spreading along the coast and Columbia River. Indeed, native place names also show the movements, as from Kittitas below, of people and speech communities which often continue to use prior names out of respect for land and its spirits.

Place name lists, often done with maps now lost, are best when there has been transparency of motivation and recording, with careful listings of the alphabet of letters used to capture native sounds, and intense involvement with skilled native speakers able to pronounce, interpret, and translate meanings. Some schooling, especially at college universities, also helps. George Gibbs's 1860 list, the first presented herein, indeed set a standard, and later listers deferred to him, such as Eells and Ballard. Moreover, Gibbs provided guidelines for word lists and spellings in 1863 Instructions for Research Relative to the Ethnology and Philology of America, *Smithsonian Miscellaneous Collections* VII: 1-51. Most recently, teams of geographers, linguists, anthropologist, and elders provide the most accurate lists, as for 2011 *Nooksack Place Names ~ Geography, Culture, and Language* by Brent Galloway, linguist, and Allan Richardson, anthropologist, working with an elders committee, who laud and cite George Gibb's 1857-62 transcriptions of places along the US-Canada border survey.

---

[1] Throughout, ~ means equivalent, same, similar, alike; = means 'translation of'

Since 2004 a reliably well informed means of understanding these names has been available, with regional linguists reporting on their own sections to William Bright, a California linguist, who edited the final book published at the University of Oklahoma Press. In addition, many dictionaries of native languages include place names, both within the text or as a separate section. For Washington and the Northwest, these are crucial *Lushootseed Dictionary* (1994 by Dawn Bates, Thom Hess, Vi Hilbert), *Ichishkiin Senwit ~ Yakama/Yakima Sahaptin Dictionary* (2009 Virginia Beavert and Sharon Hargus) and *Quileute Dictionary* (2008 Jay V Powel), paired with *Our Land ~ Quileute Territory* (2017 Kwashkwas Jay Powell Squawks).

Individual abilities and training play a vital role. For the five lists presented herein, spanning a hundred years, academic training made for better recording, as did keen interpretive skills of native speakers who were consulted in the process. For these reasons, biographies of each recorder are provided at the start of each section.

1 ~ The first, 1860 by George Gibbs, set a standard for its time by providing a master list of letters for sounds used in his spellings. Personally curious and dedicated, languages, especially native ones, were a life long concern of his since his early schooling and days at Harvard, where he took a law degree. He assembled his list while working for the US commission surveying the international boundary across northern Washington.

2 ~ The second, 1892 by Myron Eells, life-long missionary to Twana at Skokomish, where his brother Edwin, a lawyer, was agent, published in American Anthropologist professional journal. These men were sons of Cushing Eells, early, though failed, missionary to the Spokan in eastern Washington. The Eells were well educated, exposed to many native languages, but biased as Christian reformers hostile to ancient traditions. Myron attributed names to tribal languages rather than linguistic families, in part because such recognition of language stocks was in an early stage.

3 ~ The third, 1919, with 1922 article on native names around Seattle, by Thomas Talbot Waterman, a PhD trained at Columbia University by Franz Boas, then working as the first full time anthropologist at the University of Washington in Seattle. He had done similar studies in his native California, published at Berkeley, applying the highest linguistic standards of his time.

4 ~ The fourth, 1939 by Alfred John Smith, relies on Little Bill Penn, a multilingual Quileute, but Smith had little schooling and, working during the Depression, was hired to draft articles for the federal writer's handbook for Washington State, not an academic outlet. His interest in Indiens seems to have been sparked by his second marriage to a woman raised in Forks, near reservations on the coast. To his credit, he also consulted Arthur Ballard.

5 ~ The fifth, 1959 by Arthur Ballard, was a work for hire for Robert Hitchman (1985 *Place Names of Washington* by Washington State Historical Society), based on Ballard's lifetime of dedicated amateur devotion to Lushootseed language and culture. As a result, Hitchman's book is much superior to that of his mentor, Edmond Meany, a UW historian and legendary mountaineer. Waterman had provided academic and linguistic guidance to Ballard, further improving his life's work. Ballard also advised AJ Smith.

All place names vary in meanings and references, as shown by comparison of Edmond Meany and Thomas Waterman. Meany (1923: vi) lists 2813 place name entries for all of modern Washington state, with 771 cross referenced. Of the remaining 2042 names, 842 refer to individuals, 399 to physical features, 191 to towns, states, countries, 115 to crops, trees, animals, or birds; 68 to freakish ideas, 17 to American ships; and 6 to British ships, while 386 come from native languages, 33 from Spanish, and 6 are Biblical names.

Within the TT Waterman manuscript strictly of native place names, Seattle and vicinity has 323 native names, which separate into six categories, with geography and anatomy combined because the same lexicals (see below) are used for both:

113	GeoAnatomy = 33 Anatomy: nose, mouth, head, neck, lip, ear, breast, fingers, 50 Geo: prairie, lake, creek, slough, bog, marsh, rock, trail, water, colors; 20 space-shape
73	Bio-Species = animal 11, plant 36, fish 12, bird 13, shell 1
55	Actions = canoeing, paddling, sliding, digging
24	Devices = tool, clothing, construction, structure
7	Religious = taboo, spirits, rite
51	Unknown

An appalling throwback to another time is *Our Native American Legacy ~ Northwest Towns with Indian Names: Washington, Oregon, Idaho, Alaska* (2001 Sandy Nestor, Caldwell, Id: Caxton Press), who insists on listing the first white at a place as its "settler" ignoring thousand of years before him. Similarly, she quotes all sources on a native name, without any discernment among them. She is not alone in her mistakes, misplaced and otherwise.

A Klallam, Philip Hugh Howell ~ Braveheart, publisher of 1922-26 *The American Indian* newspaper then 1927-47 yearbook, assembled from Meany's book a 1948 *Dictionary of Indian Geographical Names ~ The Origin and Meaning of Indian Names*, bolstered by advice from Klallam William Hall, 83; Twana Henry Allen, 83; and Nooksack William Hunt, 55; with Ezra Hatch and Bernice Alexander of Tulalip. Separate suppliments were done for Snohomish County, for Oregon, and elsewhere.

On a happier note, the Waterman names are now part of a newer project that was years in developing because Waterman (TTW) laid a solid foundation for a place-based understanding of Lushootseed. When he came to UW in 1918, he used $200 set aside by Washington State to survey coastal Native places and ethnography. Letters imply he had some student help, which probably involved placing or coding the names on maps. After this money ran out, TTW turned with his students to library research on houses, canoes, and tools. He continued some fieldwork, however, with funds, typical of these times, from George Heye to buy artifacts for his museum in New York City (later transferred to DC to become the new Museum of the American Indian). After Seattle, TTW joined the staff of that same Heye Foundation Museum of the American Indian in 1921, and then took at job at the Bureau of American Ethnology (BAE) in DC, which sent him to Alaska. There he produced a study of local Tlingit place names, paralleling those he had done for northern California and western Washington.

As he left the US to become technical director of the National Museum of Guatemala, he wisely sold manuscripts, especially Puget Sound Geography, to the BAE for $400. He did not stay in Guatemala, teaching for a year at the University of Arizona. From there he attended the first Pecos Conference (near Santa Fe, NM in 1927) to debate a scholarly consensus on establishing the archaeological sequence for the Southwest. Alfred V Kidder, the leader of these conferences, credited TTW with first defining this series (horizons of Basketmaker and Pueblo) and publishing them from Hawaii in 1929 (Fowler 2000), as noted in his letter to Mrs Geraldine Coffin Guie (below in the full TTW biography).

By all accounts, TTW was particularly likeable, as befit potential clergy. The range of his friends, moreover, included everyone from senior colleagues such as Robert Lowie, Nils Nelson, and sober AL Kroeber to "competition" from paranoid JP Harrington of the BAE and boisterous Jaime de Angulo, a Spaniard raised in Paris and Johns Hopkins trained MD turned linguist, whose own daughter called him "Old Coyote of Big Sur". Informal gatherings of Berkeley faculty and bohemians, some raising children, discussed academic pursuits. As Jaime wrote in 1925 at Carmel, "This is a great life – especially when Waterman comes up from Fresno for a few days, and starts writing an article with the dishes still uncleared and Lowie trying to tease him into a game of chess" (Angulo 1995: 253). His second wife, Nancy Lucy Shepard Freeland, entered anthropology and linguistics after taking a class from TTW at Berkeley, subsequently enduring joint linguistic projects and a rocky marriage. A recurrent family phrase attributed to TTW warned of "being shy a kid" due to brief misplacement, life-threatening medical emergencies, or absent-minded neglect, as indeed threatened TTW Jr in Guatemala. This family banter became all too tragic when their own son Alvar de Angulo died in a car wreck, crushed under his father.

While TTW's Puget geography draft remaining at Berkeley must have been known to the faculty there, the more detailed and extensive one at the BAE seems to have been obscure until research forays extolled it during the 1974 Boldt trial on salmon treaty rights.[2] Barbara Lane, expert witness for the tribes and US, included appropriate sections from it in each of her reports on specific tribal fisheries. Similarly, William Sturtevant at the Smithsonian urged its use by Wayne Suttles while planning the Northwest Coast volume for the Smithsonian Handbook of North American Indians (projected for 1976, but issued periodically through 2008). On 17 April 1972 from Wisconsin, William Elmendorf sent a copy of his xerox of Waterman's Puget native geography to Suttles, seconding its importance for the handbook.

Vi Hilbert, a native Lushootseed speaker and writer, began recording local native place names early in her work, as illustrated by a typed list from 1977. In a long account of the Starchild epic, her aunt Susie Sampson Peter recites many place names along the way as the brothers descend the Skagit River. Then in 1984, Vi and Jay Miller began to retranscribe and retranslate local names from TTW, deadending after 40 items around Seattle. We worked in Northern Lushootseed, though the terms from Seattle south are clearly in Whulshootseed ~ Southern Lushootseed. Then as now, Whulshootseed's survival was precarious and none of the few speakers were as willing nor able as Vi to undertake this patient and frustrating work.

Efforts languished until a long Seattle winter when Miller took it upon himself to type the manuscript into a computer format since the hazy, spotted quality of all copies precluded scanning it. Entries were rearranged with the native term first, waiting for a time to work with Vi. Instead, he relocated to the East, and Vi and Zeke undertook the sustained 1998 analysis and

---

[2] By an irony of history, Fort Langley on the Fraser River noted the arrival of Suquamish with salmon in their canoe, which allowed US Federal Judge George Boldt (Finding of Fact #5, Order of 18 April 1975) to decree to their descendants fishing rights in Canadian waters, though unenforceable. Accepting this one written instance denies many other oral traditions.

rerecording in both dialects. Eventually, a new edition will correct more typos and better locate some of these sites, further revising TTW into the future and countering recent illiterate attempts of gibberish-looking spellings of these terms in an atlas ironically published by academic press.

No one can escape these mistakes and errors. They linger and compound over time, even as native speakers able to correct this faulty record pass on in tragic numbers. Comparing five lists over a hundred years, beginning and ending with one remarkably good, helps everyone understand the complexities involved and reasons why utilizing them provides a better, more reliable record for posterity.

As noted below, sounds recognized by a speaker have a consistent system. Often back sounds have a four way expression. These are written with an ordinary letter, a letter under a stroke (ejective glottal t'), a letter beside a raised W (labial -^{W}), or by both the apostrophe and the raised W (t^W t'^W). Schematically, K is said unadorned like <u>k</u>in, K' is "harsh, explosive, ejective" back sounding: gee<u>k</u>, K^W is said in front like <u>Qu</u>een, and K$^{W'}$ combines both:

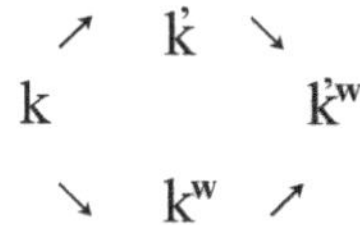

Other fronted sounds that are probably unfamiliar include ł (known as barred L), a sound used in Welsh and a letter (for a different sound = W) in Polish, said by pushing air around the tip of the tongue while it is pressed against the roof of the mouth -- something like the middle sound in Ca<u>th</u>olic ~ a<u>thl</u>ete, and ƛ̓ (a glottalized barred lambda) said with a click at the back of the throat while tapping the tip of the tongue against the back of the front upper teeth.

Knowing what to expect, aids faithful recording. Writing systems do change over time. What is now spelled with raised -^{w} was once raised -^{u} as early Ballard, though Gibbs wrote a stand alone *h* (p29 kluk 'h) and Eells spelt *-hu*. Glottal ' was once ^{3} ~ ! ~ $^\varepsilon$ unless utterly ignored. Some Northwest languages shifted from nasals M N to B D, complicating records, such as Lushootseed of Puget Sound, Twana of Hood Canal, Quileute but not Chimakum of Olympic Peninsula, and, ironically for English, Makah, Nitinat, but not Nootkan of the outer coast.

Before federal laws, tribal sovereignty, and lawyering up, cultural information, especially sensitive religious activities, was saved and recorded through the cooperation of informed elder and dedicated academic. They were concerned with the greater good of pan-human creativity, diversity, and comparative understanding. Indeed, they saw themselves as fellow Intellectuals sharing privileged esoteric data selectively available through academic outlets: journals, monographs, and memoirs held in dauntingly specialized, often research oriented, libraries.

To highlight Northwest complex morphologies, charts are included for Lushootseed Salish dialects, lexicals, locatives, Quileute verbs, and Nuxalk Salish vowelless words.

Place names have, however, been the exeption, interesting to all residents seeking to know the lay of their lands. With proper instruction on the complexities involved, all can benefit from ~ by ~ with native origins of ~ on ~ from the lands of Mother Earth ~ Turtle Island.

Languages

Native languages in the US have suffered from their oppression by English-only attitudes not shared by Canada or Mexico. For a monolingual speaker of the English language, the diversity and complexity of Native American speech should come as a welcome surprise. Befitting from long residence in Americas, many tongues evolved here. There never was a single "The Indien Language". Rather, in North America alone, over half a dozen major language stocks included thousands of mutually unintelligible languages. Within each are dialects and distinctive phrases which indicate local attachments of long duration.

Linking Amerind stocks to each other and to the rest of the world, especially Siberia, has proved difficult because a bottleneck formed in the arctic over a few centuries, allowing time for Asian migrants to develop distinct speech forms. Once an ice-free corridor opened southward, these speakers dispersed over both continents, living off game herds. Only the more recent movements of Na-Dine and Eskaleuts have echoes in the "old world", especially now that a link has been found between Alaskan Athabaskans and Ket in Siberia.

For analysis, a language's grammar has three components: sounds ~ phonology, meaning ~ morphology, and sequence ~ order ~ syntax. Distinctive and intriguing features of these emergent languages can be contrasted from the perspective of English grammar. Some forms perplex speakers of other languages. While none is absolutely unique to Native American languages, some do have limited world distributions.

Intended to be the most precise of all expressions are both languages and rituals, where an aesthetic of perfection was expected among those high born. Words and phrases were chosen with the utmost care, to convey exact shades of nuance and meaning. Evidentials in grammars of most native languages required to specify automatically whether or not any information was the result of the speaker's direct experience, vicarious hearsay, immediately in sight ~ hearing ~ senses, or out of sight ~ hearing nearby or far away. Makah evidentials are *–pi•t* = via physical evidence, *–q'adi* = via hearing ~ feeling, *-ck^w i* = via remains, *-k'uk* = via appearance, *-p'ał* = via smelling ~ tasting, *-caqiƛ* = via uncertain visual, *-wa•t* = hearsay, *–xa* … *–š* = inferred probability, *–xuča'a* … *-š* = past inferred, *-a* … *šk'ub* = belated realization (Mithun 2004: 185).

Long term residence within a community is assumed in these languages. News is conveyed by complex pronouns that require strict attention to contexts. Some pronoun referents were marked with verbal tags, such as the Algonkian *obviative* which specified the "other guy" {= B$_b$} involved with a proximate direct object in a sentence like "I gave him[a] to him[b]".

By comparison with English, Native American sound systems (phonetic inventories) include few vowels but many consonants.[3] These are often "harsh sounding" when produced at the back of the mouth and in the throat. In particular, these include glottalized consonants made by closing off the windpipe. The Pacific Northwest has one of the most complex consonant systems in the world, often stringing several consonants together without any intervening vowels. In some sound systems, the length of time that vowels are drawn out or tones fluctuated serves to change the meaning of that word. Keresan even has sounds and whole syllables that are whispered, suggesting they are slowly passing out of usage.

---

[3] Consonants are sounds made by the constriction ~ blockage of the air stream by the glottis, tongue, nose, or lips; while vowels are open with air flow shaped over the tongue or through the nose and lips.

Those trained in Amerindian linguistics learn to be sensitive to these and other possibilities. They use written characters (letters) taken by Franz Boas (1916), Edward Sapir, and others to transcribe them from the International Phonetic Alphabet (IPA) developed by French teachers of English. George Gibbs (1861, 1863), whose place names leads off this collection, published an early manual for recording native languages through the Smithsonian.

Native speakers who learn several languages modify the sound systems of each to conform to a generalized pattern. Thus, as in the past when leaders spoke many languages, grammars have continued to be modified through the historic period as natives have also learned to speak English. In even more distorting fashion, American speakers have filtered many native place names through the English sound system. Many have lost all but vestiges of their original pronunciations, as we will soon see.

Native languages are grammatically complex because, where English would use different words or sentences to convey different shades of meaning, these languages add on a sound cluster or particle (known as a lexical) to express nuance. This segment either might sound unlike any compaable full words that mean the same thing, or be formed by a standardized contraction of the whole word, as with the Lushootseed word for house *'al'al*, houses ~ village *'al'al'al* in contrast to its lexical *al'tx^w*.

Other grammatical features unfamiliar to English speakers include inflecting (if the language has verbs) for aspect rather than for tense. Aspect expresses types of actions – inceptive (starting), instantaneous, durative, continuative, cessative (ending), and so forth. Verbs can also express different modes (modalities) – indicative, imperative, negative, and so forth.

In all native languages, verbs distinguish between transitive and intransitive forms, although not all of them take accusative objects. Languages such as Tsimshian are ergative, and "work" (from Greek *ergasia*) such that what look like intransitive subjects and transitive objects are both marked as ergatives, while intransitives are lead by absolutives. In all, four sentence types are nominative / accusative like English and Yup'ik, where subject acts on direct object; ergative / absolutive as Tsimshian; agent / patient with actions by / to as Lushootseed; and direct / inverse with actions forward / backward as Kootenay, related to protoSalish.

In some languages, speakers automatically ~ inherently, without conscious deliberation, add lexical affixes that specify (like English prepositions) exact locations (beside, near, far, on the water, in the house, upward through the air, etc.), position (left, right, front, back, above, below, etc.), visibility (near, far, sensed, unknown) and shape:

For example, Navaho[4] has over a dozen inherent shape classifiers whose overall form is here indicated by interconnecting tilde ~ with examples included in parentheses (~). These are round~compact (bottle, bow, bread, candy), animal~animate (adenoids, baby, insects, corpse), long~slender~rigid (basket, cornear, dipper, gun), separate objects (dollars, sand, melons, wagons), surface (blanket, buckskin), contained substances (salt, sugar, drink), packed~consolidated material (entrails, mucus), fabric-like (paper, bag, sack), parallel objects (bridge, thigh bone), bulky objects (sled, gown), bunched-together objects (firewood), granular masses (ashes, bugs, peanuts, puppies, sand, songs), fluffy~vaporous~uncompact substances (cloud, wool, hay), long~flexible objects (belt, cable, death, feather, lightning), amorphous~mushy substances (mucus, mush, wornout hat), and so forth. Navahos delight in word games in which a bizarre shape class is applied. In a famous joke, a hunchback referred to himself as "round~compact" instead of "human".

---

[4] Gladys Reichard, *Navaho Grammar* 1951: 339-351.

Instrumentals indicate if something is done by hand, by foot, by mouth, by canoe, with a certain tool, etc. Other affixes might specify whether someone/thing is left handed, was directly or vicariously experienced, was directly seen or not, and has ever been living or not.

Some languages have different counting or number systems for enumerating manner – such as boxes, canoes, balls, people, animals, or tools – and concepts, such as offices and duties. As the great traders of the Pacific Northwest, Tsimshian used seven different ways of counting. These were either all-purpose, humans, long objects, canoes, humans aboard canoes, volume unit measures (cups), linear unit measures (spans), or animals, including flat objects like hides.

Some languages do not have the English form of plurality. Rather they recognize the singular, dual (pairs, as pants), distributive ("each their own"), and collective ("all their"). A frequent feature is two forms of the first person plural pronoun – the 'exclusive we' (first and third pronouns, s/he and I, not you) and the 'inclusive we' (all pronouns, s/he, you, and I).

Another widespread grammatical process is reduplication. This is patterned repetition of certain sounds or words. English uses reduplication in so-called 'baby talk' as an affectionate diminutive in forms such as John-John and lovey-dovey. Many native languages use it to enrich their grammars. In Lushootseed Puget Salish, varied reduplications express different meanings. For example, "American", derived from the word "Boston" as filtered through Chinuk WaWa has variants of Boston = *pastad*; Americans all over = *paspastad*, American (pejorative) = *papastad*, American child ~ friend = *papstad*, and American children = *papapstad*.

Socio-linguistics studies the social contexts of languages, particularly what are called registers. These range from personal to informal to poetic and eloquent. Usages also include argots and pidgins. An argot ~ social dialect is a speech difference recognized within a community, usually associated with particular roles ~ careers, such as distinctive speech of men from women, old from young, sacred from mundane purposes, and carpenter from fisher.

A pidgin (sometimes called a jargon) is a trading vocabulary and minimal grammar used by people of various linguistic and cultural backgrounds. Pidgins must have occurred prehistorically, but the ones we know best have blossomed and proliferated, if not originated, during the era of the fur trade and European goods. The best known spoken pidgins were each associated with a major river that served as a trade route. These are the Delawarean (below), Mobilian of the lower Mississippi, and Chinuk Wawa of the Columbia River.

Delawarean pidgin was spoken along the Delaware River, blending Delaware and Dutch with some Swedish and English. Among its words borrowed into English are wigwam from /wikwam/ 'house,' corn pone from /ahpon/ 'bread', and moccasin from /maksin/ 'shoe'.

Mobilian pidgin was spoken from the mouth of the Mississippi River throughout the Southeast. Like Creole Cajun cooking, it blended Choctaw, French, and other languages, including some from Africa. Folktales with Uncle Remus and Brair Rabbit use Southeastern, African, and European motifs filtered through Mobilian.

Chinuk WaWa ~ Chinookan pidgin was spoken by thousands along the Columbia River and throughout the Plateau and Pacific Northwest, blending Chinookan, Nootkan, French, and English, along with some Spanish and Russian. It probably began on Vancouver Island among prehistoric Nootkan (Nuchahnuth) traders of dentalia tusk shells, then developing European fur trade along the Columbia River enriched it with simplified Chinookan and European terms.

In addition to these spoken pidgins, the Plains sign language of gestures was ancient enough to have northern and southern dialects.[5]

---

[5] Brenda Farrell, *Do You See What I Mean* 1995.

More than half of the 2000 Native American languages estimated to have been spoken at contact have disappeared, and many are threatened. This does not always mean their speakers died off. Some communities have shifted to English or to another native language. These shifts in language preference reflect indigenous processes, reported from all over the world.

Western Subarctic and Plateau peoples who live along rivers emptying into the Pacific have long been shifting to coastal languages and customs, successively adopted upstream, village by village, until, to use an English suffix, they "-ized". For example, aboriginal Athapaskan Subarctic communities became "Tlingitized" and "Tsimshianized" over the past century or so.

Our understanding of the underlying semantics of these languages remains inadequate. Especially helpful in this undertaking is a small group of linguistically trained PhDs who are providing remarkable insights into their own grammars as Navaho, Nootkan, and Tohono O'otam Papago native speakers.

Understanding is growing about the profundity of semantic dimensions for some languages and stocks. For the Salishan family, a pervasive grammatical distinction indicates whether or not the speaker is in control or careful of a situation. Lushootseed Puget Salish lexicals which express control (*-t*) or the lack of it (*-du'*) provide one example. Compare /*uk^{w}alt*/ = someone poured it, with /*uk^{w}aldu?*/ = someone spilled it.

Athapaskan and Algonkian grammars include an "animacy hierarchy" based on the degree of mental discipline and willfulness of beings. According to this scale, humans are more deliberate in their actions than horses and, to an even greater degree, than bugs. Significantly, while all share minds, some beings have more mindfulness than others. This does not mean that those with more can or should dominate those with less. For example, animacy makes it impossible to say "The horse kicked the man". Instead, it has to be said as "The man allowed the horse to kick him" because he was not paying attention.

For Algic (Algonkian) languages, grammars inherently distinguish two qualities, named animate or inanimate. But this is not a clear-cut living/non-living distinction. Charles Hockett[6] noted that in a Cree story, the word for the witch skull, which chased and spoke to children, had an animate ending, arguing that the key feature of the animate was therefore the ability to communicate. But other data do not support his argument. In Ojibwa, 'airplane' is animate, as is 'knee' in Delaware, but both do not usually "speak" – even though knees can "creak" in English. Building on work by Mary Black and others, Miller[7] proposes that the key feature of the Algonquian animate is ability to move: self-propulsion, self-motivation, self-willfulness.

Recently, scholarly attention has turned to ways in which English is spoken by native peoples, leading to the study of so-called Red or Indien English. Of interest, these versions of English include grammatical features of the original native language spoken by that community. Politeness, constructions of indirection (obliqueness), and expressions emphasizing process enable these speakers to modify English to make it appropriate for existing native contexts. Native languages are supposed to caress, while English as spoken by most Americans is said to poke and prod. It is too direct and lacks subtlety.

In general, native languages are much more concerned with verbs than with nouns – with process rather than product. Indeed, they often rely on "pronoun arguments", assuming that a listener is fully aware of what, who, where, when, how something happened in these intimate communities. In this regard, native pronoun systems are highly complex, incorporating some

---

[6] Charles Hockett, What Algonquian is Really Like 1966: 62, note 10.
[7] Jay Miller, Delaware Alternative Classifications 1975: 442.

very specific forms that allow for "switch referencing" so that a hearer will always know which one of the several males called "he" is the current main topic. Such particles indicate whether that "he" is the same or different from the "he" of the prior sentence.

Language Stocks

Classifying Native American languages into smaller, closer <u>families</u> and into larger, dispersed <u>*stocks*</u> relies on the comparison of standardized word lists. Matching by means of such "lexical inspection" compares the sounds, words, and meanings. Most groupings have withstood tests of time and shifting intellectual fashions. They have become generally accepted on the basis of a consensus reached among scholars known as linguists.

A language <u>*family*</u> is constructed of obvious links showing internal similarities. For example, relationships among English, Spanish, and German is reflected in similar words – mother, madre, mutter – with regular correspondences of $th = d = t$. Similarly, Siouian speakers of the Seven Fires, east to west, call themselves Dakota, Nakota, or Lakota ($d = n = l$).[8]

A language <u>*stock*</u> has ancient ties diffused through branching "daughter" languages. Especially skilled linguists have been able to show abstract, high level, sophisticated relations between remote languages. They can reconstruct a word (as it probably was heard in an ancestral or proto-language) by a combination of lexical inspection and grammatical deduction. To do so, however, requires great insight and deep familiarity with the languages under study.[9]

After a century of coordinated research, linguists have been able to arrange the many languages of North America into over twenty major units. These are equivalent to Indo-European or Chinese in terms of the varieties of speech they encompass. Some covered huge areas, others were regional, and a few, known as <u>*isolates*</u>, were spoken in only one locale and can not be readily traceable to any other language.

General texts frequently list these stocks by name only, with no attempt to describe each of them. Linguists working within a stock have a 'general sense' of what features characterize that grouping as distinct from other stocks. These traits are highly technical and likely to confuse a general reader. Still, they bear repeating, with the help offered by the front Glossary.

Edward Sapir,[10] who was unusually qualified by his genius and many fieldwork experiences, attempted classic portraits of various stocks, although scholars continue to debate, deny, or modify it. Indeed, Morris Swadesh, Mary Haas, and Carl Voegelin later made significant strides in clarifying several lacunae. Swadesh made the most ambitious reinterpretation and re-classification. He tried to expand the value of lexical comparisons by devising a formula, using basic 100 or 200 word lists (vocabularies), to suggest lengths of time these daughter languages have been separated. Called lexicostatistics ~ glottochronology, it has since been discredited because language drift ~ fission ~ change rates are not regular.

Many of the names for these language stocks were introduced in 1800s during attempts at classifications by Albert Gallatin, Albert Samuel Gatschet, John Wesley Powell, and other scholars working for the US government or in Europe, using the names of representative tribes. Among these are Siouian (Sioux), Eskaleut (Eskimo + Aleut), Algic (Algonquian, Algonkian, Atlantic + Pacific), etc. Others are named for a word or words shared by all of its members: Na-

---

[8] Recent work, however, suggests a 5 way split among these languages, not 3.

[9] See exemplar comparison of California Ritwan to Algic by Ives Goddard (1975).

[10] Edward Sapir, Central and North American Languages, *Encyclopedia Britannica* 5: 138-141 1929.

Dene and Hokan mean 'human,' while Penutian combines shared words for 'two' and 'five.' Sapir suggested that Algic, Salishan, and Wakashan be lumped together in a stock called Mosan for a shared word meaning 'four,' but it has not withstood scrutiny. He also lumped together as Macro-Siouian both the Siouian and Hokan stocks, which others keep separate.

Eskaleut (Eskimo-Aleut) = inflective, with suffixes and greatly elaborated transitive / intransitive verbs, especially for mode and person.

Algic (Macro-Algonkian) = inflective, with suffixes, some prefixes, reduplicating (repeating) stems, weakly developed noun cases, animate / inanimate nouns, obviative, and transitive / intransitive verbs. Suggested Proto-Algonkian homeland was on Georgian Bay off Lake Huron in Ontario, as evidenced by reconstructed terms for localized species of trees, plants, animals, and fish widely shared among its daughter languages.[11]

Na-Dene = monosyllabic lexicals in a fixed order of post-positions (at the back), after abstract stems which seem to be essentially nominal rather than verbal. Verbs are active / passive, emphasizing voice and aspect over tense. Many Na-Dene languages have developed tone as a feature of their sound systems. Though the Athapaskan homeland was probably in east central Alaska, this family is remarkable for its far spaced outliers. These members have adopted cultural patterns from neighbors while retaining their own languages. Examples include the Navaho, Apache, Hupa, Plains ~ Kiowa Apache (Kilthdeen), Nicola, and Swaal.

Macro-Siouian = prefixes, active / static verbs, freely compounding stems, and nouns incorporated into the verbs. It includes both Iroquoian and Siouian.

Hokan = pluralizes most nouns by multiplying with verb suffixes, prefixes for instrumental verbs and most pronouns, and has three vowels, with both long and short versions.[12]

Uto-Aztec-Tanoan = suffixes, compounds, reduplication, noun incorporation, and distinct subjects / objects, nouns / verbs. Proposed Uto-Aztecan homeland was in the Upper Gila River or northern Sierra region of the Southwest, based on shared names for local species.[13]

Penutian = resembles Indo-European grammars with suffixes having concrete (physically specific) referents, many internal stem changes, and true noun cases. It is the most dubious of Sapir's stocks, aside from the accepted Californian Penutian Kernel ( ). Somtimes extended to include Mayan, Tsimshianic, and Oregon languages.

Major revisions regrouped Siouian, Iroquoian, and Caddoan into an overall Macro-Siouian stock. Similarly, Algonkian, Ritwan, Muskogean, and Gulf stocks can be included in an Algic mega-stock, making it more and more likely that all the inhabitants east of the Rocky Mountains may be traceable back to the same proto-stock, in contrast to the baffling diversity in the rugged terrain west of the Rockies.

---

[11] Frank Siebert, The Original Home of the Proto-Algonquian Languages 1967.
[12] Margaret Langdon, *Comparative Hokan-Coahuiltecan Studies*: A Survey and Appraisal 1974.
[13] Kimball Romney, The Genetic Model and The Uto-Aztecan Time Perspective 1957.

PACIFIC NORTHWEST Peoples

Na-Dene Stock
  Eyak
  Tlingit
   towns[2]
    Yakutat
    Chilcat
    Hoona
    Auk
    Taku
    Killisnoo
    Sitka
    Kake
    Stikine
    Klawak
    Tantskwan
    Sanyakwan
  Athabaskan
    Kwaliokwa
    Tlatskanie
    Umpqua
    Chetco
    Tututni
    Tolowa
    Hupa

Haida(?)
  Kaigani
  Masset
  Skidegate
  Kunghit

[1] sleeping
[2] tribal town (kʷaan) dialects
[3] aka Nootka, AtH̓
[4] aka Bella Bella
[5] aka Kitimat
[6] aka Bella Coola

Penutian Stock
 Chinookan
   Wishram-Wasco
   Chinook
   Klatsop
   Kathlamet
   Clackamas
 Oregon Penutian
   Takelma
   Kalapuyan
    Yamhill
    Tualatin
    Santiam
    Yonkalla
   Coosan
    Miluk
    Hanis
   Yakonan
    Yaquina
    Alsea
    Siuslaw

 Tsimshian (?)
   Coast-Southern (Sküüks)
   Niska-Gitksan (Gitxsan)

Chimakuan Family
  Chimakum[1]
  Quileute

Wakashan Family
 Nootkan
  Makah
  Nitinat
  Nuuchahnuth[3]
 Kwakiutlan
  Northern
   Heiltsuk[4]
   XaiXais
   Owikeno
   Haisla[5]
  Southern
   Kwakwaka'wakw

Salishan Family
 Nuxalk[6]
 Central
  Comox
  Pentlatch[1]
  Sechelt
  Squamish
  Halkomelem
  Cowichan
  Musqueam
  Chilliwack
 Straits
  Lummi
  Songish (Lkungen)
  Sooke
  Klallam
 Nooksak
 Lushootseed (Puget)*
 Twana
 Tsamosan
  Quinault
  Chehalis
  Cowlitz
 Tillamook

Goals and techniques of linguistic prehistory have been discussed with care and insight by Edward Sapir,[14] Mary Haas,[15] and in several summary assessments.[16] Lifework of Haas deserves special mention because she was largely responsible for clarifying the broad framework for several East stocks, especially Algic and its Gulf component of the Southeast.

While linguists and archaeologists rarely work together to trace the prehistory of these Amero-linguistic stocks, some regional match ups have emerged. Shared farming rituals across the East, such as the Green Corn Busk, left similar archaeological patterns among diverse languages and cultures, such as Iroquoian, Algic, and Gulf. Mississippians, leaving truncated mounds along their namesake drainages, belonged to diverse stocks such as Caddoan along lower tributaries, Muskogean and Tunican in the south, and Siouan upriver on the Missouri. A Culture and a language were not always identical. Regional patterns blended many local ones.

In terms of lifeways, regardless of languages, the oldest American occupation involved _tenders_ who "worked **with**" their own landscapes. They did this first as big game hunters (Paleo-Indiens), then as harvesters of natural crops of plants, fish, and game. Ironically, the most recent natives of the Americas, the Eskimos, live its oldest economy, the hunting of large animals of the sea and land. Tillers who farmed ("worked **over**") the land developed later. They domesticated the sunflower and other foods, then, over thousands of years, adopted the trinity of squash, beans, and corn from Mexico.

Lushootseed Puget Salish

Around Puget Sound, Lushootseed has northern and southern dialect chains. Those of the north, with the larger population and proximity to the Coast Salish heartland on Boundary Bay and the Lower Fraser River, were Skagit (including the Sauk-Suiattle), Swinomish, and the Snohomish (including the Skykomish); while south of Whidbey Island, Whulshootseed dialects were Snoqualmi, Duwamish (including Muckleshoot), Puyallup, Nisqually, Steilacoom, and Sahewamish at the south, together with Suquamish on the west side (Suttles and Lane 1990). Important linguistic distinctions are respective accents on the first or second vowel of the basic root of a word, separate names for salmon species, some body parts, and some artifacts.

Culturally, the pattern number 4 (repetitions done four times) is used in the north but 5 in the south, as well as by Columbia River Chinooks and upriver Plateau tribes. Salishans of the inland, upriver, and southern Sound also held Plateau ideals of a kin-based society, while those of the coast emphasized class. "Southern Puget Sound culture emphasized spirit quests and had a lesser emphasis on inherited privileges than the Northerners" (Roberts 1975: 32, 35, 77).

Socially, the South Sound also stood apart because it had a smaller population, tribes without namesake rivers, less elaborated society, a large-mammal harpooner specialization, earlier European contact overland, more urbanization, and the innovative Indian Shaker Church.

While most Lushootseed "tribes" occupied a single river drainage, whose flow provided cohesion and identity to an otherwise diverse array of communities, households, and camps; three in the South Sound relied on passages – Duwamish, Sahewamish, and Suquamish.

The Duwamish once had a complex outlet like an H through the transverse Black River, since obliterated by downtown Renton and concrete walls straightening the lower course. The

---

[14] Edward Sapir, *Time Perspective in Aboriginal American Culture*: A Study in Method 1916.

[15] Mary Haas, *The Prehistory of Languages* 1969.

[16] Thomas Sebeok, *Native Languages of the Americas* 1976.

Sahewamish, merged with Squaxon Islanders, are named for the portage between the southern Sound and Hood Canal. Suquamish ancestral territory is the Kitsap Peninsula between the Sound and upper Hood Canal, without a major river.

While all men hunted, career hunters were men with talents and powers to harpoon sea mammals or undertake the arduous task of hunting mountain goats. In the southern Sound, at least, these special hunters wore clothing and used equipment, such as quivers, made of cougar skin (Smith 1940: 309). Male career specializations included those of canoe maker, hunter, story teller, gambler, and harpooner carpenter, warrior, and ritualist (Smith 1940: 34, 49), while women excelled as midwives, weavers, and basketmakers (Collins 1974: 3).

Historically, Lushootseeds and Whulshootseeds raided each other for slaves. At least one prominent northern family maintained a fortified home in the South Sound at Quartermaster Harbor to take advantage of nearby Fort Nisqually, intermarry with Puyallup women, and raid Duwamish communities to take slaves. No southern colonies are known in the North Sound, though there was intermarriage among noble families in the past couple centuries. That Whulsootseed kept NL slaves is illustrated by the life of Dr Simon, born a Snohomish, owned at Minter, and redeemed by William Tolmie at Ft Nisqually.

Native adzed-plank houses, bastions of communal life, were early targets of American authority. In 1871, Reverend Myron Eells, author of our second list of place names while missionary and agent at Skokomish, had Klallam houses on the Port Townsend beach burned in a vain attempt to force their move to his reservation. About 1874, loggers desiring lands that were already improved, burned down the plank homes at Minter Creek on the Key Peninsula, and build their own cabins. Hostilities were averted because these landgrabbers deliberately kept away from the aboriginal Glen Cove fishery where this community rebuilt (Harmon 1995: 286). The school teacher at La Push burned that native village in hopes of claiming its desirable beach as his homestead. Federal funds paid for the lumber that Quileutes used to rebuild their homes, though much of their ancient heirlooms had burned up.

Euro-American settlers established early hubs in the South Sound, preempting Fort Nisqually and Cowlitz Prairie founded by the Hudson Bay Company in 1833. Americans developed Olympia, which became the state capitol, Steilacoom, and Tacoma, which long delayed the eventually dominance of Seattle. Natives became dependent on manufactured trade goods, purchased by their trapped furs and labor. Logging became a source of funds for many native men, as cooking, housekeeping, and laundry did for native women. Some families soon became favorites of enterprising patrons, such as Ezra Meeker, who employed straw bosses to obtain and retain native workers for his hop fields.

Lushootseed, as written by linguists, has separate letters for each of its 46 sounds. First attempts to write down this language, as elsewhere, were by missionaries, particularly a learned French Oblate (Fr Eugene Casimir Chirouse) long serving at Tulalip. The complexity of its sounds derives from using different parts of the mouth to produce four different pronunciations of a basic plain sound. Routinely, these are the back in the throat (as k, q, x = German *ich*), the nose (nasals), the lips (labials), and doubling up of throat and lips.

$$\nearrow \quad \acute{k} \quad \searrow$$
$$k \qquad\qquad k^w$$
$$\searrow \quad \acute{k}^w \quad \nearrow$$

Such fourway sets include a sound that it is plain (said much like ordinary English), glottalized ~ ejective (said in the throat along with a raspy pop of air released from the voice box ~ glottis), and labialized (said in front through rounded or pursed lips). These are indicated by an ordinary letter, a letter under a stroke (glottal t'), a letter beside a raised W (labial -^{W}),[17] or by both the apostrophe and the raised W (t'^{W} t'^{W}). Schematically, K is said unadorned like k̲in, K' is "harsh, explosive" back sounding [Cf gee̲k̲], K^w is said in front like Q̲ueen, K'^{w} combines both:

Other fronted sounds that are probably unfamiliar include ł (known as barred L), a sound used in Welsh and a letter (for a different sound = W) in Polish, said by pushing air around the tip of the tongue while it is pressed against the roof of the mouth – something like the middle sound in Ca̲t̲h̲olic or a̲t̲h̲lete, and ƛ̓ (a glottalized barred lambda) said with a click at the back of the throat while tapping the tip of the tongue against the back of the front upper teeth.

Lushootseed functions with many more consonants and fewer vowels than English because many of the sounds produced at the back or sides of the mouth continue to force air through the lips and so can act as the more open, free flowing sounds known as vowels.

In rank-conscious communities, densely inhabited for centuries, special words had to be invented during certain conditions, such as a taboo on a word resembling the name of the deceased during mourning,[18] so neighboring communities usually did not share the same word for something. The status of a family was indicated by the extent and intensity with which others observed their word taboo. In the case of the highest ranks, they could insist on substituting a new word for something as common as the name for "ax" and have it become permanent.

Contrasting (55)
Northern (NL) ~ Southern (SL) Lushootseed

arm, wing əstabłax̣ad NL əsʔilax̣ad SL
bad saʔ NL qələb SL
basket (hard) spəču̓ʔ, yiq̓us NL syalt SL
black x̣ibəč̓ NL x̣ituc̓ SL
bow c̓aʔsuč, q̓əčic NL c̓ac̓us SL
breast stabidg^{w}as NL sʔilidg^{w}as SL
canoe (middle) ʔudg^{w}ił NL ʔacg^{w}ił SL
child (any) č̓ač̓as NL č̓ač̓aš SL
child (own) bədaʔ NL bədəʔ SL
children stawix^{w}əʔł, stawig^{w}əł NL wiw̓su SL
cradleboard skəkiʔiʔł (NL) sx̌altəd (SL) [–iʔł = infant, child]
dish (wood) q^{w}əłayʔulč NL s̓tək̓^{w}abulč SL
hand čaləs NL čaləš SL
hat šiq^w NL sx^{w}ayʔs SL
head -qid, sx̣əy̓us NL -ač, sx̣ay̓us SL
heart yədwas NL sc̓ali SL
how čal NL x̣id SL
hunt in forest šayil NL łəx̌^{w}ub SL
lost x̌^{w}il̓ NL wix̌^{w} SL
meat biac NL bayac SL
mink bəščəb NL c̓əbal̓qid SL

---

[17] Palatals t^y with raised ^{y} occur in other languages.
[18] William Elmendorf, Word Tabu and Change Rates: Tests of a Hypothesis 1970b: 74-85.

new, fresh x̣aẁs NL ɬaw̓t SL
nail something c̓is NL c̓əs SL
pick fruit c̓əbəb NL k̓ʷil SL
red x̣ičəč NL x̣ik̓ʷiƛ SL
rip sik̓ʷ NL x̌ʷət SL
rock č̓ƛa NL č̓əƛ̓ə? SL
salmon s?uladxʷ NL sčədadxʷ SL
      humpy hədú? NL héjdu SL
      dog ƛx̌ʷay? NL ƛəx̌ʷay? SL
      dried x̣ax̣yəƛ̓, k̓ayayə? NL k̓ʷas SL
      fermented eggs sc̓əq NL du?ayus SL
      king yubəč NL sac̓əb SL
      sockeye sc̓uwad, sči?ɬ, x̌ʷbadi? NL scəqi? SL
      silver sq̓əčqs NL sac̓əb SL
      steelhead qiẇx̣ NL skʷawəɬ̓ SL
see it šudxʷ, šuɬ NL šudxʷ SL
set nets jiq̓alad̓z̓əd NL ɬiča?alikʷ SL
shake d̓z̓akʷ NL d̓z̓axʷ SL
shell č̓awəy? NL č̓uwəy? SL with –ulč ending = a ceramic dish
shine gʷiličəbša NL šay SL
shirt pu?təd NL šxʷpiptxʷ SL
six yəla?c NL d̓z̓əlači SL
sleepy ?əxʷs?itutəb NL ?i?tut SL
spear pole č̓əsay? NL č̓əšay? SL
stand up kiis NL ɬx̣iɬč SL
star sčusad NL sčušad SL
ten ?uləxʷ NL ?ulub SL
that one ti ~ tsi NL šə ~ sə SL
this ti?ə ~ tsi?ə NL ti ~ tsiə SL
very cickʷ NL cay SL
waterfowl bu?qʷ NL əsq̓ʷaləš SL
wife čəgʷas NL čəgʷaš SL
women sɬəɬadəy? NL sɬadɬadəy? SL
year sd̓z̓əlč̓ NL sd̓z̓əladəb SL
d̓z̓əgʷa? = professional, d̓z̓əgʷə? = monster

Salishan Family

    Lushootseed belongs to the Salishan Language Family, which aboriginally spread from the Pacific shore into western Montana and Canada. It was a localized original of the Northwest, with no obvious links with the dozen or so major linguistic stocks (Algic, Iroquoian, Uto-Aztecan, for example) across the continent.

    The Salishan Family has 23 interlinked languages, separated by the Cascade Mountains, divided into Coast (16 members) and Interior (7 members) divisions. Coast Salishan branches, from the north, are Nuxalk (Bella Coola), Central, Tsamosan, and Tillamook. Central Coast Salishan includes Comox, Sechelt, Pentlatch (extinct), Squamish, Nooksak, Halkomelem (including Chilliwack, Musqueam, Cowichan), Straits (including intergrading Sooke, Saanich,

Songhees, Lummi, Samish, Semiahmoo, and, more apart, Klallam), Twana, and Lushootseed. Tsamosan, once called Olympic, includes Cowlitz, Upper (including Satsop) and Lower Chehalis, and Quinault.

Interior Salishan consists, from the north, of St'at'imcets (Lillooet), of Nlakapamuxcin (Thompson) and of Sexwepemxcin (Shuswap), and of Mid-Columbia dialect chains with "upriver" Methow-Okanogan-Nespelem-Sanpoil-Colvile-Lakes and "downriver" Chelan-Entiat-Wenatchi-Columbian, of Kalispel-Spokan-Selish (Flathead), and of Coeur d'Alene.

Over a century ago, the shift from nasals (M > B, N > D) by Lushootseeds, Twana, Chimakum, and southern Nootkans (Makah and Ditidat, still called Nitinat in English) may have been a counter-response to territorial aggression by nasal-using Straits Salish speakers such as Lummi, Klallam, and Samish (Duwaha, Nuwaha, dxa'ha). Thus, any consistently snowcapped mountain is now called _taq^woba_, which is the source for what the settlers applied as _takoma_ (Tacoma) to Mt. Rainier and a nearby city.

Kittitas Nexus

Over recent centuries, important outside influences have also impinged on Lushootseeds, particularly the adoption of the horse and of more centralized leadership from east of the Cascades. The Kittitas Valley was a hotbed of such impacts. Located near the north-south Columbia River and the east-west trade route that became I-90 in the Ellensburg ~ Vantage area, Kittitas emerged as a major contact point, pivotal in the trade of local lithic materials, especially a bright pale green jade (like Granny Smith apples) and the exchange of Coastal and Plateau products. Its lush meadows fed large game herds, and fostered the early adoption of livestock, especially horses. Increasingly mobile, leading families visited and married far and wide, founding dynasties with lasting impacts today.

The result was a region of complex linguistics, across two culture areas and along major rivers. In addition, leading families were multilingual within vast, resourceful kinship networks. For simple barter, exchange, and trading there was also a set of words and simple grammar, such as Chinuk Wawa in historic times, that fostered "skin trade" transactions. Indeed, the study of trade, exchanges, and gifting in the archaeological and ethnographic record can to trace the rise of dynastic families throughout the region, as well as material shifts due to prophetic movements.

Kittitas[19] Valley was the nerve center[20] of emerging tribal dynasties providing "high elite" leadership to coordinate the greater mobility in the later 1700s due to the spread of horses into the Northwest. Much earlier, rock art styles with rayed arcs and twins intensified around nearby Vantage (Boreson 1998: 613) helping to amass useful spiritual powers for these elites.

The Sahaptin name for the Kittitas people is Pshwanwapum[21] and "a considerable number … crossed the Cascades and settled in the Snuqualmi country, on a prairie about a mile back on the north side from Snuqualmi Falls. Here the remains of a great number of lodge-sites,

---

[19] This place name k'tɨtaas derives from Yakama k'tɨt = "hard, solid (thin in shape)" (Beavert and Hargus 2009: 72).

[20] David Munsell, The Ryegrass Coulee Site (KT88) 1968 is at the top of the bluff near the east-west I-90 rest stop of the same name, built atop 13 feet of fill, and "may represent a meeting place in the Plateau for assemblages having diffused both north and south" (1968: 3). This open camp site, dating 6900-3500 BP, had both microblades like those to the north (Lochnore-Nesikep) and lozenge-shaped foliate points like those to the south (Snake River).

[21] From _pshwa_ = pebble, rock, stone + _-pam_ "people of" (Beavert and Hargus 2009: 153).

most of them underground lodges, could be seen until very lately [1909], about a hundred in all. The name of this place is *Soxqo'ko* ("people gathered together"). After intermarrying more or less with the Snuqualmie, and becoming to some extent incorporated with them, part (or the remnants) of these people – consisting of seven families, including the chief – moved down and settled among the Snohomish about five or six generations ago" (Teit 1928: 108). A son married to the north, becoming the Skagit Prophet. A few later returned to the Psk^waws. The upper Nisqually Mishel spoke both Kittitas and Lushootseed, and a Yakama name for Mt Rainier ~ Takhoma is Pshwanwapum for snow-capped peak (Smith 2006: 23).

As Verne Ray (1939: 149) noted:

> The linguistic boundary itself in no way corresponds to cultural transitions, even of a secondary order. The Sahaptin-speaking Kittitas, for example, have far more in common with their Salishan neighbors on the north, the Wenatchi [Psk^waws in their own Salish], than they have with their Sahaptin neighbors, the Yakima [Yakama], on the south.

Its dynamism was also fueled by the overlapping of Sahaptin and Salishan language families, making the area heavily bilingual. Vast trade in a local jade, ranging from waxy white to black – most especially bright pale green – tapped into continental networks. Lush pasturage encouraged large animal herds, and the quick adoption of livestock. Larger groups on horseback – venturing into the Plains to hunt bison though opposed by resident tribes – needed more protection and hence more centralized leadership. These Salishans "through disease and wars [became] mere remnants of what was once the largest of tribes ... and commanded the Snoqualmie, Yakima, and all the principal passes through the Cascades, including those to the Cowlitz country ... the first horse seen by the Coast tribes ... was brought over by Wenatchi" (Teit 1928: 95, 97, 121). Thus, horses, pasture, and an easier communication route joined at Kittitas to aid the founding of two powerful alliances.

First, it was the homeland of Wiyawiikt ~ Weowitch, the founder of the Yakama confederation. Second, along the Columbia's Big Bend just to the east was the homeland of Split Sun ~ Suktalkosum ~ səɋtałk̓^wusm, founder of the Columbian Confederacy eventually headed for decades by his younger son, best known as Moses, also holding this hereditary Split ~ Half Sun name-title. To the immediate south were Wanapums, led by the prophet Smohalla ~ smoxala (c1815-95) and the Sohappy families, adding a religious dimension to the region.

In the 1800s, the Upper Yakama chiefly line at Kittitas included eight sons of Wiyawiikt, of whom the best known are brothers tiyayaš ~ Teias (elder), awxay ~ Owhi, and shawaway ~ Showaway.[22] Teias's daughter was wife of Kamayakin, whose own brothers were Ice ~ Showaway (named for the uncle), and youngest Shkluum ~ Skloom. These were leaders of the Lower Yakamas. Owhi and his son Qualchan, related as cousin to Leschi in Puget Sound, were killed by the US Army during the Treaty War, precipitated when Indian Agent AJ Bolon was

---

[22] Richard Scheuerman and Michael Finley, *Finding Chief Kamaiakin ~ The Life and Legacy of a Northwest Patriot* 2008. Erroneously, Anastasio (1975: 198) refers to a "failed" unification by We-ow-wicht of Kittitas when leadership passed to his eight sons about 1800. Rather, it instead broadened its alliances via many intermarriages. Indeed, his affinity diagrams consistently undervalue the vital nexus of the Kittitas.

killed and cremated by mušiil ~ Mosheel, son of the younger Showaway, and others. In 1858, Qualchan was hanged without trial on 24 September and Owhi shot 3 October.

Moses, chief of the Salish-speaking Snkyuse,[23] was married to Owhi's daughters, Quomolah and Sanclow ~ Mary. He famously had other wives and children among allied tribes (Flathead, Wanapum, Nez Perce). The family of Pat Kanim, pro-US leader of Lower Snoqualmies during the Treaty War with many brothers, also came from this area. From the north around Nespelem, by way of Snohomish, came the family of the Skagit Prophet, whose daughter and granddaughter rose to prominence in northern Puget Sound and intermarried into local leading families. Somewhere in this mix was mid-1800s Upper Snoqualmie leader Saniwa, baptized as Aeneas, with ties to Psk^{w}aws ~ Wenatchi. He is buried at Cashmere, along highway 2, with his wife and others.

Wanapums long lived at P'na ~ Priest Rapids, and claim perpetual residence there (Longenecker, Stapp, and Buck 2002). Their leaders included the Sohappys and, especially, Smohalla families. Prophet Smohalla ~ šmuxala was born 1815-20 at Wallula, the large village at the mouth of the Walla Walla River on the opposite side of the Columbia River. His mother was Wanapum from P'na. Rivalry at Wallula from Homlai, nephew of murdered leader *piupiumoksmoks* ~ Peopeomoxmox ~ Yellow Swan (Stern 1993: 268), led him to relocate about 1855 to P'na and draw in followers. Wanapums have vibrant tradition of religious leaders, with several known in the historic record (Relander 1956, Ruby and Brown 1989, Rigsby and Finley 2009), including Shuwapso ~ swapc'a = Fast Runner into old age from his *waat* (spirit patron) of *yaamaš* (Mule Deer) at Saddle Mt, as youth "taken across the sea" and returned with a book, danced on his knees until rebuked by Catholic priests and thereafter stood up. Priest Rapids is likely named for him. Today, this religious tradition is led by the Buck family.

For the neighboring Snkyuse Columbian Salish, "the only major pastoralists not in contact with a hostile area, seem to have played a stabilizing role in maintaining peaceful relations in the Plateau" (Anastasio 1975: 146). Their family of leaders, who led bison hunts into the Montana Plains once horses were adopted, peaked with the famous Chief Moses (1829-99), who carried the dynastic name of "Split Sun". Named for an 1800 eclipse, his father Split Sun ~ Half Sun ~ Eclipse ~ Sulktalthscosum led hundreds into the northern plains to hunt bison, dry the meat, and bring it back to the Columbia for winter meals. He was killed and dismembered by Blackfeet, resentful of his encroachment into their hunting territory. His short-lived sons Patshewyah and Louis Quiltenenock succeeded him, then the title was inherited by Moses, whose boyhood name was Loolowkin ~ headband and adult name was Quetalican ~ One Blue Horn (Ray 1960, Ruby and Brown 1965, Teit 1928).

For the interface at Vantage (Miller 1998), in terms of rivalry and cooperation by these communities, we have the report of Abbot Gerald Desmond (1952: 34, 35), in his study of Yakama gambling:

"Chief" Moses of the Sinkaquai'ius band of the Columbia was considered not only a great athlete but also a "great race horse man" who was willing to pay almost any price for a race horse he wanted. Smoxa'la of Ghost Dance fame, the most prominent man among the Wanapam, was also considered a professional gambler on horse racing who,

---

[23] Bruce Rigsby (in Beavert and Hargus 2009: xxix) derives the designation "Yakama" from the midColumbia Salish place name for the Kittitas Valley, further emphasizing its central importance across the languages and traditions.

in a race between his champion and a white man's horse, bet ten horses, and he and his followers added a hundred dollars to the wagers on this single race.

People also mixed together at favored root grounds in the Spring:

> As the first of June drew near, the Yakima began looking forward to the high light of the year — the "big time".   Certain roots of high quality in the vicinity of the former villages … in the Kittitas area were particularly abundant at this time of year. Practically all of the Yakima from the Kittitas area and most of those from the Yakima area foregathered there since they used the roots from this site for barter. In addition many of the Sahaptin-speaking Wanapam and a goodly number from the Salish-speaking [Psk^{w}aws] Wenatchi and Sinkaquai'ius [Snkyuse] band of the Columbia came regularly each year, and some few visitors as well from nearly any of the groups living between the Cascades and the Rockies in this region could be expected. Those living west of the Cascades were, however, prevented from coming by the snow remaining in the passes.

In addition to these obvious language differences, Anastasio and Brunton have specified cultural distinctions:

> activity was properly conducted as directed by the salmon chief [Salmon tyee] … quite uniformly for all the Salish groups…. among the Sahaptin, the ritual control of salmon fishing was less important than it was among the Salish (Anastasio 1975: 176).

> The events themselves differ in expressed orientation from one congregation to the other, the Interior Salish congregation typically having pow-wow or encampment type gatherings while the Sahaptian one typically has the feast type. The notable exceptions to this were the Nez Perce encampment at Mud Springs and the Yakima encampment at White Swan Long House (Brunton 1968: 17).

Spiritual traditions also continue to contrast, though both had men and women always sitting separately. At winter ceremonies, Salishans look outward into the cosmos, with each visionary grasping a central pole while singing a power song. Sahaptins focus inward, seeking the wellbeing of each member in turn during a *Waashat* service. "Wanapum … seem to be inward-facing … yet they produced Smohalla, who had a wide effect in the Plateau with his religious doctrine" (Anastasio 1975: 186).

George Gibbs
(1815-1873)

Eldest child of a distinguished Northeast family, George Gibbs spent an adventurous decade in the Northwest which he abundantly chronicled in diaries, letters, manuscripts, and massive publications. But his efforts took a toll. Short and burley, he suffered severely from gout as he got older. Yet even when told to keep his feet elevated, he disobeyed doctor's orders to continue writing and editing on Northwest native languages.

George was born 17 July 1815 after his parents had been married for five years. His father, Colonel George (1776-1833), was 39, and his mother Laura was 19 and daughter of federalist Whig Oliver Wolcott. The Gibbs family traced its American origins to James who left Bristol, England, in 1670, and his son George who put down roots. The grandson George (1735-1803) founded the family fortune by running 70 trading ships of the firm of Gibbs and Channing out of Newport, Rhode Island. After he died, his widow Mary (nee Channing) established the family in Boston. Living with her were two daughters, Sarah, unwed, and Ruth, married to her cousin Rev. William Ellery Channing. Sarah, in particular, was a staunch Episcopalian, and maintained the family chapel and cemetery at "Oakland" in Rhode Island. William, a brother, became governor of Rhode Island.

As a young man, the colonel visited China and Russia, with the family hope that he would learn the trade. Instead, he turned to scholarly interests in geology and mineralogy. Family funds enabled him to assemble the finest mineral collection in the US, which eventually went to Yale University. Upon marriage, he became a gentleman farmer at Sunswick Manor, on Long Island, where his children were born. He easily sailed his sloop across into downtown New York City. The family had wealth, power, and connections throughout the Northeast.

Laura's father Oliver Wolcott, Secretary of the Treasury and strong Whig, was allied with George Washington, John Adams, and Alexander Hamilton. Wolcott was head negotiator when New York Iroquois were pressured to cede homeland at the federal treaty with the US just after the Revolution, accomplishing by threat what US forces had not been able to do by scorched earth tactics. Whigs lost favor with the election of Thomas Jefferson and appointment to the Treasury of Albert Gallatin, who late in his life became famous for his study of North American native languages. Gibbs, Channing, and Wolcott family fortunes worsened with the election of populist, Irish-born, Indian-hating Andrew Jackson in the 1830s and 1840s.

Laura had seven children. George was eldest, followed by Mary (1917, died 1820), Elizabeth {Tuckerman} (1819 – 1906), Oliver Wolcott (1822 – 1908), Alfred (1823 – 1868), Laura Wolcott {D'Oremieulx} (1827 – 1902), and Francis Sarason (1831 – 1882). Elizabeth married a city businessman, Laura married a professor at West Point Military Academy, Oliver, better known as Wolcott, became an MD and professor, Alfred graduated West Point for an Army career, becoming a brigadier general, and Frank speculated in Chicago.

After some schooling by his family and occasional tutors, George was sent to newly-founded Round Hill School at Northampton, Massachusetts. Its curriculum was based on languages, mostly taught by European native speakers. The boys were also allowed to set up "Crony Village" where they lived outdoors and hunted with bows and arrows. This training with its freedoms had a long lasting impact on George's scholarship. He graduated at age sixteen.

From this prep school, George went on to enroll at Harvard Law School, delaying his degree until 1838 by taking a grand tour of Europe with his Aunt Sarah in 1834. He served as law librarian, completing an inventory and catalogue that also set a standard for the rest of his life. He joined a law practice in New York City, but soon turned most of his attention to the New York Historical Society, where he mixed with the great Americanists of the day. They included Albert Gallatin, Henry Schoolcraft, and John L Stevens, who traveled through Middle America with the artist Frederick Catherwood recording Maya sites. In 1843, George became librarian of the society, completing an inventory of manuscripts and maps. He also urged that they concentrate on American materials, doing that well instead of scattering their energies. As a result, the fame of this organization has been assured for over a century.

With news of gold in California, the withering of his law office, and a sense that life was passing him by, George and John Ruggles left on 20 March 1849 for Fort Leavenworth, where his brother Alfred and the Mounded Rifle Regiment, marching west, provided safe escort. George carried the map drawn by John Fremont in 1845, amending it as he saw the need. Later, he also added details from an 1828 map by Jedediah Smith he inspected at Fort Vancouver. When his invaluable document was discovered in the American Geographical Society in 1953, it received great cartographic fanfare.

The overland journey ended at Oregon City, and George looked around for a local base. He chose Astoria, made famous in the history of the fur trade by Washington Irving, to set up a law office. He soon became assistant collector of customs, earning $2000 a year, and invested in lots, hoping the tiny port would grow but it did not.

Ever the lawyer, he damaged his career in 1850 by insisting that the Hudson Bay Company pay duties on shipments from Victoria to Fort Nisqually, though the customs office was far away at Astoria, at the mouth of the Columbia. He insisted the new Oregon governor and judge take passage on an American vessel instead of the free passage offered by HBC. During resulting bitterness, he wisely resigned his lucrative job, which later allowed him to return to it a few years later.

He next joined the treaty commissions set up for the Willamette Valley tribes of Oregon. George used his fluency in Chinuk Wawa (pidgin, jargon) to collect vocabularies from many of these badly decimated communities. He prepared a useful map of the Willamette with Edward A Starling, soon to be briefly the first BIA agent on Puget Sound.

Many of his relations had settled in San Francisco, providing him with a base there. In 1851, George finally went to California, intent on finding gold. Instead, he was repeatedly diverted by his academic talents. He was hired by the California treaty commission, serving with Redick McKee's delegation assigned to the northern territory between Golden Gate and Oregon west of the Sacramento Valley. Local conditions were harsh. Clear Lake Pomo were living in naked squalor. After his initial shock, he recovered enough to take down word lists and ethnography. Local ranchers were no better. Vaqueros entertained the commission's detachment of dragoons by tying grizzlies to bulls to force a fight to the death. Yet his research interests remained foremost. His diary was filled careful notes on local geology, flora, fauna, and habitats. Along the Klamath River, he could finally use his WaWa to good purpose.

Only once did Gibbs try to turn his research interests into business ones. The ancient Pacific trade valued dentalia (tusk) shells, dredged from deep water off the west coast of Vancouver Island. Fully aware of the high regard natives along the Klamath had for these tapered, tube-like tusk shells, George sent samples to his brother, who was in business in Shanghai. He asked Frank to find Chinese to make enough porcelain copies to string 5000 fathoms but nothing ever happened.

In 1852, the departing Whig President Millard Fillmore (VP before the death of Zachary Taylor) appointed George to be customs collector at Astoria. Though he knew he would soon be replaced, Gibbs used this steady salary to pay off debts. His luck held.

In 1853, he was hired by Captain George McClellan for the survey for the northern route for a US transnational railroad. McClellan was a classmate of George's brother Alfred. The large survey staff included Gibbs as geologist and ethnologist, Lt Johnson K Duncan as draughtsman and assistant astronomer, Joseph Minter as personal aide and engineer; Lt Henry C Hodges as quartermaster; Lt Sylvester Mowry as meteorologist, Dr James G Cooper as surgeon and naturalist; and AL Lewis as guide. Remarkably well equipped but over cautious, this survey accomplished little.

Yet George was tireless at collecting word lists wherever he went, carefully interviewing long residents like Fr Marie-Charles Pandosy at the Yakama mission and Fr Joset at Fort Colville near Kettle Falls. He fully inspected any documents, books, and personal archives he encountered.

In January 1854, Governor Isaac Stevens hired George to prepare a topographical report on Puget Sound. Alexander Anderson, an aged HBC employee then in Seattle, provided background information for the larger region.

George himself took a donation homestead (T 19 R 2E S 11-14) on 17 May 1854 near Fort Steilacoom, close to friends in the Army and the Masonic lodge. He named it *Chetlah* {čəx̌ə? = rock}. Like his father, he was a gentleman farmer, hiring the family of William Lane to do the actual labor. This land was still claimed by HBC as part of Fort Nisqually, and Gibbs would end his public career under attack by the HBC seeking legal reparations for their lost land, improvements, and revenues.

To fill in language gaps, he kept up a barrage of letters requesting information from informed locals such as missionaries, doctors, traders, and military. He relied on William Tolmie at Fort Nisqually, William McNeil at Fort Simpson, Dr George Suckely at Fort Dalles, Seth Lount at Fort Orford, UG Warbass at Cowlitz, and James Swan at Shoalwater Bay.

By the end of the year of 1854, Gibbs was serving on his third treaty commission, having drafted the form used by Gov Stevens throughout Washington Territory in 1855. Based on treaties with the Omaha and Missouria, George is credited with adding the clauses about native rights to salmon, shellfish, plants, and hunting as a way of allowing Indians to feed themselves and hold off destitution and damage on the expanding frontier. In the immediate aftermath of these hasty treaties, the Treaty War flared up. Concerned Army friends removed George's writings from Chetlah to the fort for safekeeping.

Gibbs held ironic public offices in Olympia. He briefly was acting governor between the time Stevens left for Montana and Charles Mason took over. The legislature elected him brigadier general of the Washington militia, but, at the outset of the Treaty War, Mason put a career army officer in charge. Gibb's seeming inactivity was later used against him.

In 1855, as though for relief, Gibbs helped concoct a naturalist hoax that amused readers of several newspapers: The prock (*Perockius Oregoniensis*) was a newly discovered mammal that had adapted to steep mountainous living by having shorter legs on one side.

When visiting his homestead, his worker reported criticism of the war by local Métis men, HBC employees married to native women. Ever the lawyer, Gibbs had Lane swear out an affidavit on 9 March 1856. Stevens later misused it in accusing the Métis of disloyalty. This malicious campaign helped to drive Steven's aide Doty, son of a Wisconsin governor, to suicide.

George felt even more compelled to uphold the letter of the law when Gov Stevens had the chief justice arrested while presiding in his own courtroom and declared martial law in two counties.

Thereafter, these two became embittered and Gibbs lost his official support. He retired to Chetlah, intending to farm and write. The Lanes tended his fields, and a Nisqually named Jack was cook. It is also likely that Jack was the main source for the words that later became Gibb's Nisqually Dictionary.

For a fourth time, Gibbs joined a survey, this time a joint US-British venture along the border with Canada, under Archibald Campbell. Staff included G Clinton Gardiner, John Grubb Parke, and Caleb Kennerly. Many staffers had been "snakers", naturalist students of Spencer Baird before he took charge of the Smithsonian. The military escort included Lt August V Kautz, a German-born army officer with descendants enrolled among the Nisquallys; and Lts George Pickett and Philip Sheridan, of later Civil War fame. Indeed, several of these men left children behind among local tribes, particularly while camped at Chilliwack (Chiloweyuck). Son James Pickett, in particular, became locally famous as an artist and newspaperman. In 1858, Gibbs finally went up the Skagit River, having previously relied on interviews with locals to learn about upriver conditions before the treaties.

The boundary survey shipped specimens of all kinds to the Smithsonian in bulk. Among them, unknown until a few years ago, was Mutton, the 18-month old wooly dog pup that had been Gibb's pet until it chewed up one too many mountain goat pelts and was itself collected, prepared, and sent by Kennerly.

When the field survey disbanded and moved to DC for the write up phase, George went along, returning to the Northeast after eleven years. He arrived at his mother's home in New York City on 10 January 1861. He wrote up his portion in DC until 30 May 1862, and was released after five years devoted to this federal effort.

He turned next to working on native language materials at the Smithsonian, while offering advice and publishing a pamphlet to guide philological [ethnographic] research, including a basic 180 word list. He also edited and published his own materials on Lummi and Klallam, Straits Salish languages, as well as a Yakama grammar by Fr Pandosy. He assembled dictionaries of Chinook WaWa and of Nisqually (southern Lushootseed).

An 1864 treaty between the US and Britain allowed for payment of indemnities for the loss of Ft Nisqually and surrounding lands to Americans who had crowded in, Gibbs among them. These funds were to be paid to the Hudson Bay Company (HBC) and its subsidiary Puget Sound Agricultural Company. The British claimed $4,281,936 but the 1869 final settlement was for $650,000. By the end, Gibbs produced fourteen volumes of testimony and accounts. He finally had to defend his role as a homesteader at Chetlah {"rock"} after an attack by the HBC late in the proceedings.

Two years before he died, following family tradition, he married his first cousin, Mary Kane Gibbs, on 11 April 1871. They moved to New Haven, in the Yale neighborhood, where he intended to finish many projects. Instead, his wife became his nurse until he died 9 April 1873 and was buried in the Rhode Island family cemetery beside the chapel kept by his Aunt Sarah.

Over 58 years, Gibbs was predominately a scholar who supported himself in governmental employments which drew somewhat on his legal training. He was gifted with the ability to organize the diverse materials of himself and others, though he failed to publish all of it. Childless, his materials passed back to their original institutions or went to collateral family lines, such as the manuscript heavily edited in 1877, passed on with other family papers to the Wisconsin Historical Society in Madison by a niece living in Milwaukee.

Thus, despite being assembled by a life-long organizer, the Gibbs family materials are today scattered from the Wisconsin Historical Society to archives at Harvard, New York Historical Society, and DC (several locations). Coming from the East and returning there after his decade in the Northwest, he was driven by great insight and scholarly motivation. His friends shared his concerns and protected his papers during the Treaty War. Eventually they became valued gems in major archives of the East.

Located in DC archives, his place name lists continue to be used, most recently for 2011 *Nooksack Place Names ~ Geography, Culture, and Language* by Brent Galloway, Allan Richardson, and elders committees, whose overlaps with George Gibb's 1857-62 transcriptions are cited below by their assigned # numbers, map #, possible < translation sources, and internal page (2011:#) if there is room on the line, otherwise as :#.

Gibbs was a more-than-adequate artist, surveyor, map maker, and tracker. He left an extensive collection of artifacts, augmented by family travel in Mexico and elsewhere. Native languages were ever his keen interest, supporting related work on place names, literature, and cultural traditions that have not survived in their own communities.

Overall, Gibbs was an organizer; building on his talents as observer, artist, surveyor, map maker, interviewer, archivist, linguist, and lawyer.

Stephen Beckham 1969 George Gibbs, 1815-1873:
Historian and Ethnologist. UCLA: History PhD Dissertation.

Major Works

1834 *The Judicial Chronicle.* Cambridge, MA: J Monroe & Co.

1846 *Memoir of the Administrations of Washington and John Adams*, edited from the papers of Oliver Wolcott, Secretary of the Treasury. NY: W Van Norden.

1853   Indian Nomenclature of Localities in Washington and Oregon Territories [West of the Cascades]. 14pp. ms # 714. [SI 248] DC: National Anthropological Archives.

1853 California Languages. Henry Schoolcraft federal report in five volumes, Volume III.

1854 *Pacific Railroad Reports*: Reconnaissance of the Country Lying upon Shoalwater Bay and Puget Sound 1:465-473 (1 March); Geology of the Central Portion of Washington Territory 1: 473-486 (1 May).

1862 *Grammar and Dictionary of the Yakima Language* by Fr Pandosy. NY: Cramoisy Press.

1863   Instructions for Research Relative to the Ethnology and Philology of America. DC: *Smithsonian Miscellaneous Collections* VII: 1-51.

1863 A Dictionary of the Chinook Jargon, or Trade Language of Oregon. NY: Cramoisy Press. DC: *Smithsonian Miscellaneous Collections* VII (10).

1863 Alphabetical Vocabularies of the Clallam and Lummi. NY: Cramoisy Press.

1863 Alphabetical Vocabulary of the Chinook Language. NY: Cramoisy Press.

1873 Physical Geography of the North-Western Boundary of the US. *Journal of the American Geographical Society of New York* 3, Part 1: 134-157; 4, Part 2: 298-415.

1877   Dictionary of the Niskwally. *Contributions to North American Ethnology* 1: 285-361 (Appendix). Smithsonian Annual Reports 1866, 1870

Washington Boundaries Place Names

Method of Pronunciation

a   as a in "father" except that at the end of a word it has the same sound as in peninsula

aā   as a in the word "mass"

eh   as a in "mate"

e   unaccented as in e in "merry" "when"

i   as e short, or as i in "magnitude"

ai   has the prolonged sound of i as in the Spanish "pais"

u   has the sound of oo unless followed by a consonant when it is sounded as in "fun" "hut" etc

ew   as u in the word "puke"

y   as in English "my" etc before a vowel it becomes a consonant as in "you"

ay   as in "may"

ow   as in "how"

au   as in "maul"

aii   like the sound of ahw or aāw

ch   before a vowel as in "church" at the end of a syllable or word it gives the guttural sound of the gaelic as in "loch" or of the German unless preceded by t when it takes the hard sound as in "scratch"

gh   at the end of a syllable is also guttural

j ~ jh   as in jail

g   as in give

s"   followed by an apostrophe signifies a simple sibilant very common before other consonants, particularly h & k as for example "s'huts kus"

h'   followed as in the preceding case by an apostrophe denotes an aspirate not guttural,, as in the word "hah'tl" "s'hah'tl"

tkl ~ tlk ~ tl   represent the peculiar clucking of the gutturals

z   as in the English "gaze"

the letters r f v are wanting. b and m are used indiscriminately, also d and n.[24] By the kwantlen's d is changed into l, as also n. [2]

---

[24] Gibbs was astute in first noting this Salishan shift away from nasals M > B & N > D.

Nomenclature
Bellingham Bay and Gulf of Georgia

what com	the outlet of the lake
squod li cum	small creek at Ind[ian] village
klik a toh nud	prairie at Military Station
chah choo sen	island in delta of Lummi River
swul leh sen	portage to straits above Pt Francis
seh liss	Point Francis
keh mook oom	outer bend of " *do* [ditto " same]
whn cht lan	under the bluff on Hale's Passage
tom whik sen	Ind[ian] village
taā la pie	white man's house above it
mah mo lie	a little above
maā chan ilp	lower mouth of Lummi
skul hah nutl	upper " *do* {ditto}
sut eh nus	bight inside Sandy Point
slai uks	Sandy Point
tuts e nuts	beach above the point
tul tul o	}
kwulch tun nus	} various points on the shore
hoo tchich hum	}
hul lech tan	point below Whitehome, rocks off is[island]
whee ess en itch	bight above the last
whul kwāan	indentation just south of Whitehome
now uk sen	Point Whitehome
tsau wuch	Birch Bay
tsult laāltch	within Pt Whitehome
shkwaām	small creek on SE side of bay
klun kun nup	locality East of last
tut kum aā la	creek in Birch Bay
shka ahl	}
ma lach han	} other localities in the bay
hoi a mit hlaā la	small bight on N side

Gibbs places

mook mook kwch kun	west of " *do* [3]
kwul luk an	}
hoos chaā kutl	points on shore, above Birch Bay
al aā alum	Stony Point visible from Camp
salleht lus	Ind[ian] vill[age] at upper end of Sand Spit
she litsh ~ tcheh litch	Sand Spit, Simiahmoo Bay
sim i ah moo	Name of the tribe
kluk 'h	brook inside of the bay #9 Tl'eqx̱ < soggy Map 5 (2011: 58)
kwul lah hoom	creek at head of bay #10 Dakota Creek < dog salmon (2011: 59)
see es sus	Shaw's Point
tah ta lo	creek at Camp Simiahmoo
pe kahlps	present Indian Camp
kwo ma is	Pt west of camp "~~slight ocare~~" Slytscans ᴊ sʜ
too wahk	the Sandy Point inside
no ku meh hil	creek heading in Langley Prairie
tsum tun num	" " " near Fraser R
kwus so wutl	" " " tule swamp
taā na kun	bight inside Pt Roberts
chul tun num	Point fishery
smah kwuts	prairie at Pt Roberts
che was sen	(properly S'cho ah sen) Ind[ian] vill[age] outside?? [Tsawwaussen]

Interior Custer's Route[25]

sow el loh wuch	pr[airi]e at head of no ku meh hil [Nicometl]
tsaāts kwai yem	branch of creek at the prairie
tsut laāng	branch where Ind[ian] house is
stul tuch til	fork of Tsutlaāng
ta ang ten	branch at beaver pond
ho hwah kwutl	first branch of Tahtalo
pehl han	potato patch
ahnowutl	little prairie on " *do*
ha pai elt hu	larger " " "

---

[25] Henry Custer, a German speaking Swiss, was official topographer.

so sai	head of Tahtalo #19 Map 5 Campbell River (2011: 65)
se es sys	Shaw's Point
tuch tuch hum	first large branch of Kwul lah hoom ~ con lahm
ka lah wul leh	second " *do*
kal kalk ku	first creek running to Nooksaak #16 qalqalqx^w < 'roses' Bertrand Ck
she ku mich	second " " " #15 c'ik^{w}əmæx^y < 'get moss' (2011: 61)
tsah nung	creek running to Seh ku mich #17 Map 7 (2011: 63)
noo kope	larger fork of " *do* #23 nox^{w}q^{w}o'pay < 'crabapples' Fishtrap Creek
kwool laām	~~creek~~ fork of the last #30 x^{w}k^{w}əlɛm < 'scouring rush' (2011: 74)
kweh sa litsch	first prairie on Nooksaak
kwo las ta meh	second " *do*
mah moo koom	prairie at Skul leh itl house #18 Map 7 Bertrand Prairie (2011: 64)
koh kwoon nes tum	branch of seh ku mich above #20 Map 7 Howes Creek (2011: 65)
set she no wa	branch of kwool laām
ko kwa ahm	an upper branch of Kwool laām #41 k^{w}ak^{w}ə'ɛm < 'fishtrap' (2011: 84)
pehp she	[ ] Fishtrap Creek #42 Map 7 (2011: 71)
seet leh whutsh	head of kwool laām #43 syiłexič < 'mid 3' (2011: 85)
noo ko kwum	small lake at head of 'kwaachem
see it leh hu	1st creek running into Soomass
tah ta la o	riv[er] entering Soomass Lake [Sumas river] #69 totəlæw < 'creek' :104
skum mehn	}
swah leh whai	} points or localities on the creek, coming in from the west, from the ?? up [3b]
stuk ah niss	} heading in a swamp
ne oh ku nooch tan	} three heads on the last creek
hood maāts	} small house on it
shahs ma koom	the swamp #68 šx^{w}moq^{w}em < 'marsh tea'
tsech lehm	small stream from mtn [mountain] into lake
shwum mut	place of Custer's camp
seetsh tan	high peak ascended?? by him
klaā lum	creek emptying into lake beyond tahtalao #70 łalem < landing camp :105
kwud stanss	another " *do*
yuch wun neh ukw	1st small prairie on tah-ta-lao #60 yux̱^{w}uniq^w Sumas (2011: 96)
hoo mah so snelp	2nd " *do*
kwil tel lum un	prairie near Nooksaak #55 ?? Everson (2011: 92)

koh yohtl	creek running through it #58 kʷəyuɬ 'died prior' (2011: 94)
tum mehw tan	creek entering *tahtalao* below pr[airie] #62 təmi•xʷtən < 'earth device':97
chah a la sum	prairie on head of it
ne see sa ahk :99	small pr[airi]e at mouth of tum mehw #63 noxʷsisæ'æq < 'bracken fern'
ne oh ku nooh tan	2ⁿᵈ prairie on " *do* #64 nuqʷnuxʷtan < waving :100

Fraser River & C[anyon] (Kwantlan Language)

kuk a teh niis	the Cowichan fishery near mouth
keh kait ~ keh kite	the skwaunish " *do* south side
cheh tch lus	small creek opposite <added as insert>
kwio kwut lum	stream behind Misskweum [Musqueam] village
miss kwe um	small village on the island
keht sie	Pitt R and Lake
hul chahm	buttes at mouth of Lake
chul chul	site of old Ft Langley
kwai e tass ~ kwi e tass	stream opposite " *do*
chil o wheh ying	stream below present Fort
sah na satl	a tributary of Pitt R
skwah lutsh	Ind[ian] vill[age] opposite Fr Langley
silts ahss	the Langley Buttes
sai yah al ten	small stream above Ft L[angley]
hai yuks ~ s'hai yuks	Kwantlen R
kwa ah num	small stream above " *do*
mams hweh	lower Masskwee [Matsqui] R
pook chen nus	fishing villages on island
kwaā chem	Upper Masskwee R [Matsqui]
yeht sehm	first branch of " *do*
skow ak sen	Mass kwee [Matsqui] Prairie
oke iaā koonw	high point on prairie
me maāk teb	} branches of kwaa chem R
klaht hlo	}
skwah na watl	}
so mo sakw	}

shum a hum set	prairie at camp No 5
skah na	masskwe [Matsqui] vill[age] on Upper pr[air]e
haāt suk	a stream on N side Fraser R, above the Kwaa chum
hul whai elt hu	prairie on Masskweh R
stehtch	} right hand branch " *do* ascending
o weh tum	} right hand branch " *do* ascending
yeech yill	} two below Soomass
tsah mahtl	} two below Soomass [4b]
klatl hwass	a large slough on N side Fraser R
tso ho mass	a stream putting into it
stuch kehn	Soomass mtns [mountains]
kwee ah matsh	stream on N side Nukatsum territory ??
mass li tel la	a creek
hel hul ahss	a mountain
laā how ic	creek & mtn [mountain] above Soomass flat
ko meh litsh	center hill of the map, mouth of Chik [k] ??
ko mut hoom	mountain on N side Fraser's R
swehl tcha	mountain between Pekosie & the Lake
sehs kul la kun	slough on northern side
skow un nicts	village a mouth of Isehniss } Harrison's R & L
tseh niss	Harrison's river & lake
nuk um men	a small stream running into little lake
steh mwa	higher peak on west " *do*
kweh kwuch hum	mtn between Harrison's & Fraser's R
kluk tuk sen	the small lake
choo choo waā sen	village at head of rapids
yaalsh tun [ā]	large village on the strait
shu pah peh lum	upper village
s'hah ha	creek from west at upper vill[age]
tsuk wil la	sloping rock on right bank of river
kwah lis	stream at camp no 8 ??
saāt sla	snow peak & creek on lake
sho waātl	small lake on trail to Fraser's R
h'kwai ukw	first island in lake

Gibbs places

hwehw kwaā sun	the Persis ?? island
noos kah la	first creek about camp No 9
kt chess ~ kul chess	island, opposite camp 9
hoot sah lo ka litsh	mtn east of the peninsula
sip shum	a stream on west side behind klchess I
ne huk wutsh	mtn seen up gap of lake fr[om] C[am]p 9
le laā le wutsh	mtn east of lakes seen?? Fr[om] C[am]p No 9
h'tasm a hoom	*do* {ditto} west " " " [4c]
nooksh kwum wutl	} creek at camp No 9 on Harrison's L
what hoom	} creek & cascade west of S point Kulchess
shpet kehl	} little I[sland] west side of Lake
shoo up ohls	} creek at place of Musi obs N c[am]p 10
choo choo wulp	} brook at gravelly flat, W side of Lake
koo what sew	} " opposite head of first island
shook shook o meh	} " "the birch trees" Camp No 10 I?? three
s'haalt chum [ā]	} the rapids of Harrison's R
shmah lakw	}
shpah pel tum	} creeks putting into W side ?? below s'hah ha
ass hu	} "the seal"

Fraser R continued

tum me a hai	}
la yome sun	} two mountains S of Chiloweguk R
kleht lw keh	"snow peak"
s'yeh yuk	point of rocks at Camp No 11
kech keh shum	creek entering slough above C[am]p No 11
hach tcha	Pelalthu village on the island
semehn	creek on south opposite it
kwaiss	small lake at its source
keh ka la hum	mtn on Soomass lake S of stuch kehn
see ah la	Camp No 12 on island
kum kweh niis	mtn opposite it
skah met shin	high mtn between Harrison's & L Francis

skah ka enet shin	village on opposite Island
kwa lee ta kum	village on the slough under the mtn
she am a wis	island below, coming out of trail fr[om] lake
shweh lits	village opposite
show hah mil	mountain over it
hwa leht	village / on island / at place of ?? kur obsn [observation] Mch 21st
shnah se la	exit of trail from the lake
ka hahl 'hs	high peak below the trail behind hill
yuk kwah la wun	stream moving into slough from trail [4d]
see sa sum	creek on N side
skwah wahl kum	high bluff mtn above L before it
skow aāl hu	Ind[ian] vill[age] next above that of mtn?? observ[atory]
ko kweh niss	a stream on South side
stet hwaā sum	very precipitous mtn over it
se shehk	high mtn on south side
~~ks kweh~~ ~ wa hus sum	Camp No 13
keh ka al	mtn opposite Camp 13
ts'kah lis	site of Ft Hope
wool kum mech	hill on island of camp 14
ai h'yew	" " " opposite
kleh kwun nuw	stream below Ft Hope
nuk a lah woom	snow mtn [mountain] in gap of " *do*
koomt seh niss	mtn behind Ft Hope
ste teh mia	mtn on S side up & below Ft H[ope]
slept h'yel luk	" " " kusikwunnum
kwee kwee ah len	stream fr[om] south above Ft
hooks hah sum	branch of Nooksahk [Nooksack]
noo teh a kwoom	" " " " #109 nox^{w}t'iq'^{w}əm < 'always murky' :144
noo whai yum	south f[or]k Nooksahk
ko la wheh	north " " "
te ko meh	Mt Baker[26] #71 k^{w}elshæn :105
smamt lek	mtn between Chiloweyuck & Nooksahk
ee shal tul luk	mtn in gap of kwee kwee ah len

---

[26] Nooksack pronunciation of Tacoma since they retain M & N.

Gibbs places

kleh lah woom	East fork of " " also a mtn & lakes of the same name
skehm	small creek ~~on left~~ near C[am]p Mch 28th behind Pt of rocks
kwee ach	snow mtn between Ft Hope & Yale S riv
kwāat se tose [ā]	{ park of same name
whee ah koom	{
klehs kum kum sum	knob on NW end of koomt seh niss
ktitl tah lits	Ind[ian] vill[age] at mouth of kwu kwe ah la [5]

Fraser R continued

s'haht la koom	rapid stream fr[om] west Mch [March] 26[th]
tsim e kwehm	hill below Ft Yale
hwah hu lalp	at the Ft
che wehlp	above the creek & the creek
sche inn	last Ind[ian] vill[age] on right b[an]k below falls
me tul la	Ind[ian] house opposite chewehlp
s'hen niss	mtn on right bank above Ft
hut lalh	" " " in center ?? of gap
kl patl	" " on left bank
lahs kotes	a mtn seen down the river, also from lake
shoot leht luts	small stream from north riv (April 1)
skwaala [ā]	a prairie on it
ten eh scii	"leaning mountain" S of Chiloweyuck
smehm ku	} a range of snow mts east of kleht la keh {visible at mouth of Fraser's R
mam ook wum	large prairie between Soomass & chilow[k]
skwo aā litsh	"signal peak" <added at end> [6]

Adopted Spelling Of The Names Of Camps Etc (Official)

man sel pan ik	creek heading with Chuchehum
kle sil kwu	" " " klehkwunum
wai haist	mtn on upper Skagit
shah wa tum	" " " Skagit
ne po pe eh kum	creek, branch of " *do*

che cheet hu	Skagit cache
ho zo meen	mt [mountain] near Camp Skagit
chu chu wan ten	creek of Haig's camp
skwai kwi eht	mt at head of " *do*
pa say ten	creek of Harris camp
yakl to le min	mouth of Pasayten
nais nio loh	south fork Similkameen
si mil ka meen	
okin a kane	
tcho pahk	mt back of C[am]p Similkameen
haip wil	the lake " " "
o so yoos	
sah lilt kwu	the forks
te kum whehl tin	Archer's (Camp of Oct 9th)
se hai yak kan	Camp of Oct 10th
se hai uks	the creek
twai yeep	upper forks of Ne hoi al pit kwu
ne hoi al pit kwu	
in chu in tum	
stat a poos tin	
en chahm	} lakes below Statapoostin
sin pail hu	creek running south to Columbia R [Sanpoil]
show yet pi	Kettle Falls
stle kehm	Mill Creek
pep tah shin	creek at Depot
chow a wee za	Fool's prairie
an i aht wha	kamass
che laws kan	Little Pend Oreille
chem a kane	Walkers prairie & creek
kai seet lin	crossing of Spokane [crofsing]
kal is pelm	Pend Oreille Lake
yome tsin	White Sheep Creek
en kwool ch la	mouth of Clark's Fork

[7b]

NW Boundary Com   Jno G parke
Colville Depot W T   chief act & sec
Jany 7 1860   [8]

kit lat laā nook   creek heading east of Mt Wilson, empties into lower [lake]
a kwote katl nam   name of the upper lake
kin nook kleht nan na   creek running east from divide ?? to lake
a kam i na   east fork of kish e nehn ka min na a watushi ??
kish e nehn
kish ne neh na
kint la
a kin is sahtl   Flathead River
a kin kwo nah ki   branch of " *do* heading with Tobacco River
kat lak woke   creek running to Flathead through pass
kaisin   a branch of the last
yak in a kahk   name of the pass
ak o no ho   creek running to Kootenay
skits ooh nan na   small creek running to Kootenays above it
ak swak   creek from south at bend of Kootenay
yaks koo nak he   first creek below bend of " *do* from north
ak kaph kleh   falls of Kootenay
yak took i na   third creek from north
ka yak ka   creek from south below falls, a large lake on it
yakh
moo yie
yak kwoo kah keh   } the Chelemta cache
skwoots kose   }
chuk kose   the Mooyie lakes
ha cha atl   Ind[ian] village below Aklew cache
aktlaka   creek above kishenehn [9]

Adopted Spellings of the Names of Camps etc (Official)

Simiahmoo

Sumass

Chiloweyuck

Tummeahai

Chuch che hum

Skagit

Similkameen

Okinakane

Fraser

Nooksahk

Swehl tcha

Pekosie

La yome sin

Sen eh say

En saaw kwatch

Grays Harbor – Rivers, Creeks, Streams, and Features

North Side of Bay

Pt Brown

  Oyhut

  Sampson

North Bay

  Campbell Slough

  Jessie Slough "named for an Indian, who rafted logs on the slough, and whose nickname was
      'Humptulips Jesse'" (Hitchman 1985: 137).

  Humptulips = xʷəmtulapš < /apš/ 'stream' (Bright 2004: 175)[27]

  Burg Slough

  Gillis Slough

  Chenois Creek = čənus, name of a Lower Chehalis leader (Bright 2004: 93); qi'əsqalʔux
      (James and Martino 1986: 44)

  Grass Typso Creek {Latin name for cattails}

  James Rock aka Neds Rock, Lone Rock, Point New, Brackenridge Bluff; shoreline there is
      named = ɬəmiṁ (James and Martino 1986: 44)

Pt. New

Bowerman Basin

Hoquiam = x̣ʷəqʷyamc < x̣ʷəqʷ- 'hungry' + yamc Douglas fir, wood = driftwood 'hungry for
      wood' (Bright 2004: 173)

---

[27] The angled bracket < means "derived from".

Gibbs places

Fry Creek chominim (James and Martino 1986: 42; Van Syckle 1982: 370)

Cow Pt

Big bluff near Aberdeen = qaysáləbeš, questing site for wealth spirit who gifted sons of chiefs
   with the song to summon whales to beach themselves

Wishkah = xʷəšqaɬ < xʷəš- stink + qaɬ water = 'stinking water' (Bright 2004: 572). Refers to a
   legend where a Thunderbird dropped a whale into this river. See Eells next

South Side of Bay

Pt Chehalis

  South Bay

  Andrews R

Elk River Nushiatska (James and Martino 1986: 40)

Beardslee Slough

Dempsey Creek

Redman Slough

John's River < "Uncle" John Hale land claim, Wilkes called it Dinsmas River (Hitchman 1985:
   138); two cabins, burials, prairie above high tides (James and Martino 1986: 39)

Beaver Creek camas beds (James and Martino 1986: 40)

Stearns Bluff a/k/a Roundtree Point, Judsons Point, Crabapple Point, Jones Point, South Arbor
   (James and Martino 1986: 39)

O'Leary plankhouse, weir (James and Martino 1986: 39)

Stafford < a settler; Wilkes called it Typha Creek (Hitchman 1985: 267)

Indian

Chapin

Newskah = "good water", with tidal weir nearby (Van Syckle 1982: 370)

Charley

Riverine

Chehalis River mouth from Cow Point to Cosmopolis = nsulapalucn

Chehalis River nsulapš

Cosmopolis = qaysalməs

Gibbs places

North Side of River

Elliott Slough

Max Slough

Higgins Slough

Peels Slough

Wynoochee = xʷənuɬč ~ 'shifting sands'? (Bright 2004: 576)

Camp

Sylvia Creek

Satsop = sacapš < /sa'a-/ 'make, do' + /capš/ stream = 'made stream' (Bright 2004: 422)

Newman Creek

Mox Chehalis < Chinuk Wawa 'two, twin, double' + Lower Chehalis 'sand' (Bright 2004: 299)

Porter

Gibson

Shelton

Cedar

Black

South Side of River

Blue Slough

Preachers Slough < 1859 transit of Rev JS Douglass, a Methodist Episcopal minister (Hitchman
    1985: 240)

Stevens

Elizabeth

Workman < settler, a/k/a Mason's Creek

Delezine

Eaton

Gaddis

Coastal

Quinault < k̓ʷinayɬ (Bright 2004: 405)

Wreck

Moclips = nəw̓muɬapš > beginning syllable has dropped off (Bright 2004: 292)

Joe

Elk

Boone

Copalis = k̓ʷpils < /-ils/ 'rock' (Bright 2004: 121)

Connor

Oyhut < Chinuk jargon "portage, cross over"

These native place names express inherent qualities or attributes of these spots, while the English ones rely on applying the personal names of explorers, first settlers, notables, or nostalgia for places in Europe.

Of all these names, only the Wishkah involves an epic with profound spiritual and religious consequences. Outside of Grays Harbor, Olson (1936: 17-22) recorded similar names in Quinault territory, showing that the Wishkah epic is consistent with the region. Jay Powell similarly notes Quileute named 'whale rocks' abound on their territory, comprised of petrified whales of the Mythic Age.

#714 [S.I. 248 old No {# number}] M'Film Reel #48 (NEG)
Bureau of American Ethnology Catalogue of manuscripts

Salishan and Chinookan
George Gibbs
List of Localities, with native names, in Oregon and Washington
[all w. {west} of the Cascades]

{his} Title: "Indian Nomenclature of localities in Washington and Oregon Territories"
oval: manuscript vault Mar 1926 Chinookan = sh-18-19 Salishan = sh − 50

Indian Nomenclature[28]
Collected George Gibbs 1853-56

Chinook Language
Columbia River

Cape Disappointment	káh-use
?McKurgies' head	no-hóh-te
creek near Baker's Bay	wál-la-kut
at Dawson's	wáp-pa-lo-chie
Dawsons'	nose-whói-nulhs
Pacific City	káh-so-lit
McCartys'	noshe-ootl <u>*or*</u> no-shootl
Chinook Point	nóse-to-ilse
Pt Ellice	no-wíhtl-kai-ilse
Deep River	kéhm-tsa
Grays' River	móhk-ho <u>*or*</u> mó-hool
Yellow Bluff	na-kahtl-kwaiu
Pillar Rock	kweht-sa-kas-nac
Scarboro's hill	no-se-misp
Jim Crow hill	wa-kai-a-túm-a
Skesmahquesip's village	wa-kai-a-kum
Creek near Birnies	e-ló-ka-min
Birnies (Cathlamet)	kwil-loo-chinl
Pt Adams	klāat-sop (Clatsop)
Raymonds	nai-áh-ak-sten
Creek at Clatsop Plains	skip-pa-nósiin
Lewis & Clark's R	néh-tul
↕ Young's River	↕ inserted

---

[28] edits: titles have been indented instead of under listings in the interest of more space per
line; <u>*or*</u> was originally only underlined but is now both <u>underlined</u> and *italic*. Unreadable
words or syllables begin with ? a question mark; ↕ marks Gibbs insertions. Footnotes and
{curved brackets} explain additions to the original 714 list.

First fk {fork}	wa-toos-ki's *?or* nak-e-któw-a-nok
Second fk	klúts-ka-nsii
Astoria	a-wák-atl
Adairs'	nóht-la-quok
Shortess'	a-wák-sil
Tongue Pt	soo-kum-its-ėák {2}

Coast of Oregon (?Milhan & Kautz)

ne-a-húm-tuk	vill{age} at mouth of Alseya R
scius-clau	
kal-la-wát-set	Umpqua R below the rapids, above which it is the Umpqua, *or* as called by them ten-na-woot-tay
me-luk-itz, how-nay-setch	Coose *or* Kowes bay, the name "Coos" signifies in the too-too-ten language a lake, lagoon, or inland bay. De Mofras absurdly translates it R des Vaches
kas-o-a-cha	village at Flores Creek
te-cheh-quut	" on Sikhs River. This last word I presume to be the jargon word for Friend, probably given by whites, just as I see "win-chuck" creek, win-chuck being lower Klamath *or* Aliquah for woman.
yah-shoots	village at mouth of Rogue's R. The too-too-ten village from which it takes its name is a little further up.
chet-léss-ing-en	village on Pistol Creek
Chit-ko	stream of that name {2b}

Shoalwater Bay – Chinook Language

a-teé-so-will	Bear R S end of Bay
táh-lilt	cr{eek} at Tarlict P.O. {post office}
chík-lis-ilh	Pt Leadbetter
tee-choots	the peninsula
nass-tōō	Sand Island
mo-kwol	S side o Nasal R {Nasel R}
néh-sal *or* leh-soolt	Nasal R
cl-a-mée-a-kolt	cr above the Nasal
péh-luks *or* co-péh-luks	Palux R
na-wáu-kum (? Chehalis) }	two small creeks above last
quil-quil-im (? Chehalis) }	
qwul-qwul	Ind Vill{age} at Swan's old house
kwal-so-wilh	Russels'
wah-hótes	Champ's beach
qum-áp-tilh *or* quil-úp-tin-?lilso	Stuarts point
will-o-pah	name of the River

Gibbs places

amps-kome	Vail's place
kah-kilch	creek west of Willapah
nek-o-man-chie	North River (or noo-hu-mín-i-ke)
aih-aih	above the last
quahpt-sum	Toke's Point
áh-se-hat	} neighboring localities to Toke's Point
no-ít-woo	} /
klo-milt	} /
too-it-tum	} /
chi-hual-sta	under Cape Shoalwater

Coast above Gray's Harbor

	Chihalis language	Makah language	
Next stream north	co-péh-lis	~~kwi-nee-tut~~	
	Quin-ái-ūtl	qum-áitl	
	Kweéts-hu	lóh-whilse : kéh-chen-wilt	
Hooch, the vill{age}	hooch cháh-latt	kwáak-sat	{Hoh}
Chahlatt, the R			
	kwilléhyute	kwi-née-tut	

Makah villages

(Note: Classet, Klaizzart of Dewatte	o-sétt	at Flattery rocks
is probably the Nootka name for	tsoo-yéss	at a creek in bight
the Makah tribe)	wá-átch }	bight south of Cape
	hatch-áh-wat }	bight south of Cape
	teh-da-kom-it	"Classet" village
Nee-ah & klehs-sid-ats-oos	the two western villages in Neah bay	
beh-da	the two eastern village	
séh-loks	two sisters in rocks a few miles east of Neah, a legend concerning them {3a}	

Coast below Pt Adams   Chinook Language

stream at ?foot of Clatsop Plains
tíl-a-mooks	the correct name, not "Killamook"
ecola (ékoolie)	creek of Lewis & Clark – a creek below Tillamooks head.

The word means "a whale"

The word Neacoxie refers to the small pine trees at its mouth

ne-a-car-më	Head, false Tillamooks ne-a-káh-nie
ne-káh-,na-hum	a creek emptying into the sea, at head of Clatsop plains
wa-hun-ni	creek & small lake at Perry's head of Clatsop plains

Coast   from S{ilas} H Smith, Clatsop Plains

Kilamook river	káh-ha-léh-tchie
another bay south of Kilamook	na-hats _or_ natahats
two small streams running }	na-wug-ga
into the coast below the last }	nes-tug-ga
another stream, a promontory	
intervening }	ne-ches-nie
Celetse R just below it	nes-lah-chie ("flood tide")
ya-?kód-na	still south

Grays Harbor Chihalis River Chihalis Language
{modern place names inserted between curved brackets}

1 Ind. Vill. at mouth (Kakowan's) {Westport} Tsi-héh-lis (Chihalis), the word means "sand"
  "Sites of villages on the South side of the bay" {is written vertically in the middle space}

2	klum-ái-tumsh	abandoned
3	noo-hoo-ulīch	'''
4	noo-si-átsks	'''
5	kl-kóh'tl	'''
6	tseh-chie	'''
7	tsah-koo-lin-tń	abandoned
8	mil-lúch	
9	noos-kóh	Creek opposite Whis-kah River
10	noo-ách-hum-milk	Vill{age}. on the ocean

"Sites of villages on the North side of bay" {is written vertically in the middle space}

11	noo-kált-hu	
12	koom-tóh-lupsh	
13	kish-kal-len	
14	klim-mím _or_	Wch-ta-mich
15 {Hoquiam}	ho-kwa-im-its	
16 {Wishkah}[29]	hoosh-kal	abandoned
17 {Wishkah}	whísh-kah	a pretty large stream on the N. side of bay
18(Cosmopolis}	kai-sáh-lumsh	Pilkenton's place on S. side of river
19{Wynoochee}	wan-noól-chie	stream from North, above Pilkenton's
20 {Satsop}	saāt-sop	The Satsop branch; from north
21	ts-po-áh _or_	S. side a little below Cedar Cr, ab. vill.
	kula-kwul-lum	{ = abandoned village}
22	Sa-quát-lum	a stream 4 m.{miles} above Satsop {3b}

---

[29] This listing has been numbered and coordinated with modern names; Wishkah is a better
  spelling of the actual native name {x^{w}əšqaİ}.

Grays Harbor   Chihalis River   Chihalis Language cn't

chahnitot   Cedar River (Armstrongs')
tsh-chol   Creek S side just above Cedar
klak-wáh-mihl   Vill{age} *do* " *do* {ditto}
Saht-sall   Black River at mouth
ta-ow-wun   On N side above Black R
kluk-ái-a-kl   Mound prairie
téh-a-woot-en   Skookum Chuck vill{age}
noochts-saal   mouth of Nawaukum
nich-yeó-nuchtl   Tho{ma}s Ford
tah-lal   Boisfort Pr{airi}e   } Owillapah {Swaal}
tsa-wháh-sen   Above the forks   }   villages
noo-so-lup = word means 'rapid water'   Upper Chehalis, above Ford's
shé-kwi-ukl   Mt St Helens
ne-sháh-kwi-ukl Mt Rainier
nah-chal   Small prairie on W. side R. below Ford's, where noises are heard.

Clallam going up the Straits (noos-klái-yum)

Sn-góh   a river some 12 m{iles}. from Nee-ah trail over to Kwilliyutt
óke-ho   another steam very near it, a village at its mouth
klat-láh-was   Ind vill{age}
pisht'st   (Camel R) at Pillar Pt & village
kwa-ha-mihs   (Lyle R) fishing station
el-wha   a river west of False ?ness villages
tse-whitzén   } two villages at False ?ness
yínnis   }
steht-lum   vill{age} at New Dungeness
shqueen   vill{age} at Sequim Bay
kah-quaitl *or* squáh-quihl   do {ditto} at Pt Discovery
kah-tói   Pt Townsend vill{age}
chem-a-kum   creek & vill{age} at head of Bay   {4}

Columbia River (Chinook)

cath-láh-met
Wa-kái-a-kum   Skemah-que-up's vill{age}
e-ló-ka-min   stream below Bonnies
kuch-nak   Oak point Indians, Franchére calls them Kreluits / Tolmie Kahniac

he-kís-ti-koke   Abernathy's Mill stream
chim-is-tik-ky   small creek above it
ník-wal   creek below Cowlitz R

se-ah-mis-tie	below m{outh} of Cowlitz ?ghum's ?tikky
cow-a-litsk	Cowlitz river. See infra
ka-láh-ma	thla-ka-la-mah Francère's Pretty Girls R, called *pshwat-ka* by the Klikatats, from *pskwah*, a stone in allusion to this burial place on Coffin rock.
?Klikatat wílt-kwil-luk	village a little below Rainier (?yaho towit) , nai-a-kook-wie, ne-ah-ko-twi *Tolmie* village of St Helens
scap-poose	the creek at Milton, emptying into the Willamit Slough. It was formerly ka-se-no's {Cassino's} village.
na-mun-ne-min	S. side Souvie's I{sland}
wilt-kwi (*Klik*)	vill{age} at mouth of Cathlapootl or Lewis R and also the town part of the river how-ilt'h {of} Tolmie Cow-ilkt {of} Francére Tolmie makes Well-tuks <u>Klik</u>{atat} & how-lick <u>Chinook</u>
wah-wa-chéh-as	"the oaks" <u>or</u> "place of oaks" <u>*Tolmie*</u> Around Lewes house, near the Cathlapootl (Klikatat)
cath-la-pootl	Franchère give this name to the vill{age} at mouth of the wilt-kwu Tolmie thinks it is the mouth of Lake river. It is Chinook not Klikatat. The name has obtained for wilt-kwu river.
cha-láh-cha	"fern". The prairie on the Cathlapootl
ya-kohtl	south fork of Cathlapootl
múlt-na-bah	(mult-no-mah) two villages below mouth of the Willamet <u>Franchère</u>
willamette R	(infra) properly spelt wa-lamút
cath-la-nam-i-nim	(yahotwit) a vill{age} a little below where Portland now stands.
wa-kan-a-sis-se	village on the N side Columbia, nearly opposite mouth of Willamet
skits-oot-hwa	*Tolmie* site of Ft Vancouver
at-a-shu-kas	("place of turtles") the low ground above the fort *klik* *Tolmie*
wat-se-ai-as	*klik* Mill Creek *Tolmie*
was-shoo-hul	Washugal R
is-áh-lich	the prairie a little above Switzler's opposite Ft Vancouver *Tolmie klik* {4b}

Cowlitz River (Cowlitz languages)   Dr Warbass {14 Nov 1858}[30]

<now-oo-tsou	Monticello >
cow-ee-men <u>or</u> coweema	(*Klikatat* cow-ím-in-in) the stream called Eobar's R
nu-che-lip	in lower Cowlitz river
<tsalkh	'lake' >
now-oo-tsoo	(*Klikatat* wish-ham) site of Monticello {Longview, WA}
<tsop>	
ts-ka-lump	the lower rapids
neth-wee	creek below Eagles'
ne-yám-a-titch	rapids above do {ditto}

---

[30] Warbass's original letter to Gibbs has been integrated into this 714 list as marked between <angle brackets>.

tse-qual-i-sen	"forks" at Gardiners' (séhkwu was given me as the name at the forks)
< tun-ta-malk	Grand Rapids >
se-a-kt	south fork, on Touttles River
cow-mat-tsen	next creek above on left
mock-kaults	Mill creek tun-ta-malk Grand Rapids
cla-quil	Lakamass creek
klak-olks	Cowlitz Landing
ma-tep-paɫ-lu	cr{eek} opposite
ow-well-kewkh	("paint ground" so called from a plant which they use for paint) The small prairie behind Landing
now-ok	"the prairie" Cowlitz farms
cho-wap-pow-lik }	two small creeks at upper end of prairie
sol-kum }	
nulk-tsulk	the Nawaukum River
quailt (*klik*{itat})	the Klickitat prairie
scow-wow-woulk	upper south fk {fork} of Cowlitz
cha-chin	northern branch of the last
tai-tin-a-pam	Klikatats of the Cowlitz (Klik)
wah-nookt (Cowlitz)	also the upper Cowlitz, above the Kl{ikatats} prairie
te-quil-í-pam	cha-wash (i.e. water) *Klik* Cowlitz R below do {ditto}

note: The original location of the Cowlitz tribe was 2 miles above the H. B. Co. {Hudson Bay Company} farms {Puget Sound Agricultural Company}.   {5a}

Cowlitz to Olympia & Steilacoom

nook-tsahl	Nawaukum R
kwái-ai-ilk	people of Ford's Prairie
téh-a-woot	Skookum Chuck people
tahtl-shin	Ford's prairie
chis-le-táh	Boisfort prairie (*owhillapsh*) {Swaal} {columns reversed}
too-táh-pa	Upper Chehalis R
klak-ái-a-ktl	Grand Mound Prairie
te-nal-quet : Te-nal-quuhl	Prairie at Linklater's
kl-ko-mínn	Chambers Prairie
muck	creek from plains
kwod-kwoi : kwun-kwie	Gravolus' prairie Canadian plains
s'guk-e-kwus	Quiemuhl's house
te-téh-lukw	the cold spring back of chuck
span-o-way	?Labouchelier's
klit-hlow	Dean's
tsa-tsáh-weh	"place of pine trees" from tsah-weh a red pine (P. ponderosa) the woods, back of Dean's
súk-a-towkh	Minson's {Gibb's neighbor}

Gibbs places

yelm	prairie at Edgars
tán-wut }	
o-wháp }	branches of Nisqually
mishawl }	
skó-kwit-át-chie	lake near Nisqually
spoót-sinlh	Gravelly lake
whee-át-chee	Bird's Lake
kúl-kub-leh	back Squally plain
mit-súk-wie	village at Salmon trap on Squally

Hood's Canal &c {6}

mats-mats	the cove above Port Ludlow
nook-nahn-atl	Port Ludlow
tee-ka-let	Port Gamble
kwul-seen	Colseed bay {Quilcene}
do-se-wai-lupsh	Lylopish R of Wilkes
hum-hum-ái	{Hama hama}
lilo-wap	creek at McNeah's {Lilliwap}
duwatto	creek in bend of Canal
sko-kó-mish	river entering the bend
to-an-hooch	tribe occupying Canal. Toando of Wilkes

Upper Inlet

S'quahk-sen or skwawk-sen	portage to Case's Inlet
sa-héh-wa-mish	tribe on Hammersley's
ta-pek	Totten's Inlet
squái-áitl	Eld's Inlet
stéh-chass	Olympia
noo-séh-chatl	South bay. Henderson's Inlet
kláh-che-min	Island at mouth of Totten's Inlet
sho-nah-nam	"medicine place" McAllister's creek
Nisqually River	the name Squally _or_ n's-qually, belongs strictly to the Indian village at the fish dam on it.
se-qwal-li-chew	the mill creek near Ft Nisqually
steilacoom	the mouth of the creek about the town
s'noh-tlam	Carr's Inlet
puyal-lup	name of the river at the mouth
choo-choot-luts	("the maples") inside of Pt Defiance
téh-la-kwuts	site of the Block house
t'kwahk	the forks of Puyallup
soo-éhkw	the prairie at the forks

schó-wah	south fork of Puyallup
ke-pów-sim	Lake of S. fork
swa-tehnts _or_ sáh-hum-alt-hu	("place of dancing" from sáh-hum to dance lower ford on Puyallup)
stuck	the slough connecting White R with the Puyallup. In the Nooksahk "Stuck" means a raft {6b}

Duwamish & White River

deetch-táh-litsh	the village of Seattle So called after see-āā-lth, the chief of the Duwamish & Suquamish
me-kwáh-mooks	Alki point
dwamish	is properly the tribe on the outlet of Dwamish Lake _or_ Black River, called Nahomish by Wilkes
pup-sholk	blockhouse at Dent's Camp
te-lál-kwo	village below the forks
skóhmshl	Porter's pr{air}e N side of White R.
ste-káh-mish	Indians of White R.
te-nál-quet	Williamson's pr{air}e S side White R.
cle-álp	Daniel's pr{air}e between White & Puyallup
smálh-ko	Ford on the Emigrant trail the sma-tochs of Wilkes
kla-quot	the "Bare prairie" above, not la Tete {boulder 'head', see p146} ("a plant of the angelica tribe")
noos-cope _or_ scope	north f{or}k of White R called also Green R
mukl-shootl	pr{air}e between Wh{ite} & Green US Mil{itar}ty Station
&	
skwówh	("Raven") the lake east of Dwamish L
sa-máh-mish R	the outlet of it
soos	a tributary of the lake
tudow	Cedar R heading in Yakama pass
shul-shole	outlet of a small lake below Seattle
tah-choo	Blake I{sland} or rather the low land on it

    [note: Wilkes' names of Sakpam & Tuxpam as applied to White River & his Snohomish are of Klikatat origin]

noos-sóh-kum	Port Madison
sno-hó-mish	the name of a tribe. Properly applies to the river only below the forks of Skywhamish
kwult-see-na }	a creek coming in at its mouth
kwilt-she-da }	
mukl-te-óh	Point Elliott

50

tu-lā-lup	(tu-léh-lúp _or_ hu-lé-lup) a small bay above it

sky-whá-mish	name of a tribe, also the N fk of Snohomish R
sno-qual-moo	(sno-qual-mewh) name of tribe & S fork
tolt-hu	a branch above the Skywhumish
kwéht-lum	" below " {7}

d'gwatsk _or_ n'whát-sa }
skulhts (Skagit) }   Skagit Head

hahd-skus	Point no Point
steil-a-gua-mish	(?) sto-luk-wha-mish, ie, "River People"

cho-mahlst _or_ s'cho-bahlst	SE Pt Penn's Cove ? kamass
to-ho-wall	Sneetlum's point
hai-ha-náb-sum-	Bartow's Penn's Cove

k'tóte-sid	Oak Harbor
sh-tó-sud	Crescent Harbor
te-cháh-gwup	Martin's Point N end do {ditto}

shais-quil	Fay's house, Perry's i{sland}

kik-i-ál-lus	vill{age} on southern mouth of Skagit
skagit	the river & tribe
sin-a-áh-mish _or_ squs-náh-mish	vill{age} on north mouth
	(for tribes & forks on Skagit R see notebook)
nuk-púk-kum	next stream above Skagit
chál-cha-uk	small stream above last
swin-a-mish	tribe on the canoe passage {slough}
samish	tribe & river at foot of Bell[m] {Bellingham} Bay
sí-a-mán-na	("Hunters") name of southern lake
núch-wugh	band of Indians on lake
s'huts-kus	Samish Point
choo-áh-utsh	Samish village in the passage {7b}

Bellingham Bay[31]

chúk-a-nuts	the inner bight
sis-hit-chum	Thomas's place
ma-mó-sie	Pattles' >
squlicum (kwab-hi-hum)	creek above Whatcom
what com	"noisy water" the outlet of lake
<squod li cum	small creek at Ind{ian} village >

---

[31] Gibbs's original list as marked between <angle brackets> has been integrated into 714.

klik a teh nus   prairie at the Military Station
<chah choo sen   island in delta of Lummi River >
swul-éh- sen   portage <to straits> above Pt Francis
lum-mi , ha-lum-mi _or_ nooch-lum-mi (the latter their own name)
                    that of the tribe & town part of river
cháh-choo-sen   Part of the Delta of the river
seh liss   Point Francis
<keh mook oom   outer bend of _do_ {ditto, same} >
<whn cht lan   under the bluff on Hale's Passage >
tom-whik-sen   Winter <Indian> village on the passage
<taā la pie   white man's house above it
<mah mo lie   a little above
<maā chan ilp   lower mouth of Lummi
skul hah netl _or_ slah-yuks   mouths of Lummi River on _do_ <upper _do_ {ditto} >
<sut eh nus   bight inside Sandy Point
tut-se-nuts }   Sandy Point beach above the point
slai-ek-sen }   Sandy Point

          Lummi Island [mum-míh-uk] mam-íh-uk mountain on S end

chów-uks   southern end of I{sland}.
skáh uk-shun   fishery on W side
kleh-kwan-nie   rock off the S.W. side, It is a demon

Reverend Myron Eells
(1843-1907)

Myron, the younger of two sons of pioneer missionaries Cushing (1810-1893) and Myra Fairbanks Eells (1805-1878), was born in 1843 at the Tshimakain Mission they founded near present-day Spokane, Washington. After nine years, Cushing had made no converts. When missionaries Marcus and Narcissa Whitman were killed in 1847 at the Waiilatpu Mission, near present-day Walla Walla, Washington, the Eellses relocated to the Willamette Valley, where they homesteaded and Cushing taught. Missionary and other families left inland region, while Catholic priests were allowed to remain. In 1859, when eastern Washington reopened for resettlement inland, Cushing obtained a homestead and a charter to establish a school to memorialize them at Whitman College at Walla Walla, where it thrives.

Myron graduated in the second class in 1866 with an AM from Pacific University in Forest Grove, Oregon, then worked on his father's farm in Walla Walla for two years, deciding to study for the ministry. He went east, graduated from Hartford Theological Seminary, as had Cushing 34 years before, in Connecticut and was ordained 15 June 1871 to return to the Northwest to lead a Congregational Church in Boise, Idaho. He married Sarah Maria Crosby 18 January 1874, and they had five sons: Edwin Fayette 1874 - ?, Chester Cushing 1874 - ?, Arthur Herman 1876 - ?, and two living to adulthood: Roy Whitman 1890-1879 and Walter Crosby 1885-1963. His children helped him make regular reports to the US Weather Bureau.

Restless in 1874 and visiting his brother Edwin, new agent for Skokomish, at the elbow of Hood Canal just west of Puget Sound, the "hand of Providence" urged him to stay as missionary for 33 years. Myron also served nearby Congregational churches at Seabeck, Dungeness, Mt Constance, and Holly. Both brothers were dedicated to a mission of Christian reforms, often relying on school boys to keep them informed of local events and transgressions.

Edwin, also born at Tshimakain 27 July 1841, served for 24 years, married Abigail A Foster (1844 - ?), and had six girls and a boy: Ida Myra Eells 1871- ?, Eva Alice Eells 1871-1898, Gertie Fairbank Eells 1877-1961, Gracie Foster Eells 1871- ?, Abbie May Eells 1871-?, and Edna Eells 1871-1890, and Edwin Eells 1893-1959. When the family moved back to the area around Walla Walla, Edwin helped his father establish a small school, which ultimately became Whitman College. After reading law in Seattle, Edwin was appointed Indian Agent of the Puyallup and Skokomish, serving with various agencies until 1895 when he moved to Tacoma, where he helped found a Congregational Church and the State Historical Society, where he gave his papers. He died in Tacoma in 1917.

Myron found time and stimuli to conduct research on various religious, historical, and anthropological topics. Beginning with his responses to the questionnaire sent to his agent brother to gather information for the Centennial Exhibition in Philadelphia, published in 1877 by a DC agency, Myron pursued painstaking investigations into the written and unwritten records of the native people and history of the Northwest. His literary output included over 1,250 articles for newspapers and magazines, some 50 pamphlets, four books, and a number of unpublished manuscripts. For his church, he published *Ten Years of Missionary Work Among the Indians at Skokomish, Washington Territory* in 1886 during a period of great change, building on previous work and contemporary events such as the origins of the Indian Shaker Church.

In order to pursue his studies, Myron assembled books on Northwest history, a historical-manuscripts collection, and a collection of Native American artifacts. He gained a national reputation as both a scholar and a collector, receiving an honorary Doctor of Divinity from

Whitman in 1890. In 1892, he was appointed superintendent of the Department of Ethnology for the Washington State Commission for the World's Columbian Exposition in Chicago. On 5 May 1896, the Seattle Post-Intelligencer ran a feature on his Northwest library.

Though Myron wrote about local native languages, especially Chimakum which is unique as an isolate with Quileute, he had not training or skills at languages, struggling with only the English alphabet to write down these complex sounds. Edwin was much the same.

Myron was a trustee and avid supporter of his father's Whitman College, as well as Tualatin Academy and Pacific University at Salem, Oregon. In 1882, he gave 10 bound volumes, 15 pamphlets, and $25 to start a Whitman library. After his death in January 1907 he donated to Whitman more than 1,600 Native American artifacts and hundreds of historical manuscripts that substantially changed the size and nature of the college museum, and the college library grew by more than 10 percent with the addition of Myron's 1,800-volumes. One-third of these volumes, forming Myron's Northwest history library, became the first significant special collection. Myron's materials are now held in the Myron Eells Library of Northwest History, the Whitman College Northwest Manuscripts Collection, the Whitman College Archives, and the Maxey Museum.

Myron died 3 January 1907 at Tacoma and is buried in the Masonic Union Pioneer Cemetery at Union, Mason County, Washington.

Bibliography

1877   The Twana Indians of the Skokomish Reservation in Washington Territory. *US Geological Survey Bulletin* 3 (4): 57-114.

1878 *Hymns in the Chinook Jargon Language.* Portland: George H Himes. [expanded 1889]

1878 Mounds in Washington Territory. *American Antiquarian and Oriental Journal* 1 (1): 13 April.

1880 The Chemakum Language. *American Antiquarian and Oriental Journal* 2 (10). October.

1881   *History of the Congregational Association of Oregon and Washington, The Home Missionary Society of Oregon and Adjoining Territories, and the Northwestern Association of Congregational Ministers.* Portland: Publishing House of Himes the Printer.

1882   *History of Indian Missions on the Pacific Coast: Oregon, Washington, Idaho.* Philadelphia: The American Sunday-School Union.

1883 Catholic Missions: Recent Changes. *The American Missionary* 37 (7): 211-12 July.

1883 Marcus Whitman, MD: Proofs of His Work in Saving Oregon to the United States, and in Promoting the Immigration of 1843. Portland.

1884 Census of the Clallam and Twana Indians of Washington Territory. *American Antiquarian and Oriental Journal* 6 (1): 35-38 January.

1886 *Ten Years of Missionary Work among the Indians at Skokomish, Washington Territory, 1874-1884.* Boston: Congregational Sunday School and Publishing Society.

1887   The Indians of Puget Sound. *American Antiquarian and oriental Journal* 9 (4): 1-9 January. In 6 articles.

1889 The Twana Chemakum and Klallam Indians of Washington Territory. DC: *Smithsonian Annual Report* for 1887: 605-81.

1890 Worship and Traditions of the Aborigines of America: The Sinful Soul. *Washington Magazine* 2 (2): 49-51 April.

1892   Aboriginal Geographical Place Names in the State of Washington.   *American Anthropologist* 05 (1): 27-34 January. {see 1985}
1894 Chinook Jargon. *American Anthropologist* 7 (3): 300-312 July.
1894 *Father Eells*: Or, The Results of Fifty-Five Years of Missionary Labors in Washington and Oregon; A Biography of Rev Cushing Eells, DD. Boston: Congregational Sunday School and Publishing Society.
1909 *Marcus Whitman, Pathfinder and Patriot.* Seattle: Alice Harriman Co.

1985 Myron Eells *Indians of Puget Sound* ~ The Notebooks of Myron Eells Volume 4, Chapter XVIII ~ Names 275-287, Meaning of Place Names 277 - 287. George Pierre Castile, ed. Seattle: University of Washington Press for Whitman College.

1976 Myron Eells and the Puget Sound Indians. Robert Ruby & John Brown. Seattle: Superior Publishing Company.

Aboriginal Geographic Names in the State of Washington

Almata [Eells 1892: 27] is a corruption of the Nez Perce word *allamotin*, signifying "torch-light fishery".

Alpowa is a Nez Perce word, and means "the mouth of Spring creek". The Indian name of the creek is *alpaha*, which means "spring creek", and was so given because of the numerous springs there.

Asotin is from the Nez Perce word *hashotin*, which means "eel creek", from the abundance of eels [lampreys] in it.

Cathlamet is written Cathlamah by Lewis and Clarke, and was the name of a tribe of Indians as well as a stream. It evidently comes from the Indian word "*calamet*", meaning "stone", and is believed to have been given to the river because of the fact that it has a stony bed along its whole course. See Kalama.

Camas — see La Comas.

Chehalis, the name of a river, county, and city, is pronounced by the Indians Tse-ha-lis, and by some early writers was written Chi-ke-lis. It means "sand", and was given to the Indians about the mouth of the river because of the sand there. Hence the early settlers gave the same name to the river and the upper Chehalis Indians, though originally neither was called by this name.

Chewelah is a corruption of the word cha-we-lah, which is the name of a small striped snake {gartersnake ~ *sčew'íl'e'*}. It was applied to that place either because the snake abounded there or because of the serpentine appearance of the stream.

Chimakum was the name of a small but brave tribe of Indians, which is now as a tribe extinct, who lived near a place bearing the same name. Its meaning I cannot learn.

Clallam, the name of a county, bay, and river in the northwestern part of the State; originally the name of a tribe there. It is also written S'Klal-lam; said by Clallam Indians to be a corruption of their name for themselves, Nu-sklaim, meaning the "strong people". A Twana Indian says that it comes from the Twana name for the tribe, Do-sklal-ob, meaning "the big brave nation", which [28] is essentially the same as given by the Clallams. Judge JG Swan is of the opinion that the term is derived from the Makah name for the Clallam, which means "the clam people", from *klo-lub*, "clam;" *aht*, "man". Although his opinion is entitled to great respect, I incline strongly to the former origin of the word.

Conconully is a corrupted Indian name, meaning "cloudy", but was applied to the lower branch of Salmon river. The proper Indian name for the valley where Conconully lies is *Sklow Ouliman*, which means "money hole", on account of the number of beaver caught there in early days, when beaver skins were money to the Indians.

Dewatto is from the Indian name *du-a-ta*, for the reason that in their mythology certain imaginary pigmies or sprites used to live there, who made folks crazy if once they entered them. The names of these sprites was *tub-ta-ba*, and the name of their home in the spirit world, which was within the earth, was *du-a-ta*, and this place was called by the same name because here they came out of the earth.

Docewallops, the name of a river and mountain in Jefferson county, is from the Twana word *Dos-wail-opsh.* In Twana mythology the mountain of that name was long ago a man, while Mount Solomon, opposite it, was his wife, and an apparently small but noticeable mountain far up in the valley between them was their child. Mount Tacoma was another wife of the same man, who lived at the same place, but the two women quarreled so badly that after a time the big woman, whose name was *Tu-wah-hu,*[32] which is the native name of that mountain, picked up a basketful of the heads, tails, and parts of fish and left to find a more peaceable home. She traveled up Hood's canal and intended to stop at Skokomish, but the place was too small for her; so she went on, dropping, however, as she crossed the Skokomish river a piece of silver salmon and apiece of hump-backed salmon into the stream, and this is the reason, they say, why these two kinds of salmon ascend only these two of all the streams in the region. She then went on until she reached the Nisqually; but that place was also too small; so she moved on, dropping a piece of silver salmon into the river, and hence, they say, that kind of salmon ascend only that stream in that region. When she reached the place where Mount Tacoma now is she found room and settled down. About that time a mythological being called Do-kwi-balth, the changer, came along and on account of their quarrels changed them all into mountains. The name of the man, Dos-wail-opsh, [29] has been perpetuated in the name of the mountain and river there.

Du-hlaylip, the aboriginal name of the region around Clifton, in Mason county, means "the head of the bay". Another pronunciation or corruption of the same word is *Tu-la-lip*, the name of a place in Snohomish county.

Duk-a-boos, the name of a river in Jefferson county, is corrupted from the Indian name *do-hi-a-boos*, and means "a reddish face", because the bluff or mountain near that place has a reddish face or appearance.

Duwamish, or *Dwamish*, comes from the name of a tribe of Indians, and signifies "the people living on the river", the same as Skokomish and Stilaguamish, but in a different language.

Elhwa is said to mean "elk".

Hama-hama is a corruption of the Twana word *Du-hub-hub-bai*, and the place was so called by the Indians because a certain small rush, called *hub-hub*, abounded there.

Kalama is believed to be simply a corruption of calamet, "stone". See *Cathlamet.*

Kit-sap is derived from the name of a chief. The Indians, however, in pronouncing the word accent the last syllable very strongly, and pronounce the first syllable as if the *i* were omitted — thus: *Kt-sap'.* In this case the name is said to mean "brave", as the chief was a brave warrior.

Klasset — see Makah.

Kumtux, Whitman county, is a Chinook jargon word, meaning to know or understand. The Nootka word is *kommetak*, the Clayoquot word *kemitak*, and the Tokwaht word *kumituks*.

La Camas is the Chinook jargon name for an esculent root. It comes from the French *la* and the Nootka word *chamass*, which Jewett says means "fruit, sweet, pleasant to taste".

---

[32] Spelt *–hu* as here Eells attempts the $-x^w$ suffix.

La-push is a Chinook jargon word, meaning "mouth", as the town of that name is at the mouth of the Quilleyute river. It originates in the French *la-boos* ~ 'mouth'.

Lilliwaup, the name of a place, creek, and falls, is from the Twana word *lil-la-wop*, and is said on Twana authority to mean "inlet", because of the small bay there. The "West Shore" several years ago gave "falling water" as the meaning; on what authority I do not know, nor have I been able to verify it among the Indians. [30]

Makah ~ *Mak-kah*, a tribe in Clallam county, signifies "the people who live on a point of land projecting into the sea", or "the cape people". This tribe lives at Cape Flattery, the farthest point in the northwestern part of the State; also called *Klasset*, which bears the same meaning in another language.

Neah, the name of a Makah chief, *Dee-ah*. The Clallams on the east pronounce it *Neah*, as theirs is a nasal language.

Okanogan, spelled *Oakinacken* by Alexander Ross, *Okinaken* by G Franchére, *Oakinagan* by W Irving, and *Okinakane* by ?Dr George Gibbs,[33] the name of a county, signifying "rendezvous". It was given to the head of the Okanogan river, where it takes its source in the lake of the same name. It is here that Indians from various parts of the State and British America often met for their annual potlatch, and to lay in their supply of fish and game.

Osooyos is from the Calispel word *sooyos*, and signifies "a narrow place" or "the narrows". When it came to naming the lake, an Irishman who was present suggested that *O* be prefixed in honor of his native country, which was done.

Pataha is a Nez Perce word, meaning "brush creek", from *paton*, "brush", because formerly the brushes were very thick on it.

Quil-ceed is a Twana name, from *quil-ceed-o-bish*, the name of the band of the Twanas who lived on Quil-ceed bay. It means "salt-water people", in distinction from the *S-kaw-kaw-bish*, or "fresh-water people", another band of the same tribe.

Seattle was the name of an Indian chief of the Duwamish tribe, who was very friendly to the whites.

Se-quim ~ *Seguin*, is a corruption of the Clallam name for the place, which is *Such-e-kwai-ing*.

Siwash is the Chinook jargon word for "Indian", and is a corruption of the French word "sauvage".

Skokomish is a corruption of the Twana word *S-kaw-kaw-bish*, pronounced *S-kaw-kaw-mish* by the Clallam Indians, and was the name of a band of the Twana who lived about the mouth of the Skokomish river. It means "river people" – from *kaw*, "fresh water" — as the river mentioned is the largest that flows into the canal. The termination *mish* or *bish*, very common on the Sound, means "people", the Skokomish word for people being *klo-wal-bish* and that of the Lower Chehalis being *a-lah-mish*. See *Duwamish*.

Skookitm Chuck is a Chinook jargon term, meaning "strong or swift water", and was applied to the stream which bears its name, [31] because of its swiftness. The word *skookum* comes originally from the Chehalis word *sku-kum*, strong; and *chuck* comes from the word *tl-tsuk*, in the old Chinook language, which meant "water". In the Nootka language the

---

[33] Gibbs was a lawyer not an MD, as wrongly indicated on the title page of the Smithsonian report assembled by Dall, so this had to be the source used by Eells.

word is *chauk*, and in the Clatsop language it is *tl-chukw*. The name Skookum has the same origin, and was applied to the bay because the tides rush through it with great swiftness.

Snohomish, the name of a city and county, is also the name of an Indian tribe and a style of union among them.

Snoqualmie is "not of much account, but they were strong Indians", so MB Hallam, an intelligent Snohomish Indian informed the present writer. A recent newspaper article gives its meaning to be "plenty of waters".

Sooyoos — see Osooyos.

Spokane has some reference to the sun. Ross Cox says that in 1812 he met there the head chief of the Spokane tribe, whose name was *Il-lim-spokanee*, which he says means "Son of the Sun". *Il-li-ini-hum*, however, in that language, means "chief", while *skok-ult* means "son". *Illim* is evidently a contraction of *illimihmn*, and I think that the name, as given by Ross Cox, means "chief of the sun people," not probably the name of the chief, but his title.

Squakson [Squaxin] is derived from the Squakson word *Du-skwak-sin*, the name of a creek at North Bay, meaning "silent" or "alone," because it was the only stream of any importance in that region. When .the treaty was made with the Squakson Indians an island was selected as their reservation, which was some distance from the creek, and as the name of the band or tribe was *Skwaks-namish*, the name has been transferred to that island, but originally it referred to the region near North bay.

Steilacoom is a corruption of the name of the Indian chief *Tail-a-Itoom*.

Stillaguamish (more properly *Stil-a-qua-mish*), like Skokomish, means "river people". See *Duwamish*.

Tacoma — The origin and meaning of this word is as yet unsettled, and considerable discussion has been had in regard to it. A very intelligent Puyallup Indian, whose reservation is near the foot of the mountain, told me that it means "the mountain", being pronounced by his people *Ta-ko-ba*, but that this was not the name by which the Indians originally called it, as their name was *Tu-wak^{hu}* or *Twa-hwauk*. Mr GW Travers, in his "Tacoma and Vicinity", [32] gives the meaning as "near to heaven", on what authority I do not know. To me this definition seems very doubtful, as the Indian idea of the land of happy spirits, before the coming of the whites, was not above the world, in the heavens, but below, in the earth. Mr PB Van Trump, of Yelm, says:

The first Indian I heard pronounce the name of the mountain was old Sluiskin, who guided General Stevens and myself to the snow-line, where we made the first ascent to the summit in 1870. Sluiskin's pronunciation, as near as I can represent it by letters, was *Tah-ho-mah*, and in his rendering of it there was, besides its music, an accent of awe and reverence, for Sluiskin was very imaginative and superstitious about Tahoma, believing that its hoary summit was the abode of a powerful spirit, who was the author of its eruptions and avalanches and who would visit dire vengeance on any mortal who would dare to invade (if that were possible) his dread abode. When Stevens and I were encamped at the foot of the snow-line we would often be awakened by the thunder of falling rocks or the deep thud of some avalanche. At such times Sluiskin would start from his blanket and repeal a dismal dirge-like song as though he would appease the mountain spirit. Mishell Henry, another old Indian guide to the two-named mountain, prides himself in giving its true name and its correct pronunciation. He has several times drilled me in pronouncing it, always smiling gravely and dignifiedly at my ineffectual attempts to give his deep chest notes. Henry was the first to mark out the present route to the snow-line, by which the tourist can now reach the snow-line and even ascend it for two miles without leaving the saddle. He guided our party (the Bayley party) in 1883, and himself ascended to the 8,000-foot level. Beyond that nothing could tempt him, for beyond (in his view) lay danger, folly, rashness; for even Henry, who is intelligent and much more of a philosopher than the rest of his tribe (*Khikatals* {Klickitats?}), associates the sublime summit of Tahoma with awe, danger, and mystery. Your correspondent gives the meaning of "*Tacoma*" as "the mountain", an interesting interpretation, considering the pre-eminence and grandeur of this noble peak. I have questioned the Indians as to their meaning for the word *Tah-ho-mah*. The answer of some showed their ignorance of the meaning. Others, with that reticence and suspicion peculiar to the savage mind, were stoically non-committal. One interpretation I have heard given is "nourishing breasts", the idea presumably being that the eternal snows of the twin summits have given origin to the streams and have occasioned the glacial deposits that have enriched the valleys, thus nourishing and sustaining vegetable life there just as through the ages the maternal breasts have nourished and sustained youthful human life.

Hon HW Scott, the editor of the Oregonian, who lived on Puget Sound from 1854 to 1857, says that he knew hundreds of the [33] Indians intimately and learned much of their language, yet he never in those days heard *Tacoma* or *Tahoma* spoken either by Indians or white persons, had never met any one who had any knowledge of the name until after Theodore Winthrop's book, "The Canoe and the Saddle", appeared, in 1862, and he is certain that the name was invented by Mr Winthrop {see footnote}, and, being a euphonious and delightful name, is a credit to his genius. I cannot agree with Mr Scott as to its origin, but believe it to be of Indian origin, as among the numerous tribes which live in sight of the great mountain and which speak various languages hundreds of words are used which Mr Scott doubtless never learned or even heard in three years. Mr MW Walker, who has lived much among the Indians on the east side of the Cascade mountains, is confident that the word originated among some of those Indians, probably the *Tahamas*, was originally *Tah-ho-ma*, and means "the gods".

{In 1893 the Tacoma Academy of Sciences published a pamphlet of sixteen octavo pages prepared by Hon J[ames] Wickersham of that city {soon federal judge of Alaska}, of which a second edition was printed the same year, enlarged to thirty-four pages, devoted solely to this name.

In it Colonel BF Shaw, interpreter at the treay of 1854, Commander of the Washington Volunteers in the Indian war of 1854-56, and a member of the State Senate in 1893, says that Tacoma is a Skagit word and means "plenty of food or nourishment", first applied to a "motherly woman" (*tacoma sladah*), then to her breasts as the source of nourishmen and lastly to the snow-capped mountains, from their resemblance to her breasts, whereupon it came rather to mean the "snow-capped mountains".[34] Hon JG Swan, quoting from Dr WT Tolmie, John Flett, Judge Francis Henry, Hon Edwin Eells, and Jacob Kershner agree in the main with the foregoing.

---

[34] In Lushootseed, *takoba* ~ təqʷubəʾ refers to any and all permanently snow-capped mountains, as Dr William Tolmie taught Theodore Winthrop, who introduced it widely in his 1862 *Canoe and Saddle*, made famous when he became the first Union officer killed in the Civil War.

Toma, Tacoma, Takob, and Tacobet are the different pronunciation given by the Puget Sound Indians to the name, and Ta-ho-ma is the Klikitat-Yakima name, which some of those Indians say means "a rumbling noise" < added from page 280 *Indians of Puget Sound ~ The Notebooks of Myron Eells 1985: Chapter XVIII ~ Names 275-287, Meaning of Place Names 277 - 287}.

Ta-hoo-ya, the name of a creek in Mason county, is from two Twana words, *ta*, "that", and *ho-i*, "done", thus meaning "that done", but why it was applied to the stream I cannot learn. One person surmises that something especially notable was done there long ago.

Ta-toosh is a Chinook jargon word, meaning "milk" or "breast". It is originally from the Chippeway word *to-tosh*. Possibly, however, it may be derived from *To-tooch* or *Tu-tutsh*, the Makah name for the Thunder bird, as the *Totoosh* island and light-house are in the Makah country.

Taxsas is a Nez Perce word, signifying "moss-covered rock".

Tee-ka-let, the former name of Port Gamble, in Kitsap county, means "the brightness of the noon-day sun", because the sun at noon shines with peculiar splendor on the sand at Port Gamble bay.

Tshinakain is a Spokane word, meaning "plain of the springs". It is applied to a small valley which is a plain and has a number of springs.

Tu-la-lip means "wide bay with a small mouth", and has been transferred from the bay to the post office and Indian reservation. See *Du-hlaylip*.

Tumwater is a Chinook jargon word, meaning "water-fall". It originated from the English word "water", and "tum" by onomatopoeia, as the water-falls reminded the people of that sound; so *tumtum*, the Chinook jargon word for heart, was given to it, because the noise of the beating of the heart reminded them of those sounds. [34]

Twana is the name of the tribe of Indians who live on Hood's canal, which was composed of three bands, the *Quilceed, Skoko-mish*, and *Duhlaylip*. It is a corruption of the original name *tu-ad hu*, pronounced *tu-an-hu* by the Clallam Indians. It is said by ?Dr George Gibbs to mean "portage", because of the portage between Clifton and North Bay, but I have never been able to verify it among the Indians, though I have inquired many times. Most Twana Indians have been unable to give me any meaning for it, but one says that the original name was *Twa-dak^{hu}* or "hard-language people", because their language is one of the most difficult to learn in the region. This fact is true.

Walla Walla, written *Wolla Wollah* by Lewis and Clarke, is a Nez Perce and Cayuse word, the root of which is *walatsa*, which means "running;" hence "running water". Two meanings of it are given, one being "a small stream running into a large one" – that is, the Walla Walla river emptying into the Columbia; another is "ripple after ripple", "fall after fall". These meanings were given the writer by Mr PB Whitman and Dr WC McKay, who have lived among the Indians most of the time for over forty-five years, and speak the Walla Walla language as fluently as they do the English. The Walla Walla Union, however, of November 29, 1890, says:

There has always been dispute as to the origin and meaning of the name Walla Walla, most people clinging to the idea that it is an Indian term meaning many waters. In a recent number of St Nicholas, Joaquin Miller gives a fresh interpretation of the origin and meaning of Walla

Walla, which is at once probable and beautiful. He says: "The lover of pretty names will easily trace this Walla Walla back to its French settlers' 'Voila! Voila!'

> "No man can look down from the environment of mountains on this sweet valley, with its beautiful city in the center, whose many flashing little rivers run together and make it forever green and glorious to see, without instinctively crying out, Voila! Voila! It is another Damascus, only it is broader of girth and far; far more beautiful".
>
> For our own knowledge and gratification we interviewed a proficient French scholar as to the pronunciation and meaning of "Voila! Voila!" He uttered a sound that was as near like the common pronunciation of Walla Walla as it seemed possible to come without uttering those words, and explained that the French word means "there", and is used as the words "see there", "look there" are used in English, as the means of attracting attention of other persons to something beautiful, attractive, or noticeable, seen for the first time.

I, [35] however, sincerely doubt the French derivation of the name, as Lewis and Clarke, who came in 1805, before the French did, and who were the first whites to cross the continent and enter the Walla Walla country, called the tribe the *Wolla Wollahs*.

Wallula, means the same as *Walla Walla*, but is in the *Walla Walla* language.

Wish-kah is a corruption of the Chehalis name *hwish-kahl*, which means "stinking water".
> {The Wishkah river in these days is shunned by all Indians. Under no considerations can they be persuaded to go further up the stream than the Smith place, three miles from the mouth. Even when crossing from the Quinault or Humptulips country to the Cynooche [Wynoochee], they avoid crossing the Wishkah by going around to the north of its source. Their tradition is that many, many ages ago some great eagle [condor] captured an enormous whale on the sea coast and carried it to the headwaters of the river, and that the whale's decaying body poisoned the entire river, so that a great epidemic came and killed all the Indians living along the stream, and that the waters of the river are dangerous even unto this day. From this tradition the beautiful river has taken its unsavory name, which in the Indian tongue means "stinking waters" {< added from page 278 *Indians of Puget Sound* ~ The Notebooks of Myron Eells 1985: Volume 4, Chapter XVIII ~ Names 275-287, Meaning of Place Names 277-287}

Yellow Hawk, the name of a creek in Walla Walla county, comes from a Cayuse Indian chief whose name was *Petumromusmus*, signifying "yellow hawk or eagle".

The following come from the names of Indian tribes who dwelt in the region, but their meaning I have not been able to learn:

Puyaliup or *Puyallupnamish*, as the Indians called the people living there; Nisqually, from *Squally-o-bish*, Wahkiakum, Skagit, Klikitat, Yakama, Lummi, Samish, Quilleyute, Quinault, from Quinaielt or Qui-dai-elt, and Pa-louse.

Thomas Talbot Waterman
(1885-1936)

Waterman was one of the giants pioneering the ethnography, especially in terms of places and abodes, of the Pacific Coast from Alaska to California. When he died in Honolulu on 6 January 1936, he was eulogized as a "vivid figure" and "great teacher", though his fieldwork, especially his ethno-geography, is what has stood the tests of time. For both Puget Sound and northern California, he carefully plotted place names, described the major ritual localized within that terrain, and traced the distribution of house types and other artifacts of human manufacture.

Born the youngest of ten on 23 April 1885 in Hamilton, Missouri, TTW was the son of John Hayes Waterman, an Episcopal priest, and Catherine Shields Church, of Mississippi. His childhood was spent mostly in California, usually around Fresno. When his older brothers avoided holy orders, Thomas took up this family obligation and graduated from the U of California Berkeley in 1907 with a major in Hebrew. He had taken one course in experimental phonetics with Pliny Earle Goddard, himself a Quaker lay clergyman who switched from being the missionary along the Klamath River to becoming its ethnographer. In time Goddard joined the staff of the American Museum of Natural History in New York, where he became known as a comparative Athapaskanist, and closely collaborated with Gladys Reichard of Barnard College, who was from a Pennsylvania Dutch family.

Waterman went along with Goddard on at least one fieldtrip to record materials from Hupa (California Pacific Athapaskan) and, in short order, resolved to switch from the study of divinity to anthropology. He entered Columbia University to study with Franz Boas in 1909-10, finishing his PhD in 1913 on "explanatory element" in folklore. His was one of three interrelated dissertations probing major themes in Americanist folklore. Another was "test theme" by Robert H Lowie (1908).

His earliest fieldwork was in southern California among Diegeño and other Mission Indians (1908), then he shifted back to the Klamath River in the far north of that state. There he mapped Yurok places and later situated the rites at the Kepel Fish Dam to renew their world. In 1911 his mechanical recording of Northern Paiute speech was a first. Coming to Seattle, he visited throughout the Olympic Peninsula and Puget Sound, using $200 set aside in the summer of 1918 for an ethnographic survey of the state. When such funding ended, with a core group of enthusiastic students, his UW classes plotted the distribution of houses and canoes along the West Coast. His genuine fondness for local Lushootseed elders encouraged them to describe the Shamanic Odyssey to him, resulting in the clearest eyewitness overview of this ceremony. It remained unmatched for almost sixty years. He complemented this description of old beliefs with one on the Shaker Church, which was founded shortly before he was born.

This "brilliant, incisive, colorful teacher, rarely systematic and sometimes erratic, but extraordinarily stimulating" (Kroeber 1937: 527) held a series of jobs. At the University of California, he was Museum Assistant (1907-09), Instructor and Assistant Curator (1910-14), Assistant Professor (1914-18), and Associate Professor (1920-21). He set up foundational courses in anthropology, and, with co-author Alfred Louis Kroeber providing "framework and ballast", published the first textbook, *Source Book in Anthropology*, in 1920, revised 1931.

The most famous event in his life was arriving at the jail cell in 1911 at Oroville, California, to read long lists of native words to a forlorn man who had just materialized outside of town. He was *Ishi*, the last Yahi, and Waterman narrowed his choices to local languages until eventually they were able to achieve recognition of the Yana word *siwini* for "yellow pine" by tapping the pine frame of the cot they were sitting on in the local jail. Thus begin the long process of communicating with this thoroughly native man who took up residence in the Anthropology Museum at San Francisco (before it moved to Berkeley) until he died of TB in 1916 (T Kroeber 1961).

At the University of Washington, TTW was Associate Professor (1918-20) when he produced the draft study of the western Washington native place names that has never been equaled, and, now, never can be. His study of Makah whaling equipment has suddenly become extremely relevant again.

His interest in ethno-geography resulted in the published Yurok study, along with unpublished, but equally detailed, studies of Puget Sound along with the Straits of Juan de Fuca, and of southeast Alaska Tlingit.

In a manuscript he finished in 1921 about the artifacts he collected around the Sound, Waterman (1973: x) acknowledged the "reputable people" who had already collected in Puget Sound, such as "Lewis and Clark, Wilkes, Boas, Culin, [George] Dorsey, Tozier, and (more recently) Haeberlin". He noted that the Tozier materials had once been on display in Seattle but then were sold and moved to Heye Foundation in New York, the parent of today's National Museum of the American Indian in DC.

Letters in the Bancroft Library of the University of California at Berkeley reveal his life long, bemused outlook on life. Writing from Fresno, 30 Dec 1908, he warned, "a urinary analysis always shows up albumen on me", suggesting health problems limiting career choices. On 29 Sept 1909, he wrote from his graduate studies at Columbia University in New York City. Back at Berkeley, 18 June 1915, he was aware of the small academic world of jobs, noting "One of Merriam's men was ready to bite, but now he is offered an instructorship at the U of Washington".

The arrival of Ishi was not reported, but the aftermath is. Because Edward Sapir had worked on Yana, he was anxious to work with Ishi and so came from Ottawa to spend the summer at Berkeley. On 2 July 1915, "Sapir landed here with ten dollars in Canadian money and needed $150 at once". Kroeber was gone, and both Waterman and Edward Gifford were poor, so it became a "real circus" to scrounge up the money. By 7 November 1915, he was reporting details of Ishi's declining health, and, by year end, 23 December, "I am still anxious to fly away from Berkeley".

The new year began with a most improbably proposal from John Peabody Harrington, the brilliant but unsocialized linguist of the Bureau of American Ethnology whose life of single minded (paranoid, compulsive) research has been traced by his ex-wife of 1916-22, Carobeth Laird (1975), who then married George Laird, a Cherokee living among the Chemehuevi. Harrington wrote to Berkeley to claim the southern two-thirds of California for his own research. Letters of 13/21 January 1916 explain that Harrington was willing to exchange his notes on native Californian moieties (mutually sustaining halves of these societies, often named Buzzard/Coyote) in return for J Alden Mason leaving off fieldwork among Salinans. The consensus (23 January) was that Harrington, trained only as a linguist, knew nothing of moieties and so would not have useful materials. A telegram on the 24th ordered Kroeber to write Gifford immediately to compose a 16 page paper on the Tachi so that his work would not be scooped by Harrington.

All this tempestuous wrangling over fieldwork and data led Waterman to muse, I February 1916, "I consider myself a hell of a fine teacher if that counts for anything. I will shine in the reflected light of the investigators I am training up, like [?] Outhwaite, [Will Carleton] McKern, and [Malcolm] Rogers".

Sadly, he reported the death and cremation of Ishi in a letter of 31 March 1916. Against the will of Kroeber and all other anthropologists involved with Ishi, an autopsy had been done, and his brain removed, only to be located and repatriated eighty years later from DC.

On 26 June 1917, he wrote that he was in the army and sending his wife to drafting classes so she could support their family if he is killed or "dies of boredom".

Waterman married twice. In 1910, to Grace Goodwin, and their children were Helen Maria in 1913 and TT, Jr in 1916. In 1927, he married Ruth Dulaney. In a 25 August 1994 tape recording,[35] Helen recalled the family's trek to Seattle.

Actually when they left Berkeley, we had an old model T Ford and we drove up what is now the … the Redwood Highway up through redwood country and up to Portland, then went into the middle of the Warm Springs Indian Reservation in Oregon, stayed there several times … weeks. He was employed by the Gustav Heye museum, and was buying artifacts from the Indians. [But he did not get an impressive leather outfit because the old man intended to be buried in it.] Then we came on to … Seattle, stayed there for about 2 years, then went back to Berkeley, then went to NYC where he was working I think at the Heye Museum, and it was at that point when my parents separated…. My father … had gotten a position in Guatemala as the curator of state archaeological museum and he had taken my brother with him to Guatemala City. They lived in a boarding house. My brother got sick with dysentery, so mother and I left NYC by boat to Guatemala picked up my brother, went over to the Pacific coast, and took a boat back up to California – Berkeley, Oakland – until I moved up to Seattle in 1958. [On weekends the whole family would camp on a beach at Suquamish] I can remember that my father would go off in an Indian canoe with Indians and perhaps one or two of his anthropology students from the university. I now know he was making studies of languages, place names, and so on.

In 1918, TTW wrote from Seattle he was teaching Evolution of Culture 70 and American Indians 18. More ominously, 23 September 1919, reporting that UW is "busted and insolvent", he added "I can get along here cordially with the business offices, but I have a bad time with the 'scholars'." Indeed, his critical comments, in his own native place names study, on Edmond Meany's work about Washington place names indicates the level of ignorance he was up against. Still his teaching carried him through, with 400 in his Introduction to Sociology class as of 11 October 1919. Still unsettled, 3 November, he pleaded "When you go east, look around for a job for me, will you. I can't go myself, they've withdrawn the allowance for research". Unable to go into the field, he turned his classes into research outlets, reporting 14 November, "I've got a group working on Indian Houses".

Among these students was Geraldine Coffin Guy, who co-authored the study of canoes with Waterman. Near year end, 10 December, he sought a familiar source of funds and outlet for research, "I'm writing Heye to see if he wants some Puget Sound Baskets, canoe-bailers, etc" setting the stage for his manuscript on local artifacts, eventually published in 1973, and a job at the Heye Foundation, Museum of the American Indian in New York.

Among the manuscripts he left behind at Berkeley are Puget Sound Marriages and Geneologies (20 pp, # 100), Puget Geography (260 pp, #106), Geographical Ideas (22pp, #108),

---

[35] Audio tape OH 173 at Bainbridge Island Historical Society, Winslow.

Eskimo and Puget (#110), and the mythology he coauthored with Arthur C Ballard (72pp, #107). The Bancroft also holds the manuscript by Erna Gunther (311pp, #) on Culture Element Distribution: Puget Sound (Duwamish, Skokomish, Klallam, Makah). Not a typical distribution for the Sound, by any means, though the key Duwamish entries came from Julia Siddle.

After 1921, he became "restless", shifting to the Heye Museum of the American Indian, and then the Bureau of American Ethnology. In the same BAE volume publishing the posthumous work of Haeberlin and Teit on Salish basketry, finished by Helen Roberts, the Administrative Report for 1922 (BAE AR 1928: 63, 73) lists Dr TT Waterman as temporary ethnologist from March 1 when he was sent to Alaska "to scrutinize certain native towns in southeastern Alaska. He collected data on totemic monuments and hundreds of place names before he returned on 15 June. On July 1, he was detached for six weeks to lecture in the Columbia University summer school.

Next he became technical director of the National Museum of Guatemala, and then, until 1927, taught at Fresno State College, where he offered geology, geography, and anthropology. Under appreciated is his summarizing, drafting, and publishing (1929) of the series of time periods known as the Pecos Classification setting the chronology for the Puebloan Southwest at a 1927 conference at the ruin of Pecos, New Mexico.

He moved on to the University of Arizona for a year, then to Honolulu to teach at the Territorial Normal College and the University of Hawaii, shifted to newspaper and public relations writing, and, months before he died, became Territorial Archivist.

Since his Tlingit place name study remained at the BAE in DC, and he began moving about, he sold his Puget Sound Place Names manuscript for $400 to the BAE, as mentioned in his letter of 21 March 1929 (below).

That the Puget Sound geography remained unpublished in manuscript seems to be due to a parting shot, honest but ill-advised, he gave his nemesis at UW, Edmond Meany, a local legend of state boosterism and self professed authority on Washington place names and history. In their feud over the reputation of first Governor Isaac Stevens and local history, pioneer Ezra Meeker often left the Y off his last name.

AN ESSAY ON GEOGRAPHICAL NAMES
IN THE STATE OF WASHINGTON
American Anthropologist 24 (4): 481-3
1922 by T T Waterman

The derivation and meaning of geographical names of Indian origin is always a matter of interest. An essay dealing among other things with Indian names, by Edmond S Meany, is now being printed in installments in a publication known as the Washington Historical Quarterly, issued, according to the title page, by "The Washington University State Historical Society". Acquaintance with the region in which this publication appears indicates that "Washington University" means in this case the University of Washington. The essay began with volume 8 of this quarterly (1917), and with the issue of January of 1922 extends as far as the letter S.

Every effort to account for the origin and history of geographic names is a move in the right direction and is to be received with due thanksgiving. This is especially the case in the Northwest, which is [p482] an extremely interesting region; and is more especially the case where names go back to Indian expressions. Our author is therefore to be applauded for his effort.

There is, however, no great amount of care or scholarship evident in any part of his work.[36] The essay is somewhat unsystematic, rather diffuse, decidedly anecdotal, and tiresomely sentimental. The author exercises himself with a mass of letters and books, to find explanations for the occurrence of certain geographical names. In this process he makes many slips and blunders – blunders both of fact and in presentation. No great amount of confidence can be inspired in the reader by such a work.

A few examples may not be amiss. The French expression Nez Perce is said by our author to be "an Idaho Indian term". The Welsh name Bryn Mawr is said to be "Scotch". The Spanish expression Sierra Madre becomes Sierra Madras. The Spanish word *orilla* is said to mean a "lesser bank". These slips occur in connection with the easiest part of the author's task. The effort to give an account of items running back to a native Indian origin is a rather more difficult matter. As would be expected from what has just been said, on such points the essay becomes totally unreliable. The errors existing in the literature prior to Meany's essay are faithfully reproduced, I think without missing one; and numerous others are added through misquoting the older authorities and through quoting half-informed and careless correspondents. The principal weakness in this part of the work lies in the fact that the author has made inquiries of Tom, Dick, and Harry, concerning the meaning of Indian names, but has never, curiously enough, consulted a single Indian. This helplessness and lack of enterprise is hard to understand.

The most instructive part of the work is the account which the author gives of numerous silly and trivial considerations which lie back of our present-day geographical names. Thus the name Ralston was given to a place by the following process. A certain railroad official, during the survey of the road, was sitting in a cook house selecting names for what were to be the future stations. Having run out of ideas, his eye suddenly lighted upon a package of breakfast-food standing on a shelf; so he promptly put down the name of the next station as Ralston. The name thus inflicted on the site may very likely remain there for a thousand years and be an offense to all thinking men for every moment of that time. Meany's [p483] account of this incident conforms exactly to what was recounted to the present writer by the hero of the occasion himself.

The geographical names published by Meany are thus a quaint and curious medley of words from the most unexpected languages, and from the most incongruous sources.

We ought, I think, to feel grateful for this essay, which represents at least a beginning. If properly revised and edited by some competent person, it would be an important contribution to our knowledge of this interesting region.

As a consequence, Meany scuttled any plans for the University of Washington to publish Waterman's work, after TT had founded an anthropology publication series that began with his own study of Makah whaling equipment. Later faculty such as Erna Gunther, Melville Jacobs,

---

[36] Meany actually sent printed fill-in-the-blanks questionnaires to interested locals, hence these less than rigorous folksy responses. These thick files are not among Meany's papers but in those of his successor in place name research, Robert Hitchman, who was more thorough and knew to consult Arthur Ballard on native terms.

and Verne Ray, students such as Ronald Olson, and devoted amateurs like Arthur Ballard published classics in this series, now available on line since no copyrights were ever claimed.

Gerry Guy, the former Geraldine Coffin coauthoring with TT, graduated, married newspaperman Dean Guy, and lived her life in Yakima. There, in the 1930s, she was host to Christine Quintasket, a Colville woman who had written a novel and an autobiography under the pen name of Mourning Dove. Jay Miller visited with her and she gave him the Mourning Dove manuscript, eventually editing it for publication in 1990.

In addition to the manuscript, Mrs Guy also gave him two letters that Waterman had written to her. She recalled him very fondly, often quoting the worst criticism he could give the work of another anthropologist, "His work reads like a hardware catalog". His letters are included because they convey a wonderful sense of the man, reflecting on his life at Washington years decade later.

Writing from State Teachers and Junior College in Fresno California on 18 January 1926, he says

Happy New Year to you. I am in the last stages, but seem to be coming out of my dreams + showing symptoms of getting back to normalcy.

Herewith a treatise on the Phonetic Transcription of Indian Languges by Kroeber, Boas, Goddard + Sapir. It was performed by these intellectual heavyweights, but is quite idiotic. I hope it helps you. Write me about your difficulties.

The vowels ought to be arranged like this

{beside a diagram arranging these phonemes inside a mouth}
machine, pin /
fate, pet fool, full /
that / back
front father ought /

Back vowel occurs in two forms, open + closed (the dropped for the "open" sounds. The letters are put in the position in the diagram where they are produced.

Yours, hastily but with fond remembrance
+ warm regards TTW

Send pamphlet back when you are through, will you ??

Without letterhead on 21 March 1929, he wrote

Answering the last remark in your letter first, it's NEVER safe to mention marriage. You know the wise crack

If you want to stay slender reach for a Lucky instead of a sweet.

Here's another one
If you want to stay single, reach for a Lucky instead of a sweetie.

I wish to God I could go out go out digging roots with you and the other Yakimas. A fellow wrote me a letter from Denver about basket designs. Such things make me positively hurt. Why the devil didn't I do some of this work when there was a chance. There were four hundred million place names around Puget Sound, also, that you and I and Ruth Greiner should have gotten. The Government paid me four hundred dollars for the manuscript, but it wasn't {wanst} complete.

I had some fun in the Southwest. A paper by your little friend will be in an early issue of the Anthropologist, on the sequence of cultures here. Clever, if I do say it. Your dear friend Leslie Spier (may the devil fly off with him) is full professor at the University of Oklahoma.

A former student of mine is Chief of the Bureau of Ethnology, Matt Sterling. I was in northern California last summer, and got some more material on Yurok, to complete some notes I got in 1909. I am writing the paper up now, except that I am writing to you instead. Is Margaret single still? If married, is she married to an Indian or a white? I sure was glad to see a snap of Hazel Jones. God. Those were the days.

I'll have to send you some snaps of myself and this house. It's a Japanese house on the hill side. Gosh, what a view. This [page 2] island is all the books say it is, and then some. Honest, it's the cat's. If you will promise to come over and visit, we will promise to stay over a week extra, or even more, and receive you.

I wish you would write to me from time to time. I put in too much energy, I guess, and get depressed from time to time. Also, I'm a bit lonesome, wife et al to the contrary notwithstanding. If you will get rid of your husband even temporarily I will come over and put my head in your lap and die. Then you can tie a knot in a string record. I would like to feel that I left a mark somewhere. Keep after that string record stuff. You can get it. All so far collected are barren of the stories.

Also I wrote up a good little collection of Puget Sound tales (a la Dean's labors), with a map, lost the map, found the map, and lost the text. It's still lost. Damn. Who John Collier is I don't know, but if he admires me, he ought to be preserved in alcohol. Maybe he was preserved in alcohol when he expressed the admiration.

Well, this is all right, but that manuscript is calling me. Be good, keep after the roots, get some photographs of anything Indians are doing (but get some good ones, five by seven). The new invention called the Justaphot, price ten dollars, will enable you to get perfect negatives. If your dealer hasn't got it, send for one. If necessary, charge it to me. It's absolutely the cat's whiskers for time and diaphragm. It is I tell you this.

God bless you and regards

TTW

In particular, driven by a "passion for flaming clarity … he loved concrete facts and sharply defined findings, both presented with the same clean-cut picturesqueness which characterized him on the lecture platform and in intimate conversation" (Kroeber 1937: 528).

Thomas Talbot Waterman's Publications and Drafts

1908 Diegeño Identification of Color with the Cardinal Points. *Journal of American Folklore* 21.

1909 Analysis of the Mission Indian Creation Story. *American Anthropologist* 11.

1910 Religious Practices of the Diegeno Indians. *University of California Publications in American Archaeology and Ethnology* 8.

1910 Collections from the Hudson Bay Eskimo. American Museum of Natural History, *Anthropological Papers* 4.

1911 The Phonetic Elements of the Northern Paiute Language. *University of California Publications in American Archaeology and Ethnology* 10.

1914 Explanatory Element in the Folk-tales of the North American Indian. *Journal of American Folklore* 27.

1916 The Delineation of the Day-Signs in the Aztec Manuscripts. *University of California Publications in American Archaeology and Ethnology* 11.

1917 Evolution of the Chin. *American Naturalist* 50.

1917 Bandelier's Contribution to the Study of Ancient Mexican Social Organization. *University of California Publications in American Archaeology and Ethnology* 12.

1917 The Yana Indians. *University of California Publications in American Archaeology and Ethnology* 13.

1920 Yurok Geography. *University of California Publications in American Archaeology and Ethnology* 16 (5): 177-314. [Transmitted 21 June 1918].

1920 Whaling Equipment of the Makah Indians. *University of Washington Publications in Anthropology* 1.

1922 The Geographical Names Used by the Indians of the Pacific Coast. *The Geographical Review* 12 (2): 175-194.

1922 MS Tlingit Geographical Names for Extreme Southeast Alaska. With Historical and Other Notes. National Anthropological Archives, Bureau of American Ethnology Ms 2938. 66pp.

1923 Conundrums in Northwest Coast Art. *American Anthropologist* 25.

1923 Yurok Affixes. *University of California Publications in American Archaeology and Ethnology* 20.

1924 Houses of the Alaskan Eskimos. *American Anthropologist* 26.

1924 The Subdivisions of the Human Race and their Distribution. *American Anthropologist* 26.

1924 The Shake Religion of Puget Sound. *Smithsonian Institution, Annual Report* for 1922, 499-507.

1924 North American Indian Dwellings. *Geographical Review* 14.

1925 North American Indian Dwellings. *Smithsonian Institution, Annual Report* for 1924, 461-85.

1925 American Indian Poetry. *American Anthropologist* 27 [with EL Walton].

1925 Village Sites in Tolowa and Neighboring Areas of Northwestern California. *American Anthropologist* 27.

1925 The Feathered Snake of the Winds. *Art and Archaeology* 20.

1927 The Architecture of the American Indian. *American Anthropologist* 29.

1929 Culture Horizons in the Southwest. *American Anthropologist* 31.

1930 The Paraphernalia of the Duwamish "Spirit Canoe" Ceremony. New York: *Indian Notes and Monographs, Museum of the American Indian* 7.

1930 Ornamental Designs in Southwestern Pottery. New York: *Indian Notes and Monographs, Museum of the American Indian* 8.

1973 Notes on the Ethnology of the Indians of Puget Sound. New York: *Indian Notes and Monographs*, Miscellaneous Series 59. [1921].

Thomas Talbot Waterman and Geraldine Coffin

1920 Types of Canoes on Puget Sound. New York: *Indian Notes and Monographs, Museum of the American Indian* ?.

Thomas Talbot Waterman and Ruth Greiner

1921 Indian Houses of Puget Sound. New York: *Indian Notes and Monographs, Museum of the American Indian* ?.

Thomas Talbot Waterman and others

1921 Native Houses of Western North America. New York: *Indian Notes and Monographs, Museum of the American Indian* ?.

Thomas Talbot Waterman and Alfred L Kroeber

1920 *Source Book in Anthropology.* University of California Syllabus Series 118.

1931 *Source Book in Anthropology.* Trade Book.

1934 Yurok Marriages. *University of California Publications in American Archaeology and Ethnology* 35.

1938 The Kepel Fish Dam. *University of California Publications in American Archaeology and Ethnology* 35 (6): 49-80.

Ms 1935 The Sons of Ham

Ms 1935 Side-lights on the American Indian

Other Sources

Franz Boas, Pliny Earle Goddard, Edward Sapir, and Alfred L Kroeber

1916   Phonetic Transcription of Indian Languages: Report of Committee of the American Anthropological Association. Washington, DC: Smithsonian Miscellaneous Collections 66 (5).

George Herzog, Stanley S Newman, Edward Sapir, Mary Haas Swadesh, Morris Swadesh, and Charles F Voegelin

1934   Some Orthographic Recommendations; Arising Out of Discussions by a Group of Six Americanist Linguists. *American Anthropologist* 36 (4): 629-631.

Carobeth Laird

1975   *Encounter with an Angry God.*   Banning, Ca: Morongo Indian Reservation, Malki Museum Press.

Robert Lowie

1908 The Test-Theme in North American Mythology. *Journal of American Folklore* XXI (81): 98-148.

Alfred L Kroeber

1937 Thomas Talbot Waterman. *American Anthropologist* 39: 527-29.

Theodora Kroeber

1961 *Ishi in Two Worlds*. Berkeley: University of California Press.

Seattle Vicinity

Names along the shores of the Sound (Map A??)

1 Tet³a'iyEb "bullheads", a kind of fish with a large head, eaten in times of scarcity, for a slight projection in the coast line north of the town of Edmonds. A much smaller fish the sculpin (sxwEdi <stəqʷu' = bullhead>) is also called bullhead locally, but this place takes its name from the bullhead proper. <?? = ??>

2 S'baL "a person undergoing the ministrations of a shaman, a patient", for a small creek just north of Edmonds. <sbał = shamanizing>

3 Stuᵘbus Edwards point, the promontory south of Edmonds. <stubus = man face>

4 IᵘtL³EtL stu'bus "this side of stubus", Wells point, sand promontory just south of the preceding. A pair of nearby promontories not infrequently have one name, modified in this way. <'əƛ̓əƛ̓stubus = like a man coming>

5 Q³e'q³ewa:dEt "kinnickinik, Indian tobacco", a vine with leaves like those of the huckleberry, for a beach south of Richmond Beach. This plant has red berries called Sq³e'wald. <k'ayu'k'ayu = kinikinnick plant>

6 Qaa'dEb a small creek. <kaadeb = has mouth open>

7 Xwe'E'xwEdziᵘls "rocks sharp on the edge", for high bluffs south of Spring Beach composed of sharp cliffs. <xʷəxʷədᶻilc = sharp edge rock>

8 Tca'lkwad1 Bitter lake, southeast of Spring beach. <?? = ??>

9 S1sa'LtEb a small pond southeast of the preceding. <?? = ??>

10 Qwa'tEb Piper creek, the first creek north of the city of Seattle. <kʷaatəb = leave it alone>

11 Qe'¹LᴱbEd (suggests qe'lb1d "canoes"), Meadow point, a sandy promontory north of Ballard township. <qəlbid = discard>

12 Tci'dkedad "lying curled on a pillow", for a small curved promontory in Ballard, just at the entrance of Salmon bay, referring to the shape of the sand spit, which is curled around on itself and used to be a fine place to dig clams. <?? = ??>

12a C1lco!lutsid "mouth of cilco'1 Salmon bay" (below). <šilšulicid = Shilshole mouth>

13 C1lco'1 "threading a bead or something", Salmon Bay (See list of villages). <šilšul = threading>

14 B1t¹da'kt "a kind of supernatural power", for a very small creek entering the north side of Salmon bay, above the Fremont bridge, occupied by the "power" which enabled one to go to the underworld to regain a guardian spirit. Shamans formerly held their dances at this creek. <bətətdaq = Redeeming Rite>

15 Qw³ula'stab "a small bush with white flowers and black berries", an even smaller creek than the above #14 entering the same tiny inlet. Not the dogwood, as might seem likely, but some other plant. <?? = ??>

16 Hwiwa'iqᵘ (said to mean "large, having lots of wate", for a creek draining down a straight gully into the south side of Salmon bay from the neighborhood of Fort Lawton. (hikʷ = big) <?? = ??>

17   Pka'dzEl "thrust far out" (stem PaLkt, "to thrust ahead, to push one's way through the bush"), West point, a promontory ending in an elongated sand spit just north of Seattle harbor or Elliott Bay. Name is also used of leaves "pushing out" in the spring, and refers to the way in which the point seems to thrust itself forward into the Sound. ??I also obtained this term in the form Pka'dzELtsu. [Dates from this archaeological site confirm its long use.] <?? = ??>

18   LE'plEpL Fourmile rock, a great boulder standing in the water at the foot of Magnolia bluff, also recorded in the forms La'pub and TcE'tla <čəƛə'>, which is sometimes used to mean simply "rock, boulder". A myth recounts that an ancient hero named Sta'kub could take a gigantic drag net, made of cedar and hazel branches, and throw it over this rock while standing on the distant beach. <?? = ??>

19   TLo'xwatL-qo "land otter water", for a small creek draining down a gully, now occupied by a paved road from Ft Lawton, flowing only in wet weather. <?? = ??>

20   Silaawotsid (said to mean "talking"), for mouth of the creek draining into Smith Cove. <s'ilqucid = water edge mouth, talking>

21   T^{3}E'kEp "aerial net for snaring ducks", for a creek formerly entering the Sound south of Smith Cove. Ducks "started up" on Lake Union always flew over the low place between Queen Anne hill and the business district of Seattle, so duck snares were accordingly set at this camping place. <təqəp = aerial duck net>

22   Baba'kwo "prairie", an open space or series of spaces in the forest which formerly grew over the north side of what is now the business district of Seattle. The earliest white settlement at this point was called Belltown, just north of the present water front with its wharves. <babak^{w}ab = prairies>

23   Djidjilal^{3}1tc "a little place where one crosses over, portages" (See village list). [This is the source for the native name for the later City of Seattle.] <d^{z}id^{z}əlalič = little portage>

24   ^{Tux}pa'ctEb little "spit" or beach at the edge of the easternmost of the mouths of the Duwamish river. <dex^{w}pačəb = place for setting out items>

25   Tata^{3}lks small promontory on an island, said to have been used as a lookout point by the Indians, who built a stockade there. <tətal<u>x</u>qs = little strong point>

26   Slu'wiL (slu applied, for example, to the holes bored to test the thickness of a canoe hull, literally "for a canoe perforation") for slough passing to the south of the above, referring to a grassy marsh intersected with channels, into and through which canoes can be pushed as a "short cut". <slu'wił = short cut>

27   XwEq^3 "slough", for largest of the branches into which the Duwamish river divides at its mouth. <?? = ??>

28   Q'ulq'ula'di "shaggy, tangled", masking the shore so no one could land on the west shore of the above slough. <qəlqəladi' = shag>

29   Ts^{3}E'kas "muddy", Harbor island, a flat surrounded by watercourses and rather marshy. An old ~~informant~~, George Si'towaL, lived in a float house here with his ancient wife until they starved to death in the year 1920 [due to Seattle "development"] <c'əqas = dirty>

29a Ha^{3}a'pus a small creek draining across a flat on the west side of the river. <?? = ??>

30 Tul³a'lt^u "herring house", old village site on the west bank of the Duwamish, at the foot of the bluff of West Seattle. <t'u'əlal'tx^w = herring house> [today's Duwamish official longhouse]

31 Tua'wi "trout", Longfellow creek draining into Young's Cove in West Seattle. <sk^wəspł = trout>

32 ^Cuxu tsE'xud "something to split with", for a trickle of water draining down a little gully near Luna park in West Seattle. <səx^wučəxəd = by means of spilling>

33 SqwEdqs "promontory at the foot of something" (sqwEd "any underpart" + -qs "nose, promontory"), Duwamish head, descriptive of the sand spit, which juts forward from the foot of an abrupt overbeetling headland, once heavily timbered. <sq^wədqs = waterfall point>

34 SbEkwabEqs "prairies" (ba'kwob), Alki Point, named because the flat, sandy promontory jutting out half a mile from the shore line had many open places among the trees. Alki is not Indian, consult Meany [correctly, for jargon "by and by"]. ["Birthplace" of Seattle, landfall of the Denny Party]. <sbaq^wabqs = prairie point>

35 ^Tux qo'tEb at top of the plateau with a former cranberry swamp in a depression a mile or more inland from Duwamish head. <dəx^wqutəb = place of disease>

36 T'EsbEd "a winter house" (t³as "cold"), for a small creek south of Alki Point, untranslated, where there was a brickyard some years ago. <t'əcold weather placesbid = >

37 GwEl "to capsize", for another small creek south of the preceding. <g^wal = capsize>

38 Tc1xha'idus "crowded, tight", Point Williams. [-us = face] <ƛ̓əx̱aydus = crowded face>

39 Psaiya'hus "horned snake", Brace Point, considered the abode of one of these monsters regarded with supernatural dread because they appear as an enormous snake with the antlers and forelegs of a deer. <psayahus = horned snake spirit>

At the base of this promontory is a big, reddish boulder weighing half a ton or more, where it was formerly believed that anyone looking at this boulder would become twisted into a knot. The boulder itself was believed to change its form. Certain people had this boulder for a supernatural helper.

40 ^Tu kwa'sus "scorching the face", for a "bend" south of Brace point with a gravel pit. <dx^wk'^wasus = place of scorched face>

41 Suhu'pt1d (³asob "a pile, head"), for a small flat with a creek. <?? = ??>

42 Kwa'djaladxu "brass" (literally "pale material"), for a small creek south of the preceding near Lake Burien. <?? = ??>

43 Xwe'yEk^w "thunder", Lake Burien. <x^wiq^w(adi') = thunder>

44 Sq³olEb "loading things into a canoe", Three Tree Point (Point Pully), referring to a girl who married a Squally man, but did not like him, so ran away to come back home. The man, dressed in his marmot skin robe, came after her. When he saw her running northward along the beach, he threw his robe on a boulder so as to make more speed. The woman, almost overtaken, looked far up the beach, saw her mother and father loading their effects into a canoe to go away, and called to them to wait. At that moment the transformer turned them all to stone. The "loaded on" canoe itself became this point. The woman became a white rock near Des Moines. The blanket which her husband tossed on the

rock "is still there", seen as the folded, crinkled surface of Blanket rock near Redondo (plate 5). On each side of the promontory, the sand and gravel formerly rattled down. People said a great snake lived inside, shoving the sand down when people disturbed him. <sq'ilab = loading a canoe>

45 Kaka³a'di "where crows live" at a spring on the south side of Three Tree Point. Crow was the slave of the people in the story just recounted. She was getting ready to put aboard a basket of water when the transformation changed it into a small spring, which was always hard to find. It has now *dried up and* ?? <k'a?k''adi' = where crows gather>

46 S1gwa'lit'tcu "a large space, open expanse", for a big bend or bay with a creek below Three Tree Point, where extensive sand flats are exposed at low tide. <shig^walic'a' = large female space>

47. Number not used.

48 XixEda'l³os1d "mat smoother, creaser", for a small creek on the promontory north of Des Moines. <x̲ix̲ədalucid = mat creaser>

49 Tsike'ib swift and cold stream just north of the present town of Des Moines. <cik^wib = jerking place>

50 D1Lko'k branch of the above stream. <?? = ??>

51a Qw³ab "kelp", Bow lake, with a boulder on the beach near Des Moines known as White rock. When the Snake people were going on an expedition to Vashon island, Lizard woman stayed behind and sunned herself on this rock, so, accordingly, lizards are plentiful in this vicinity. <q'^wa'əb = >

52 Baxkwab "prairie", open space in the timber, present Des Moines. <baq^wab = prairie>

53 Tca'gEqks (said to mean "the first one in"), for small creek just south of Des Moines. <čag^wqs = first one toward water>

54 Tca'xgwEs a small creek halfway between Des Moines and Stone's landing. <čəxg^wəs = half way place>

55 Tso'Lkob1d "underground stream" at Redondo, where a subterranean channel in mythic times was used by whales to connect the Sound with Steele lake. A young man made a raft, weighted it with stones, sunk it in the water so it drifted into the sunken outlet, and, with a noise like thunder, blocked it up. Ever since, whales cannot go to Steele lake, and the creek now runs above ground. <cəłq^wu'bid = bleeding water>

55a Biskwa'd1s "where there are whales", Steele's Lake, according to the story just recounted. <bəsq^wədis = place has whales>

56 Qa'qahwEts "crabapples", for a very small creek at Buenna. <qa'qa'x^wac = crabapple trees>

57 Kokowi'ltsa "blanket of marmot skins" (marmot, skoi-skoi = sq^wiq^wəd), Blanket Rock, as recounted for above #44. <?? = ??>

57a Stsoxwa'bats "chokecherry" (locally "Indian peach"), for a stream just west of Blanket rock, named from a low cliff topped with chokecherry trees. <sc'əx̲^wəbac = choke cherry bush>

57b Mi'man Katsax "little Katsax", Dash Point (see 57c). <?? = ??>

57c Katsa'x "a cape", Brown's Point, the headland north of Tacoma, where a woman who constantly uttered improprieties was changed to stone with an open mouth. If anyone puts a stick in this hole and rattles it around, a rainstorm will come. This stone lies today near Jerry Meeker's place. Another name for this locality, or one nearby, is Tcaiya'l-qo "hidden water" <?? = ??>

Names of places around Lake Union and Lake Washington

58 Gwa'xwop "outlet", on Lake Union draining into Salmon bay to supply the [Ballard] locks of the government canal. <?? = ??>

59 Ctc1wa't-qo "place where onie whips the water", for a small creek just east of the railroad bridge in the Ballard district, where people used to hit the water with sticks to drive fish into the narrow brook to be easily captured. <ƛ̕axʷadqʷu' = whip water>

60 Ste'tciL "a prop", for a promontory occupied by the gasworks [park], jutting into Lake Union from its north shore, as though it were leaning against the opposite shore. <?? = ??>

61 Baqwob "prairie" open space near Lake Union at the former north abutment of the Latona bridge in the city of Seattle. <baqʷab = prairie>

62 Waq³e'q³ab ('waq³e'q³ "frog"), for a small creek entering Lake Union just east of the Latona bridge. [frog = waq̇waq̇] <waq'waq'q'ab = like a frog>

63 Sqwitsqs "little promontory" jutting into Lake Union where the boat house of the University Boat Club now stands. <sqʷicqs = downriver point>

64 SLuwi'L "perforation for a canoe", in the marsh [Union Bay] lying between Laurel point and the buildings of the University of Washington, referring to its intersection by channels into which a canoe could be thrust. Ravenna Creek, which enters the bay through this swamp, flows out of Green Lake through a conduit into Ravenna park. A large aboriginal fish trap intended for salmon and made of poles stood in this bay ??. <slu'wił = canoe peg hole ~ canoe thickness gauge>

65 ᴰᵘtLEc Green lake, which furnished quantities of suckers and perch taken in basket traps. <?? = ??>

66 A'did an exclamation translated as "dear me!", for a little cove on the west side of Laurel point, formerly the property of a certain Joe Somers and previous to that set aside as a camping place for Indians. <'adid = gosh sakes>

67 Cebultᵘ "dry", Laurel Point. <šabal'txʷ = dry house>

68 ᵀᵘtsa'xwub "beating," for shore of Lake Washington north of Laurel Point where a fine cliff, overshadowed with heavy timber, overhangs the beach. <dxʷč̓axʷab = place of whipping ~ clubbing>

69 T³lels "minnows, shiners", otherwise called tomcod, on the beach north of the preceding. <?? = ??>

70 BEbqwa'bEks "prairies", for flat, open area, without timber, south of Sand point. <babqʷabqs = prairie point>

71 Tc³aa'Lqo "channel, watercourse" which drains a pond south of Sand point treated in a myth Waterman did not obtain. <ƛa'alqʷu' = channel of water>

72 Wisa'lpEbc pond at Sand Point. <?? = ??>

73 SqʷsEb Sand Point, an extensive, very flat promontory. <?? = ??>

74 T³uda'xEde a plant with small, inedible, white berries growing on the north shore of Sand Point. <?? = ??>

75 Sla'gwElagwEts "cedar bark + where it grows" in a cove at the inner end of the promontory. <slagʷlagʷac = cedar barks>

76 XwExwi'yaqwais said to mean "pulling on a line which is made fast to something", for shore north of the preceding. <?? = ??>

77 ᵀᵘxu':b1d creek north of Sand Point [?dxʷx̌ubəd]. <?? = ??>

78 Slo'q³qed "bald head", for cranberry marsh some three miles from the lake shore drained by one branch of the creek just mentioned. <słuq'ʷač = bald head>

79 Ts1xts1x-a³ltᵘ "eagle's house" where eagles (tsitsis) nest in a tree. <c'ixc'ixal'tx = fish hawk house>

80 Xwiyaqwa'd1-a³ltᵘ "Thunderbird's house" on the lake shore at the edge of a bluff where mythological fowls, supposed to cause thunderstorms by clapping their wings and winking their eyes, were believed to nest in these trees. <xʷiqʷadi'al'txʷ = thunderbird house>

81 StL³Epqs "deep promontory", very dangerous, at the edge of the lake where anyone swimming was formerly "taken away" by something supernatural. <sƛəpqs = deep point>

82 ᴮˢtcE'tla "rock", for an enormous boulder on the lake shore. <bəsƛəƛə' = place of rock>

83 S³a'tsutsid mouth of McAleer Creek (see #84). <s'acuscid = face mouth>

84 S³atsu "face", McAleer Lake. <s?acus = face>

85 Sts³kE³l "a certain small bird," at a small creek. <?? = ??>

86 Sta'tabEb "lots of people talking", where a sawmill stands at the north end of Lake Washington. <statabəd = a conversation>

87 TcEtca'L small creek. <?? = ??>

88 Ts³Ebta³ltᵘ "elderberry's house" (ts³abt, "elderberry"), for level flat at the mouth of Swamp Creek [red = sCabt for "red house"]. <c'abtal'txʷ = elderberry house>

89 TuLq³a'b variously translated, Swamp Creek. Lq!ab means "the bark of a dog," and another ~~informant~~ said that the present term means "the other side of something," like the opposite face of a log. <dxʷłəq'ab = wide place>

90 TL³ahwa'd1s "something growing or sprouting," for an old village site on the north shore of the lake, at its head near where Sammamish river enters. <ƛax̲ʷadis = growing place>

91 Cxa'tcugwEs "where the lake becomes elongated", as Sammamish river enters Lake Washington, referring to the way in which the lake at its northern end gradually narrows into a long estuary. <šxʷx̲aču'gʷəs = place of pair of lakes>

78

91a sts!ap, "crooked", meandering, fot Squawk Slough, otherwise known as Sammamish River. This stream was originally crooked almost past belief. It has now been dredged out and straightened so that mill logs can be floated down it from the lake. The people living here were called the sts!apa'bc "meander dwellers," anglicized as Sammamish, but this name for the *people* has now been applied to the lake and the river. <sc'əp = deep water hole>

92 Qwai'tEd said to mean "across", Peterson's Point, a headland lying south of the mouth of Sammamish river. <?? = ??>

93 Xwi'alad^{xu} "niggardly, scanty", for promontory where it was difficult to catch fish. <x^{w}i'aladx^w = not every year>

94 U^{3}a's "gravel rattling down", North Point, because gravel continuously rolls down it. <?? = ??>

95 Li'lskut Spot on the east shore of Lake Washington, south of the preceding. <?? = ??>

96 TcE':tcubEd open space near the present town of Juanita. <či'čubəd = climb upland>

97 No number. < = >

98 TE'btub1^u "loamy place" (tEb^u "earth, loam"), for creek at Juanita. <təbłtubix^w = red marked bunch>

99 Leqa'bt "paint", Nelson Point, literally "something gathered or scooped up with the fingers". The "rust" (evidently ocher) was scraped from this cliff, underneath a bonfire, and the reddest portions were picked out for use as face paint. <?? = ??>

100 S-ta'LaL beach north of the town of Kirkland. <?? = ??>

101 Tse'xub "dripping water" on the hillside north of Kirkland. <cətx̱əb = water falling over an edge>

102 S-taLaL town of Kirkland. <stałał = fathom>

103 Tc^{3}utsid "mouth of Northup Creek", south of Kirkland. <?? = ??>

104 tc^{3}u Northup Creek. <?? = ??>

105 Txwa'bats "pulling something toward one" through a swamp at the head of Northup Creek. <tux̱^{w}abac = pull a solid object>

106 Sli^{u}Li'uqs "three promontories" (Liux "3"), Hunt's Point, Fairweather Point, and a third which has no official ?English? name with narrow inlets between them. <słix^{w}łix^{w}qs = 3 points>

107 Tca'bqwEsEbtsa small creek at the head of Anderson's Bay. <čabq^{w}əsəbəc = become added to>

108 Duq^{3}tusa Small marsh at the head of the inlet west of #107. <?? = ??>

109 CtcE'gwus "place where a trail descends into the water" on Groat Point near Peterson's Landing. <čag^{w}us = by water>

110 Number not used. < = >

111 Tlhai^{3}si named for a certain species of very bony fish (tLhai for a stripe on the side [bony sqwak?]) that "ran" in great numbers in this little creek at head of Meydenbauer inlet. <?? = ??>

112 Lcwild promontory south of Meydenbauer inlet. <?? = ?? >

113 Tl^{3}utsa^{3}lus "tying mesh" at a promontory west of Mercer slough. <ƛ́ucalus = tying mesh>

114 SqE'bEqs1d Coal Creek. <?? = ??>

115 Sa'tsakaL "water at head of a bay", old village on Mercer slough. [staging place for the native attack on Seattle in January 1856.]. <?? = ??>

116 Cbal³t^u "place where things are dried", referring to redfish on May Creek. <šabal'tx^w = dry house>

117 Kwa'kwau small promontory. <?? = ??>

118 P³E'swi³ "pressed, crowded back" opposite the south end of Mercer Island, at the foot of Lake Washington. <?? = ??>

119 Spapa'Lxad "marshes" at the south end of Lake Washington to the east of Black River, also in the form Spa'pLxad, "several little marshes" <spapɫxad = marshes, bogs, wetlands>

120 ^Tuci'tsabd^u "to thrust, shove", especially push one's canoe into the brush at a little promontory on the lake shore at the middle of the marshy flats just mentioned. <dx^wšicabdx^w = thrust ~ shove into it>

121 Ciqe'd "head, source" where the Black River starts flowing out of Lake Washington. <šəqqid = above head>

122 Tcitc³o'yaq^w probably the small island near the head of Black river. <?? = ??>

123 Sext³itc1b "place where one wades" at an old village site now called Bryn Mawr. <səx^wt'ičib = by means of swimming>

124 Tsi'ptsip "duckling" (literally "something which emits a squeak, peep" [peeper]), for a small creek north of Bryn Mawr. <?? = ??>

125 ^Tuxwoc'kwib "loon", for a creek draining into an inlet north of Rainier beach surrounded by a deep swamp or marsh where loons nested. <dəx^wwuq^wad = place of loon>

126 TL1'Ltcus "small island" for a promontory west of the south end of Mercer Island separated from the mainland by the #125 marsh. <ƛiƛcas = small island>

127 Xaxao'Ltc "taboo, forbidden [xa'xa = sacred]" at Brighton beach where some supernatural monster lived. <?? = ??>

128 Cka'lapsEb "the upper part of one's neck" employed regularly in the sense of "isthmus," here connecting Bailey peninsula with the mainland. <cqalapsəb = neck>

129 SkEba'kst "nose" (bE'k:s1d, nostril) for Bailey Peninsula, especially its north end. <?? = ??>

130 Sqa'ts1d "choked up mouth," (Astqo'tsid is the expression for closing a door, or blocking up an opening) since a lot of snags blocked up the mouth of this creek emptying into Wetmore slough. Formerly abounding in silver salmon, it was later a hopyard. <stqucid = choked up mouth>

131 Ska'bo "nipple, milk", for Wetmore slough, or a place on its shore. <sqəbu' = milk ~ breast>

132 Saiya'hos "horned snake" lived on a point along the lake shore opposite the north end of Mercer island. <s'ayahus = horned snake spirit>

133 Hwoqwe'yEqaiEks "rushes" (sqweqwats, smaller than cattails also used for a certain kind of matting), growing slightly north of preceding. < = >

134 B1sti'Exq³e'u   untranslated but suggesting st1k³a'iyu, "wolf", in very deep water near Yesler Park. <?? = ??>

135 XEtL "where one chops" (with ax) at Madison Park then at the end of the Madison street cable line. <?? = ??>

136 B1skwi'kwi³L "skate", for the southernmost of two promontories forming Union Bay because this very level point is upturned at the tip, like the nose of a skate. <bəskʷi'kʷil' = place of skate fish>

137 Sti't¹tci (diminutive form of StEtci, "island"), Foster Island in Union Bay where Indians of this part of America formerly hoisted their dead into trees. Elders recalled when the trees were full of boxes holding skeletons until their lashings gave way, to cover the ground with bones. [These bones were removed when the Arboretum developed.]. <?? = ??>

138 Sta'LaL (from staL, "fathom, stretch of the arms"), for a creek entering Union Bay from the south. <stałał = fathom>

139 Sxa'tsugw1L "to lift up (a canoe)" at a former "portage" from Lake Washington to Lake Union where natives, and after them the early settlers, carried their boats from one lake to the other. The spot is just south of the present Montlake cut. A little creek drained out of Lake Washington, up which the boats were pushed as far as they could be made to go. Those paddling from Salmon Bay shoved their canoes up this creek until they had to carry them the remainder of the distance upon their shoulders. < = >

The name of this place was also given as *stE'xuqwiL*, from the stem meaning "to shove," which occurs as the name of several places where canoes could be pushed from one body of water to another without lifting them up. <sxʷacəgʷił = lift ~ pull canoe>

140 Sp'Lxad "marsh, wet flats" at the south end of the bight in [Portage Bay off] Lake Union facing the University campus. <spałxad = march, bog wetland>

141 Sxwuba'bats "place where jumping occurred" on the shore of Lake Union opposite gas works park. A number of house boats were then moored along this water front, and one elder explained that the waterfront here was encumbered with logs, over which one had to jump. <saxʷəbabac = jump over solid object>

142 StLEp "deep" just south of #141 where the beach is very abrupt. <sƛ̕əp = deep>

143 Cta'qʷc1d "where a trail descends to the water" at the southern end of Lake Union from Seattle harbor and the pioneer sawmill stood belonging to David Denny ("Tabe Tuddy" according to the Indian pronunciation of his name). [David was the great protector of natives in Seattle, with the Zakuse and John families favorites.]. <ča'kʷšəd =trail down to water>

144 TL³pe'lgw1L "deep for canoes", bluff at the foot of Lake Union on the southern shore. <ƛ̕əpalgʷił = deep for canoes>

145 Nothing. < = >

145a TsEktsEk³a'bats "gooseberry bushes" at East Seattle on the north end of Mercer Island, particularly the Proctor ranch where wild roses were formerly very plentiful. <c'əq'c'əq'abac = gooseberry bushes>

145b   La'gw1tsatEb "taking off, stripping" at South Point, the southernmost promontory of Mercer Island where an old man once came in a canoe to get bark from the old dead trees, but he soon got "crazy," and had to go away because supernatural beings called swa'watiᵘt1d, "earth beings," lived in the old stumps, so removing their bark was like removing their clothing. People were afraid to go there after the old man's experience gave rise to this name. <łagʷic'təb = someone strips clothes off someone>

145c   Q³oq³o'btsi "water lilies" (plant with a large yellow flower) growing on the west shore of Mercer Island. <?? = ??>

(Hilbert, Miller, Zahir 2001: 54-110)

Alfred John Smith
(1886 - 1971)

Smith, with a rural education to the eighth grade and two years of Tacoma night school, earned his living as a carpenter and grocer, as well as rewriting within his own creative framework, materials by others, for a more general audience. By background, Alfred John Smith was raised in backwoods Wisconsin at Drywood, in Arthur Township east of Minneapolis near Menominee and Chippewa reservations, and early began writing for local newspapers. He also heard mention of the localized tribal guild of initiates known as the *Midewiwin* or shamans academy, and mixed it into his writings, though not always appropriately. Married at 20 in 1906, he moved his family to Tacoma to work in the Todd Shipyards during WW I.

Smith ran a grocery store (1919-29), though 1927 was hard on him. On July 11 a speeding car crashed into his grocery, broke the plate glass window and pushed the building back two feet. In August, he was robbed and began carrying a .32 revolver. In early November, Smith closed his grocery for the night and was crossing the street. When he heard the words "This is a Stickup!," he fired twice from four feet away but, amazingly, the robber ran off into the fog. On November 4th, in Seattle, the well-dress, talkative "Beau Brummel bandit," James Cunningham, was arrested trying to flee in a taxi after robbing a drugstore and soon was charged with ten hold ups and robberies, including the attempt on Smith. Convicted, he was sentenced to fifteen years at Monroe prison.[37]

In 1929 Smith served one term as elected Representative from the 28th District (western Pierce County) to the Washington State Legislature. He divorced in 1932, after 26 years of marriage and six children, though only four lived to marry, and began concentrating on native lore and stories.

His grocery was near what had been the Puyallup Reservation until 1906, and this proximity likely led to native friendships, especially with tribal leaders such as Jerry Meeker. When it was later learned that an accounting error had spared a few acres of their original lands, Puyallup tribal government was restored in 1936.

In the mid 1930s, working as a writer for the WPA guide to the State of Washington (flawed and last to be printed), he met with fluent elders at the United States Indian Service office at 2002 East 28th St in Tacoma to report, discuss, and translate native place names for the region. These became his first meetings with Jerry Meeker, Lewis, Henry Allen, and others, inspiring his work on the story cycle and eventual novel. In 1938, with Quileute speaker William Penn, he wrote a guide

Smith's Grocery Store today   titled "Translation of Geographic Names of Indian Origin", for 109 place names on the coast of Washington.[38]

---

[37] As reported in the *Tacoma Daily Ledger* under the headlines of "Auto Wrecked, Store Moved in Car's Wild Dash" (7/11/27), "Bandit Met With Bullet" (12/18/27); bound copies at Tacoma Public Library.

[38] Fish? Psyche? Whence Came Pysht Name? *Seattle Times* 25 September 1960, Sunday, p5. The original is in WPA files at WSHS, with copies scattered around the region, some of

Smith worked diligently as a paid writer, carefully dating and word counting everything he did (providing a "flavor").[39] In the late 1930s he polished entries for guide books to Tacoma and to Washington State, local contributions to Works Progress Administration (WPA) projects intended for every state. In Washington, it provided "emergency employment for perhaps 150 third rate writers whose literary competence was never in doubt".[40] One Smith file lists detailed pronunciations for every town in a county, including those derived from native languages. The published state guide acknowledges the advice of Drs Melville Jacobs and Erna Gunther of the University of Washington, who helped introduced Smith to a technical alphabet, setting the stage for his better transcriptions of Puyallup and other native words in his 1948 Minter notebooks.

Smith was proud and protective of his writing. As editor for the auto tours of Pierce County, he slammed, with increasing intensity, a draft of one tour (2E) passed from the state office in Seattle to the Tacoma district office, calling it a "joke," "poor crippled monstrosity" and "carcass".[41] Smith, in turn, was criticized for perpetuating the mistake that the same pioneer homestead was occupied by remittance Englishman JT Heath and then Walter Ross, when in fact these men had homesteads miles apart. Just after his death, Heath's plot became the site of Fort Steilacoom, the first US army base in Washington Territory.

During WW II Smith moved as a federal contract carpenter to Kodiak Island, Alaska, where he saw native people living close to the land and sea. Returning to Tacoma on 5 October 1946, he remarried ten days later to Margaret Peterson, a woman born at Forks and raised among Quileutes of the coast. The new couple began periodic house trailer journeys, while he wrote for leisure magazines. When he fully retired in 1956, they drove their trailer to the north in summer and south in winter. After three years of ill health, he died in 1971 and the widow moved to Sequim, returning home to the Olympic Peninsula.

In 1948, when he was 62, upon his return from Kodiak and recently remarried, he asked Arthur Ballard, Erna Gunther, and Jerry Meeker for help with a novel to describe the homelife of the native peoples of Puget Sound, especially the Puyallups around Tacoma. Interviewing Meeker, who was 86, they filled those three very informative notebooks with named persons and activities at his mother's ancestral village at Minter on the Key Peninsula across the Narrows from Tacoma. These notebooks were left with Dr Gunther at the Burke Museum and when Gunther was eased out of the newly built museum, the three volumes went to Special Collections

---

which include two extra pages on the pedigree of Mr Penn and details of the interviews. It is reprinted at the end of this volume.

[39] Working on guides for the state and for Tacoma, Smith's entries (WSHS WPA Box 8) are Water Tours 1 and 2 (25 October 1937), Ferry (7 July, 28 October 38), Gipsy Touring by Motorboat (1 November 37), Narrows Bridge (26 June 39), Education (??), Schools (5 October 38), Folklore and Folk Customs (??), Hops and Pioneer Days (15 September 38), Scrape Book (25 February 38), Batil Merman of Fox Island (27, 29 July 36), Indians of Western Washington (undated), Indians (26 March 36, with the above quote, Box 8, folder7), Vancouver Expedition (3 December 36), Archaeology (27 March 36). All have his word counts.

[40] Ronald Taber, Writers on Relief: The Making of the Washington Guide, 1935-41, *Pacific Northwest Quarterly* Oct 1970: 185-192, p192.

[41] Ronald Taber, Writers on Relief: The Making of the Washington Guide, *Pacific Northwest Quarterly* 1970: p188.

at the main library, misattributed to booster pioneer Ezra Meeker, whose hops empire relied on "straw bosses" Jim and Sally Meeker, Jerry's parents.

Like others, Smith quickly realized that the heart of the traditional culture and lifeways survives best in the literature.[42] He turned to the classic collections by Ballard and rewrote a cycle for general readers, and then worked several of them into his novel *Old Lukh* — named for the town's storytelling shaman and set at the village at the mouth of the Puyallup River — to provide each of them with place-based retellings at appropriate seasons and locales.[43]

In all, during 1948, he accomplished three notebooks and a novel, building on his 1935 twin collection of Transformer tales, as well as a lost poetry volume. The two anthologies relied heavily on Ballard's published 1927 and 1929 collections, as well as a few local (if dubious) classics, such as Seattle librarian Katharine Berry Judson's *Myths and Legends of the Pacific Northwest* (1910), including many photographs of native people and objects by Major Lee Morehouse of Pendleton (OR), and WS Phillip's badly-titled *Indian Fairy Stories* (1902), featuring his own sketches and drawings.[44] Smith lists these books in the bibliography appended to the novel, not to the stories themselves where they more properly belong. Along with their compatriot James Costello, whose volume has what might be considered the most racist title of all (note 10), these prior authors claimed "authenticity," though some of their tales and comments morphed into bigoted and insensitive revisions taken from federal publications by academics where, it was mistakenly assumed, "simplicity and directness had been destroyed by attempted witticisms, by philosophical remarks, or by wordy explanations".[45]

Indeed, these authors thought in terms of absolutes, seeking the most authentic, pure, aboriginal versions, which, of course, only exist in relative terms, based on context, narrators, social standing, fluency, and flare. Ballard, better educated and advised, always included variants to better represent the range of storytelling.

In tragic irony, Ballard's own life's work *Listen My Nephew*, based on fluency in the native language, original texts, and close native friendships over many decades, was snatched at the time of his death from imminent publication in Portland by his children and has been lost or

---

[42] Overviews of Northwest oral literature (Miller 2014, Hymes 1990) discuss examples, general features, motifs, and stylistics across the region. Readers interested in this subject beyond Puget Sound should consult these, forewarned that scholarly dissection often kills a good story.

[43] A prominent Nisqually named Luke seems to have inspired the shamanic characters in several literary works of the mid-1900s. Della Gould Emmons, *Leschi of the Nisquallies* (1965: 300) has "Luke, the shaman, possessing turtle power".

[44] Judson was reprinted in 1997 with an introduction by Jay Miller; ironically all of the non-Northwest stories in Smith's second volume are rewritten from her collection. Developed as a series of newspaper columns, these assembled books were James Costello (1880-1943), *The Siwash* ~ Their Life, Tales, & Legends of Puget Sound & Pacific Northwest; Seattle: Calvert Co, 1895; and Walter Shelley Phillips (1867-1940), *Indian Fairy Tales*: Folklore - Legends - Myths; Totem Tales as Told by the Indians; Gathered in the Pacific Northwest, With a Glossary of Words, Customs and History of the Indians; Fully Illustrated by the Author; Chicago: Star Publishing Co, 1902. James Costello's use of '*siwash*,' the Chinuk WaWa word for native, derives from French 'sauvage' but is now regarded as very derogatory. Phillips provided drawings for Costello's book.

[45] Judson (1997: 13).

misplaced for half a century. The Smith novel, therefore, provides a surviving if sideways look at what Ballard knew and had done.

Relying again on Ballard, Smith cites helpful, skilled elders such as Joe Young, Tom Milroy, Matthew Seattle, and Henry Sicade. He also acknowledges the use of the Phonetic Key to the Indian Language (1916) published by the Smithsonian for writing Lushootseed (Puget Sound Salish) words and other terms from native languages. Gunther and especially Ballard strongly advised him on other aspects of local linguistics, such as place names. Indeed, it is because typed letters between Smith and Ballard deal with specific local places that the novel *Old Lukh* survived among the papers of Robert Hitchman, a book collector, historian, and author of a classic study on place names in the state of Washington.

Smith's most lasting contribution is the informative Minter notebooks, whose raw and rich data inspired and drove my quest to identify their scribe. Eventually, pursuing other research interests, I opened Ballard's classic study of calendrical terms (1950) used by Lushootseed Salish speakers of Puget Sound, and found the only mention in print of Alfred J Smith. Since the source for the Puyallup month words was Jerry Meeker, and at least one phrase was verbatim from the notebooks, I was able to name the unknown scribe to be Smith, whom Ballard identified as "a volunteer student of Indian life and lore".[46] Smith gathered the month names as background for treating the seasonal food harvests in his novel, supplying this material after Ballard (1950: 85, 86, 97, 98) had drafted the calendrical article and it was in press, as explained:

(a) Since the preparation of this paper I have before me a copy of a list of Twana terms for five of the months, kindly supplied me by Mr Alfred J Smith, a volunteer student of Indian life and lore. These terms were obtained by Mr Smith from Robert Lewis, a long-time resident of the Skokomish[47] Indian [p86] reservation, who had attained his majority at the time of the treaties of 1854-55, and they may be taken as representative of Twana nomenclature....

(b) Another list of calendric terms supplied me was obtained by Mr Smith from Mr Jerry Meeker, a Puyallup of the salt water region, who is well informed on the lore of this people....

The data thus coming to my notice (through the kindness of Mr Smith) since the preparation of this paper was well along have clarified some obscurities and altered some impressions, thus forcing a revision of the conclusions drawn from the material theretofore at hand.... It is remarkable that two ~~informants~~ as far distant from each other as the Snoqualmie and the Twana, speaking different, though related, dialects, should employ the same term and both employ it as the initial term of the series.

From archives in both Washingtons (DC ~ city and state), I confirmed people and places in the three notebooks, assembling an ethnography of the native town of Minter, in several revisions and lengths. Ballard and Smith appeared in uneven detail in my explanatory footnotes, with Smith mostly the name of someone who had done ethnographic work with Jerry Meeker.

---

[46] Falsely assuming an academic career for him, my call to the UW registrar suggested a 1950 graduate of the University of Washington from San Diego, California, with the same name but he was the wrong person.

[47] Smith's contacts at Skokomish also included Henry Allen, an informed elder who worked with Edward Curtis and later William Elmendorf, who wrote the single best areal ethnography.

Then came the full breakthrough during email, phone, and letter exchanges when I learned of a collection of "Transformer myths and legends" by Alfred Smith for which a native woman was simply seeking a publisher who would make them available to tribal and other readers. My name was suggested as an editor, and, intrigued, I met with her and was amazed to see a full manuscript in two parts: an interconnected story cycle of Moon as Transformer by Snoqualmie Charlie, obviously derived from Ballard, and a much more diverse assemblage of mixed stories from western tribes (Klamath, Teton, Blackfeet, Tlingit, Puget Sound) derived from Judson's library assemblage. Following up another suggestion by the press, I learned from the UW Special Collections website that a novel, *Old Lukh*, by Smith was held in the papers of Robert Hitchman, who famously published on place names in the state and chaired the board of the Washington State Historical Society in Tacoma.

Thus, ironically, the proof that the three notebooks were indeed inscribed by Smith resided on nearby shelves in the same archives. Mercifully, correspondence between Ballard and Smith is bound in the same volume, with copies also in Tacoma. In a letter of February 3rd, 1948 from Smith to Ballard, their collaboration is confirmed:

> In line with our previous talks, I am writing you, passing on information which may be whipped into shape between us. I am going to send this material in the best way I can, in an endeavor to get across to you the stuff I have. You are much better qualified to get somewhere near the proper spelling of the words than I am, so that I am asking you to help me in order that both may share in it providing we can get it in shape. I have just completed this field work [with Jerry Meeker], and want you to join me, and share with me, the benefits we may derive. …
>
> I sincerely hope I have put this over so you can grasp what I want to tell you. It will mean so much to both of us if you can get the meaning.

Smith wrote for a popular, general audience, favoring Westerns, slice of life, and travel trailer stories. His concern, self-described, was home life, and the novel nicely captures routine activities such as the seasonal round to prepare foods and fish, as well as seemingly lighter moments devoted to games and story telling, though these had the much more serious purposes of encouraging community morality and cohesion.

In sum, my past and immediate research suggests Smith produced three notebooks and a novel in 1948 after he returned to Tacoma from Kodiak, Alaska, remarried, and decided to focus on native home life in Puget Sound as he renewed his own. In 1935, the legends, novel, and lost poetry collection had been submitted to Caxton Press in Idaho, but never saw print and passed into other hands. The twin tales went from a daughter to Bernice Morgan, who had been a missionary with her husband to Alaska tribes and later had a small museum of native artifacts in Ocean Shores, where she also served as mayor. At her death, they went to Philip and Thelma Carlson, and then to their son Bruce Carlson, who gifted them to a Lakota woman, who loaned them to Jay Miller at the recommendation of Washington State University Press. As noted, regrettably, Ballard's own magnum opus, *Listen My Nephew* was suppressed by his children.

The third figure in all these efforts was the eminent Dr Erna Gunther, long at the State, later renamed Burke, Museum at the University of Washington, who kept the three notebooks of raw data. Her own long-term academic interest was the First Salmon Ceremony, and her dedication to local natives — especially their children, cultures, technologies, and histories — was legendary. That the Salmon Ceremony is featured in a chapter of the novel can be directly attributed to her.

Fish? Psyche? Whence Came Pysht Name

"THERE are a number of subjects that just naturally generate controversy. The moment they are mentioned, logic flies out the window and emotion takes over. Pysht is one of these".

The quotation is from Robert Hitchman, Seattle authority on origins of Washington place names.

An article appearing recently in The Times Magazine Section about the Pysht tree farm in Clallam County, inspired several letters taking issue with the statement that the name of Pysht derived from an Indian way of saying "fish".

The community, which no longer has a postoffice, now consists of eight families, a total of 39 persons. It is on a rural-delivery route out of Port Angeles.

Hitchman said that the origin of Pysht's name is such a controversial subject that the late Prof Edmond Meany, in his book on Washington names, avoided discussing the place directly and wrote instead about Fish River, stating that in the report for 1862 gave the Indian name of the stream as Pisht-st.

"Samuel Hancock in his narrative, dated February 17, 1860, spoke of a small river which the Indians called Postchet. The testimony of an acting coroner at Crescent Bay in December, 1863, referred to the place as Pisth. From this evidence we can include that the name was well established a century ago".

Further bearing this out is the statement of Alfred J Smith and William Penn, in their "Translation of Geographic Names of Indian Origin", that Pysht is a corruption of the Clallam Indian words "p'he sith".

Not all Seattle Times readers seem to agree. Conner Reed, of 7737 31st NE, wrote, contending that Pysht does not derive from "fish" but from "ignorant white men's mispronunciation of the Greek 'Psyche'," originally intended to be joined with the Greek 'Sappho'" when these two classical names were conferred on two Olympic Peninsula localities.

Reed said Clallam County historians had confirmed the fact that the same man named both places.

However, Mark Wienand of Olympia heard a different version.

MANY years ago," Wienand wrote. "I traveled for the Black Ball Line to obtain material for their travelogs on the Olympic Peninsula. [From the] office they first sent in the name of Union, only to be advised that it was unacceptable, because there was already another Union in the state. The settlers met again and chose another name, which also was rejected because of duplication.

"When they met the third time, word had come that neighbors down the line had submitted the name Sappho, which had been accepted, so the motion was made to submit the name of Psyche. Nobody knew for sure how to spell the name and, furthermore, the letter to the Postoffice Department was so badly scrawled that all that could be deciphered out of it was Pysht".

Hitchman says another possible source of the name was cited by Lieut Frederick Schwatka in the following quotation from an article about the Port Angeles hinterland in 1892, mentioning the Pysht River:

"Years ago, the story runs, the ship Psyche was wrecked off its mouth. The name-board of the vessel floated ashore and fell into the hands of a goodly citizen who had not papered" his house with the college diplomas he had won. He slowly spelled it out several times and then remarked to his comrade. 'That's a hell of a way to spell fish'."

Hitchman consulted a reliable coastal marine history of the anecdote to his friend, Henry L Mencken, who referred to it in his book, "The American Language".

Mencken wrote: "Mr Lewis A McArthur ... tells me of the fate of Psyche, a town in Clallam County. The local residents, baffled by the name, called it Pysht, and in the end the Postoffice succumbed, and Pysht it is today".

Hitchman is favoring the "fish" origin, but says he is open-minded and willing to be convinced.

"Although it has been my experience in tracking down place names," he added, "that the most colorful and amusing stories are the ones that aren't true".

Sunday > *Seattle Times* 25 September 1960

ROBERT
HITCHMAN

NB: Accurately describing natural local conditions, Pysht is the name of Klallam settlement pəšc't, 'against the flow ~ wind ~ current' (B04: 401). It was bulldozed in the1930s and burned by Merrill and Ring Timber while families were working nearby at Port Angeles. Lynda Mapes (2009: 88-93), citing the family of Tim Pysht, translates it 'place where wind blows all the time'.

E Mails

From: Jay Powell
To: Jay the other one Miller
Subject: RE: Bill Penn first place name list
Date: Tue, 18 Nov 2014 05:24:09
        HAVE YOU FOUND IT?
        Yup, copies and original.
Date: Tue, 18 Nov 2014 05:47:06 -0800
        Alright, you Turkey .... How do I get a copy... PLEASE!

From: jaymiller
Date: Thu, 27 Nov 2014 20:18:52 +0000
To: jay v powell
Subject: MPR
        Turkeys come at Yanksgiving, so from US to wherever U are, here it is, not great, but a
        start for what became a more ethnographic project. Any & all of your comments
        appreciated. Happy, Thanks.

        Fri, Nov 28, 2014 11:38 AM

Reply: Well, that is interesting for a number of reasons:

1) my publication of Quileute Place names was primarily working with William Penn (Big Bill), but this one was working with William E Penn (Little Bill). Both were well informed.

2) I don't know why he called it Quileute Placenames, since there were only about 8 Quileute placenames ... but 12 in Quileute country (the other four from Jargon).

3) Many of the "Placenames" were the names of tribes. The rest were in other tribal areas as far away as east of the Sound. There was also the word for the Quileute warrior society (Tlokwali), hardly a place name.

4) Execrable phonetics and syllabification. Just awful. Examples available upon request. Even knowing the true Quileute root, which means 'Hole in the Rock place' and which everyone knew, I couldn't recognize any part of the way he transcribed it. He did the English accent issue of putting epenthetic r`s after word final vowels like *dikwodachtadar* (no r`s there or in Quileute at all, Mac!)

5) Improbable Quileute source roots and affixes using n and m, which don`t occur in Quileute.

6) A translation of the supposed Sol Duc source word meaning `sparkling water` is bullshit.

7) Quileute sourceword for Teahwit Head (complex polymorphemic root is bullshit. It comes from Chinook Jargon Teahwit, foot and means, comically, ``foot head``.

8) Archawat was NOT a village site, it was a beach, etc. on the issue of the ethnographic import of the names.

Again, why would he call it Quileute when there`s almost nothing Quileute about the word list or the information he provides. I think he fooled the US Govt and Indian Affairs into thinking he was qualified and had done something. There was nothing there that a smart man like Little Bill Penn would've told him.

Thanks for sending that along. I needed a good laugh. jvp

Dialog

Jay Powell & Jay Miller
Vancouver BC
8 16 2017

Alfred John Smith consulted Little Bill E Penn for this list, while the place names in print were done with Big Bill Penn, working with JV Powell. Both were respected elders, and cousins.

jvp Get that file, the Quileute file. Then it had all of this. So I made a copy of this for you.

jm You had to get to Dorothy Jean Ray to get this? That is why I couldn't recognize it.

jvp So I made a copy of this for you. So we can check on the various … as much as he worked, he must have had an awful typist, barred Ls ł are Ts, etc etc Or he had a real tin ear.

jm Yeah, I, we just had this problem. He, for 50 some odd years, his Lakes ethnography, he gave it to a woman who was supposed to edit & publish it. And for the 50th anniversary of NARN/JONA this woman came out of the woodwork. Oh, he also gave her, you know, culture element distribution charts of several hundred pages. That is what she came to JONA with, asking to publish it. Everyone looked at her, rolled their eyes, and said No. Then she said she also had his Lakes ethnography, and we all said What? Because he has always said the Lakes had, the most famous chief of the Lakes was a woman. And he never gave a name, never gave a name, but it turns out he did not get a name. We just know it was Gregory's mother and Gregory was a historic chief of the Lakes. So at least we have a way to refer to her at this point. It is a pretty good ethnography, but he stipulated that … anyone who published the ms could not touch a letter of this linguistics. It is abominable from start to finish.

jvp yeah   Who taught him?

jm I don't know. Dale Kinkade made the same remark. He did the all of the place names all down the Columbia River, literally, the whole length of the Columbia River. Transcribed in his wretched orthography.

jvp Well, let's … you are going to have to go soon.

jm OK

jvp OK

ARCH-A-WAT, hach is 'good' and 'awat' is beach Oh He says "good beach". Do you want me to write this out?

jm No, just tell me. That was encouraging, he got off to a good start, didn't he.

jvp OK, the name of a Makah Indian tribe?

BAABOK

jm I think it is Ba'da Its one of the villages

jvp But the $-ok^w$ on the end is a locative in Quileute $-ok^w$ = locative. So the double A must be a long A rather than ba'a'da. So Baada is Makah and the $-ok^w$ on the end, it's really k^w is Quileute. It means 'the place where it happened, where they live' OK

BOGACHIEL ~ bō qwå tchēē el   Now, just so you will know, a lot of this stuff is coming out in our next book, which just getting ready to be sent off to MakeSpace {CreateSpace}, and it is call Our Land, Quileute territory OK Because a lot of the overlap is covered in this book, that's coming out, if you want to know about it?

jm I do.

jvp OK Here are all the Sol Duc place names, the final one {list}, here are all the Dickey River place names, I just did this up for you OK Here are all the Calawah River place names, and here are all the bōqwåtchēēel. This is the last time I will ever go through with adding things, but if you need to check on spellings of things, for instance, we were just talking about bō qwå tchēē el and there is the spelling and what not. So that will make it easy.

jm exactly.

jvp OK So should I just mark the ones that we are talking about?

jm No, cause I'll do that later. That is a tedious job that I'll fold into something else. OK

jvp OK so bō qwå tchēē el that's pretty good.

jm and the river all lumped together

jvp on the other hand Bogachiel Peak has its own name, and it might be in there. He's just got there off

jm I think off a gazetteer.

jvp Yup, down at the bottom anyway

jm #42 'mountain where it begins'

jvp OK

CALAWAH it means, not the middle fork, but 'the one in the middle' yeah

CAPE JOHNSON 4 miles north of the Quillayute River. All I can say is, I don't know, but if Big Bill said it, Let's keep going through

CAMAS ~ La Camas

jm That's Chinuk jargon

jvp The Chinuk jargon word I'm loosing my nouns. How are you doing?

jm Names escape me, I never forget a face, but

jvp that's, that's interesting. I'm also, My left eye is gone, and my right eye

jm is going?

jvp is going.

jm with glaucoma or ?

jvp just deterioration. My mother and grandmother both died blind.

jm As did Vi {Hilbert} pretty much   > 10: And Harriet Turner, too, though she was getting injections and then was so upset she never went back, once she stopped the injections, deterioration took over

jvp so far I am working well, it is just that I move really slowly. OK the Quileute word for camas if you want it is k^{w}ala Rounded K + W + accented A + L + A. And La Camas simply wasn't used, though it is a known Chinuk word Camas was so important for so long

jm and the next one is where part of the novel is set, and that's why it is here

CEBALOP

and we do have that from Arthur Ballard

jvp OK

CHIBAHDEHL ~ KASHUKUDDIB is, Let me check on it, that's way up on the other side of Neah Bay

jm Um. Off the wall question. You and Dale did an article years ago on language stocks {homelands} in North America, and their likely homelands, ending with a long discussion of Cape Alava Ozette.

jvp Yeah. Yeah As part of the evidence for the fact, the clear fact, that, well, Ozette, that the whole north end of the Peninsula was once controlled by Chimakuan speaking tribes. And then the Makahs came over and pushed and unseated and wiped out the tribes on that corner, and then Klallam

jm Klallam. Everybody seems to agree that it was a thousand years ago for the Makah. I've never seen a date for the Klallam. But is it probably only a couple hundred years.

jvp The thing I, they may have at the earliest time moved across from southern

jm Vancouver Island

jvp I think they were on the peninsula before they pushed the Chimakums into the corner

jm further east yeah

jvp You have a copy of that? You want a copy of that?

jm yeah Dale gave me a copy and I've been looking for it for weeks

jvp yeah I have it. I'll give it to you

jm perfect!

jvp OK

CHIBAHDEHL ~ KASHUKUDDIB I'm having trouble …

jm I think it's more a matter, is it plausible? As a Quileute name?

jvp Oh yeah but I know that is in the, oh, here we go, the Quileute actually had a different name for this, right there #12

jm OK

jvp You are going to mark it in there?

jm I've the number #12. > 15:00

jvp Ok The next one

CLALLAM

jm is Klallam

jvp Meaning unknown. Is that true?

jm I'm sure if I asked Tim Montler, he'll have an etymology

jvp It is interesting, I've asked Tim about when, is there a Klallam tradition that they moved across from southern Vancouver Island. He said No. According to their creation stories, they were created right there.

jm yeah There is a creation spot on the Elwa, Lower Elwa.

jvp and that they moved up towards the Port Angeles area, in late prehistoric time. I tried to push him on it, you sure there's no reference on it coming from the island? No, I told you, No.

jm Oh yeah there is some Flood story, buried somewhere

jvp I wonder why, why he has that in there if this is, oh, geographical names just of Indien origin.

jm yeah that is why it is the first attempt. I mean there are other attempts, there is a part Klallam guy Totski who tried to put together place names but he had no linguistics, but he did have some journalistic ability.

jvp yeah OK

CLOQUALLAM Oh Quillayute Indian secret society

jm And there is a creek down in the Chehalis territory where Dale was always told ... by one of the Penns, not Penn, Silas Heck, was where Upper & Lower Chehalis fought to a draw and that became the boundary.

jvp Heck

jm And it is called CLOQUALLAM

jvp Oh that would explain the –am on the end. you know tloquali is used both by the Kwagiuth and Nootkans

jm yeah all the way down, but I think there is a disconnect

jvp so tloquali It says "corruption of the Quillayute Indian words" in fact, the tloquali is in fact the name of a secret society and among the Quileute it was the warrior society. Those who had a warrior guardian spirit and were that warrior spirit Sings: ha my yi The tloquali spirit song that everybody sang uses the _xap_ root, which means Eat in

jm Eat, in Wakashan, I think, kwakwala

jvp yeah Wakashan root, when the tloqualis are coming out, being tamed, they shout <u>X</u>AP! And have to have 2 guardians to keep them from rushing out into the audience, and biting people.

jm nibbling on the audience.

jvp OK

COMAX ~ CUMTUX

jm kumtux is the End in Chinuk

jvp kumtux is a Coast Salish word, I think and it is not from jargon kamux the word for 'dog' Comox is a real tribal name

jm Comox is a real tribal name > 20:00

jvp OK

COPALIS we've got that

jm and we think it is actually named for a person? Chief John

jvp I just don't know anything about it.

jm Nor I, though I've been up the Copalis to the Ghost Forest

jvp yeah

Copalis Crossing 12 miles northwest of Hoquiam Yeah, he went far & wide to get his place names, didn't he?

jm yeah. I think because he was working in the office of the WPA guide to Washington State. If they saw a word they thought was Indien, they just sort of started a file. And then he took responsibility for finding an Indien to translate words in that file.

jvp What do you suppose "COWITCHE ~ COWICHE, meaning "get hunchback" is?

jm It is the equivalent of Haboo is what it sounds like, but I have no idea what tribe would have used it, oh, I take it back, it looks like it is a Yakama word.

jvp It could might be, now

CUITIN

jm that is gyiwatan, I'm sure, which is the Chinuk word for 'horse'

jvp It is This is the way it is spelled on the north part of the peninsula yeah It is how it is pronounced.

CULTUS "worthless", "bad"; "purposeless" Now just a minute, there's a, indeed it is a kind of bad, but there are 3 words in jargon for 'bad' and cultus is reserved for 'worthless' OK

DI = DESTRUCTION ISLAND Now "Ta tchist q^{u}" ~ Tå tchist qh, the word for DI, that is a Quileute word that he's got down there that he says is Quinault. And I'm not sure if it is not also the Quinault word.

jm Quinaults have a new linguist, but they have no speakers.

jvp that is true?

jm There is a Quinault tribal member who has just gotten a PhD from U Arizona. Everybody went down for the graduation.

jvp What was the name of the Wycliff bible translator woman?

jm Who just died, you know. You were the only one who responded, nobody else knew of Ruth Modrow. It is probably 2 months since, I was in Oklahoma for a month. Yeah, no, quite the obituary for a missionary woman, naming her llama first, before her husband and children.

Ruth Modrow April 10 1922 - October 14, 2016 Despite threatening to outlive all of us Ruth graciously threw in the towel on October 14, 2016. Ruth is survived by her llama, Jeraldo, her dog, Tosha, her son, Jerald and family, a sister, Doris, cousin, Omar, and countless friends. Born to Dora and Olaf Nelson on April 10, 1922 in Petersburg, North Dakota. Married to Guy Modrow November 2, 1941 in Rugby, North Dakota with whom she enjoyed 61 years of Guy grounding her when she got excited. Ruth and Guy were missionary linguists for 50 years bringing the Gospel to people around the world. A memorial service for Ruth will be held at Christian Fellowship, 630 Cemetery Rd, Winlock WA, on Saturday, November 5 at 11:00 am.

jvp OK

DTOKOAH is {Dickey #2} the word

DICKODOCHTEDER that is really a mess, but it is in here, so it is under the Dickey, oh shit, I gave you the one that's {jumped out of the correct font, back into English}. See if they are all that way?

jm No, all are fine, except that one page. Oh, you capitalize the first letter of each name. yeah, it is only this page.

jvp It means "people who live in the first branch of the Quillayute River. OK so you can figure that out from my lists

jm so which one on the dictionary?

jvp #2 Dickey River OK OK

DUCKABUSH That is way over on the east side of the peninsula

jm That is on Hook Canal, it drains out of the Brothers, I think

jvp OK

DOSEWALLIPS the same thing DUWAMISH

jm interestingly enough he cites that DUCKABUSH source as Laqh-kla-dub ~ Robert Lewis, one of the oldest living Skokomish-Skagit Indians, Born about 1821-1825

Lewis was a hundred year old Twana, his name keeps cropping up, he left a series of interviews, in fact, interviews with Al Smith that same summer, but I can not find them, they are not in Bancroft, Bill Elmendorf's papers at Berkeley.

jvp really, OK

ELWA

Quileute call them ałkʷak I'm not sure, I think that's the Quileute version of the Elwa name for themselves. He says it is a Quillayute Indian name. Let me, can I write it here íłxʷaḵʷ Quileute

jm Here on this page under Elwa

jvp We're past Duckabush

jm OK next one.

jvp ENUMCLAW

jm It's Yakama

jvp OK

HOH Quinault word hux^w and it became, the word is in fact from Quinault hux^w H + U + back X + W but the Quileute word is ča'la<u>k</u>^w CH + A + glottal stop + L + A + back rounded K + W {ča'la<u>k</u>^w} OK But he's got it here > 30:00

Hoh Head, a promontory That has a name of its own We don't have the Hoh list here

jm That's OK

jvp OK yeah right

HOKO HOQUIAM hoko is to 'drift down the river' in Quileute 'ho' to drift is all over the coast, so

HUMPTILIPS KALALOCK Oh Song: "I was down in Kalalock, I was starting to feel no pain, did I drink, oh God, did I drink" OK so it says KALALOCK is a Quinault word

jm laughs main character

jvp yeah, it is over the boundary OK

KASHUKUDDIB "standing rocks" ten miles east of Cape Flattery OK

KLAHANEE "out-of-doors", that's Chinuk jargon

KULO KALA "kula" (bird) and "kala" (goose) No that]s reduplicated

jm reduplication, so it's jargon

jvp yeah well yeah It's the goose word.

KULTUS again, this is interesting, he puts it under C and under K

jm And he gets this one out of Gill's dictionary

jvp Here's LACAMAS again. OK

LA PUSH named by a Frenchman who established a post office on the coast and named it La Push. Oh "lå pěsh" in the Chinook jargon meant "a pole"; especially a setting pole for a canoe. Smitty, what's his name, who did the place names of Olympic Park, he suggests the least probably of the etymologies for La Push is the *la pesh* word. And I don't know where that came from {la bouche = the mouth}

jm yeah I always thought it was la bouche = the mouth French for 'the mouth'

jvp But {long pause} I don't know where in hell this comes from, and it keeps showing up,

jm Dan Pullen, is he the one who burned down the village?

jvp yeah um um I, although it is in more than one place, I, it just does not make any sense to me, why they would call it *la pesh* for poling a canoe could be the name for any place.

jm I thought this was like to stick a pole down as anchor ~ tie up. Maybe not.

jvp *la pesh*

jm Is setting a pole, setting a pole for a canoe.

jvp You don't need to take any, render an opinion, of course, both are possible, but , you know, as the mouth of the river Quileute coming to at that time because they were being kicked off their traditional territory by the holders. OK here is another of the jargon words for bad

MESATCHEE but that means 'sinful' as opposed to 'wicked', as opposed to Kultus

MOCLIPS MUCKLESHOOT Here's

IPSOOT ~ IPSUT Chinuk jargon "ĭp sōōt" meaning "to hide" I've got it in Quileute as ipswoot but that has nothing to do with it {airplane noise}

jm   NACHES that's Yakama

jvp Yyou know, he was really lucky to have Little Bill

NEAH ~ di ah ~ dēē åh It is not mentioned there since both the Makahs and the name of their village itself had nasals, but they lost all the nasals, so Neah became Diah and that's why. OK

NISQUALLY

MOWICH again from Chinuk jargon 'deer'

OHANAPECOSH glacier Ohanapecosh Park at the head of Boulder Creek, it doesn't say what language but is in Quileute territory. > 40:00

jm Which is on Mt Rainier And the native guy who lived there was a Sahaptin speaker. Again, I should check with the Yakama dictionary, Virginia Beavert is still with us, so

jvp holy cow

jm You know, she finally got her PhD at 92 at U Oregon.

jvp That's a beautiful story.

jm She comes over to Seattle every so often and works with Sharon Hargus.

jvp So

OYHUT is Chinuk jargon. Let's see what he says about that

Ozette small reservation on the Coast Doesn't mention Bill E Penn there

jm No He's down for

PYSHT

jvp The Quileute word is pixítsitaḳ^w and that suggests to me that that could be a very old word ~ name Such a different form of it in Quileute the Pysht River is just directly north of, um, Quileute habitation area at the top of Dickey River. So, and, if the Quileute s have a name so different from the Klallam based name, it leads me to think there was an earlier name that both of them derived from.

jm right

jvp of something. And that is simply another nail in the argument that Chimakuan speakers were there earlier, a long time ago. OK

jm Did you not derived at one point Chimakuan from Wakashan? Or

jvp Oh, I have a paper Chimak-Wakashan. The number of cognates, both grammatical issues and lexicals lead me to think that there is a great time depth, a relationship that could possibly be figured out. I just never did it. I gave that paper in a conference in about 1973 or 74. OK

jm I must have heard the paper.

jvp yeah, you were there then. What year did you come?

jm 1972 to 80.

jvp You know, it's such a great injustice

jm You know, we're putting together Pam's collection of essays is another reminder. All those guys are either dead or have Alzheimer's, or ALS Lou Gehrig's disease, > 45:00

vj You guys ready for a refile, or want cold beer, or ? {Vickie Jensen}

jm I'm fine for the moment.

jvp OK How much time do we have?

jm What time is it? 4?

jvp 4:00 pm

jm 5

jvp Thanks, darling, I think we are OK.

jm Thank you

jvp Are they going to come back and get you?

jm No, I'm going to have to do the bus route in reverse

jvp to get to them

jm to get to them to get to the Welsh Center

jvp Well, I'll walk down with you to the bus. I'm sorry about that.

    QUILCENE

    QUILLAYUTE The name of a tribe of Indians having a dialect or language different from all others

jm What about

    QUEETS

jvp Oh OK It says it's Queets River, um, OK, it is Quinault, Quileute is ḵ'ʷayt'soxḵʷ people who live at a particular place, but that's, that has, I don't know if that is an addition. It is surprising that William E Penn, it sounds like he knew Quinault.

jm It's possible

jvp Anyway, it's south of, south of Quileute territory, and Hoh so is there anything you might want to add to that? Or, Quileutes have used that name in a very Quileutized version. But that's perfectly understandable thing {leafing thru pages} OK How close are we here > 50:00.

jm 1½

jvp OK

jm Queets thing make sense in terms of all the K'wati stories, making human people from different substances. Like wolves, skin rubbings, and

jvp absolutely

jm I have no idea how QUILCENE ends up referring to "salt water people"

jvp Great Spirit Oh OK The Great Spirit is *c'əkati* and that's Earth ~ Nature, which is that word t'sikáti, Country ~ Land, so that's the one he has That is a serious error, so the Great Spirit is different from the transformer K'^{w}ati

jm It's still K'^{w}ati for Quileute

jvp OK back K glottalized rounded + A + T + I In the ceremonial language they have an æ̀ sound that does not occur anywhere else k'^{w}æ̀ti but that is only in ceremonial usage. K'^{w}ati is the way it happens in stories. So you have the Great Spirit, who is sometimes called the Land, so it is the Nature spirit that she ~ he ~ it is also called the Land, as opposed to the Transformer K'^{w}ati, who went around changing things into the way they are today. And incidentally creating the People, changing the People because People always existed. OK

jm yeah yeah

jvp OK saying, "From this time you shall remain on this river, and your name shall be K'witz q^u because from the dirt of the skin you were made" And I don't know how they refer to themselves {c'əkati }

jm And they have their own representative on the Quinault council.

jvp Do they?

jm Yeah, there is always a special position that is always filled by a Queets resident.

jvp Good OK

QUILLAYUTE Now, um, um, I'd love it if you'd give a little more information on this. The word QUILEUTE ~ k^{w}o'liyot'ilo, the root is k^{w}o'liy- who was the name of the chief of ancestral Wolves that were transformed in the ancestors of the Quileute, and here again is the Quileute word, and there is, and then, -o- means at a certain place + -ti- = means the people who live at that place and + -lo is the possessive. Incredibly, lovely, complex semantics, k^{w}o'liyot'ilo is the word. {pause} Lillian Pullen would pray in the morning to Land ~ Nature.

jm And yet I think she was as much Muckleshoot as

jvp She was, her mother

jm She floored Vi once by speaking Lushootseed with her.

jvp She was raised there and then came back and was raised by the chief of the Quileute

jm Oh

jvp A powerful, powerful woman

jm One of Vi's cedarbark dresses was made by her, tho it may have been Lillian working with {David} Fourlines.

jvp Say it again. David Fourlines.

jm He may have done the bulk of the work before Lillian finished it off.

jvp Yeah, he did a beautiful job with those vests.

jm This was a whole dress and for a while Vi told stories in that dress until one of the Skagits {Alice Williams} made a dress for her. And she felt it more appropriate.

jvp OK anything more.

jm No I will amend that.

jvp yeah No that, what we were talking about before, Queets

jm yeah yeah

jvp OK

QUINAULT

SATSOP Chehalis Indian word "tsa sup" (tså sup), meaning "tyee salmon".

jm Yeah I don't know where Quinault comes from, but there was a distinctive type of tyee salmon in the Satsop.

jvp OK What are Tyee salmon?

jm They {Kings} had a distinctive taste, big trade item.

jvp I did not realize that, that's neat OK

SATULICH Indian Henry We don't have to do anything with it?

jm No There is now a member from that family who is doing Yakama linguistics {at OU}

jvp Huh OK

SAMIS SAMISH Did you known Kenny Hansen?

jm Oh yeah. Not well, but y'know a force to be reckoned with

jvp Well, He actually got them recognized.

jm Him and his mother. A force of her own.

jvp God, she was a kicker. Um. Kenny was the godfather of our kids.

jm Both boys?

jvp Yeah. Oh wow. Uncle Kenny. I mean, talk about information from all over the place.

You know, Quileute word for

SEQUIM in Quileute is sx^{w}chk^{w}i'in   That is the biggest consonant cluster in the entire language. It's amazing! sx^{w}chk^{w}i'in sx^{w}chk^{w}i•yib

jm And it means?

jvp Like a lot of names, we don't know. But it is an ancient, ancient name. D'you want to put it in there?

jm Yes. Of course.

jvp What happened to Sequim, must be the next page. Didn't have room to write it. Redone. OK, Oh

SHUWA That is shówak^w I don't know where he gets OK shówak^w

jm It really was a village, a group?

jvp That is where, interestingly enough, that is where the other Bill Penn's mother came from

jm "Big" Bill?

jvp "Big" Bill's mother {pause} No I'm wrong about that, there are 2 Susies. And the Susie that grew up at shówak^w was the one that married Chris Morgenroth I the first. So that was where the first wife of Chris Morganroth came from You know about Christ Morgenroth, he was a German who came over and became the one that figured out all of the road beds on the western Olympic Peninsula by simply following the Indien trails. So when you go from Crescent Lake down to Forks the road is following the old Indien trails along the SolDuc.

jm So he was like a road engineer?

jvp What is that? He was old, some sort of, he was one of the first settlers in the whole set of river valleys around La Push. He married by an Indien ceremony Susie, then abandoned her. He became one of the most notorious early settlers, who was involved And he's the one who pushed to have the Olympic Forest set aside

jm National Park

jvp It was first a National Forest, then became a National Park.

jm He was German born?

jvp Yeah, he came from Germany. And now the Quileutes have Chris Morganroth V, and because when he abandoned Susie, she continued to use the name, and his family had a fit because he then went up and married a woman from Port Angeles, so his name is morgen + roth the German way, and Quileutes said well chuck it and changed it to morgan + roth and said if they want to be upset about it they can go crap in their hat! > 1:10:00

jvp OK

SKOOKUM SUQUAMISH OK SKOOKUMCHUCK what do you know about

SLUISKIN

jm He was a Yakama who lived on the slopes of Mt Rainier

jvp Oh, he's the one, on the east side?

jm No I think he was on the west side. He'd go home a lot. He was a guide on Mt Rainier. That's right, he was the guide for Isaac Steven's son Hazard when they made the first ascent, but he wouldn't, supposedly he would not go above the timber line. So there is all this stuff about the spirits above the timber line Hopeless junk

jvp I never heard What was Isaac Steven's son's name?

jm Hazard He wrote the 2 volume bio of his father, who could do no wrong. Even tho I'm still good friends with the family of Leschi's brother who was murdered in the governor's home office when he was guaranteed a safe night's sleep before they talked about, you know, winding up the Indien Treaty War. They {family} left Nisqually and went to Chehalis, which is how I know them. They still … this woman ran a logging company for years. That family did a collection of stories that are called Chehalis, but are really Nisqually. But it is X^{w}onné

jvp This is Upper Chehalis?

jm This is Upper Chehalis

jvp You mentioned Silas Heck and I think he was one of the last speakers of Lower Chehalis?

jm And Dale could never figure out why everyone else in his family spoke Upper, but he spoke Lower. He married several women who were Lower Chehalis, including a woman from an incredibly powerful family who set aside $8000 for her funeral. Big time.

jvp Vickie and I once found an Indien cemetery up in Haisla country with a beautiful tombstone that said "She raised good children" You have got to be proud, throw out your anchor

jm proud of your accomplishments

jvp OK

jm What about

SOL DUC ~ SOLDUC ~ SOLEDUCK

jvp Did I miss it?

jm bottom of page 17

jvp Oh

SOL DUC, SOLDUC, SOLEDUCK meaning "clear, sparkling water" That is such horseshit But the word is really sóliłt'a$\underline{k}$^{w} {plane noise} We don't know what it meant. That is an accent over the O.

jm Opaque as we say.

jvp Just a moment. "One of the tribes lived on the northern branch of the Quillayute River; the water of which was particularly clear and sparkling. In referring to the people of this village, they were called "so ls dAk q^{u}" or the "people living at the place of the clear, sparkling water". In time this tribe came to be known by that name". Sol Duc Hot Springs Do you know the origins of Sol Duc Hot Springs? Chris Morganroth wrote that up, and only later did we get Quileutes to say Yes that is one of our stories. Um I've got it written up and can send it to you if you are interested. Sol Duc Hot Springs has a myth of origin.

There were 2 incredibly big fire-breathing monsters, 1 was on the Quileute side and 1 was on the Klallam side, and they used to meet at the border between the 2, which was

Boulder Peak, OK, and they would fight, and fight, and fight, ripping and tearing, but they were evenly matched so one never actually killed the other, but they would roll around and Boulder Peak essentially has no trees around it and so they say that is because they were all knocked flat by the monsters, and finally they would stop, stop fighting, and the Quileute monster, and I have his name {named A'latkił = 'The one who cries in the woods'}, would come back to Quileute territory and crawl into his lair, wall it up, and sit and cry for years and years. His tears would roll out into the creek to form Sol Duc Hot Springs.

jm Sol Duc Hot Springs

jvp The Klallam monster did the same thing, and his creek formed the, um, the other hot springs over there. Anyway that is where the 2 hot springs come from. I'll send u the story.

jm OK Great

jvp Anyway. There really was no tribe, as it says here, no Solduc tribe, but there was a settlement and that settlement, interestingly enough, was shówa$\underline{k}^w$ that is located about 7 miles above OK So that is the band of Quileute speakers that lived on the Solduc.

STUCK > 1:20:00

jm It's Lushootseed.

jvp And

TAHOLAH Do you suppose the place was named after the chief or the chief named after the place?

jm No It was named after the chief. They began negotiating with the chief and it is still the name in the village. The Mason family holds that name.

jvp That right?

jm I have never heard anyone with that name who is not Mason family to this day.

jvp Good going.

TEAWHIT Now that is a Chinuk jargon word for 'foot' so there's a TEAWHIT Head so it is interesting that it really means 'foot head' "4 miles south of the mouth of Quillayute River, in northwestern Jefferson County" Yup promontory There's actually a Quileute name for TEAWHIT

jm for TEAWHIT itself?

jvp Yeah. That's a Chinuk jargon name that was given to it.

jm Oh it says William Penn of Clearwater, WA. Where's Clearwater?

jvp Clearwater is south of the Hoh River. For a while, Little Bill moved down and settled there because they declared to Quileute River to be a … something waterway.

jm Navigable Waterway Barbara Lane was involved as a witness in such.

jvp Navigable Quileute could not fish off the reserve, which was limited, so several Quileute including Little Bill moved down to Queets and fished on the Queets River and Clearwater is in Queets Country. That is actually an issue having to do with Little Bill Penn. {pause} Boy > 1:25:00 {plane noise}

TSA TSA DAKH, the Indian name meaning "tall, tall leaning rock". Name is of Makah origin. Doesn't ring a bell, but … OK It's TL TL kish. That is a mishearing that I could understand, TS instead of TL so Quileute tɬatɬakishxʷoʼwis {bee buzzing}

jm Quileute have the same word as Makah?

jvp I'm not sure what the Makah word is but this is clearly his mishearing of TL and TS. Let me write it down OK? OK

jm You have a black squirrel that runs your power line. Quite often.

jvp Oh, there he is. The interesting thing is, see that next pole down, this one has a … transformer on it.

jm yeah

jvp They just put a new pole up and moved the transformer. That transformer would have meant that we couldn't put anything that was combustible within 26 feet of it and that would have changed the nature of our lane way house across the back of it. So it was just shithouse luck that they came along and moved it. OK OK I haven't heard that word Can you see the accent is on the O?

jm yeah

jvp Now what did he say. It could just be a Quileute adaptation of that, with suffixes on the end. This could very well be a Makah name. If there is anything of interest to you … OK

WAADAH

jm That's a Makah village It's a long A Waaaadah

jvp Wa'ada

jm Interesting, the next one is

WAATCH That is where Isabel Ides lived

jvp There is the WA'ATCH band And the Quileute word wa'ada is their word for, it is Tatoosh Island? Just a minute … wa'ach > 1:30:00 [jm huh]

jvp I would be surprised if there wasn't a glottal stop in the Makah form of it too. Here is WA'ATCH too, they both have glottal stops. OK

WISHKAH "stink river".

jm Because there was a fight between a thunderbird and a whale and it dropped the whale in the river {to rot} which is why it stunk. Dale's papers refer to getting that text but we can't find it. Nobody at Chehalis can find it. They do remember that is why it is called 'stink' because of the whale that was dropped into the river.

jvp This was Thunderbird that did it? [jm Yes]

jvp You know Thunderbird's home was on the Blue Glacier, under the Blue Glacier?

jm Under? In a cave?

jvp In a cave essentially the Blue Glacier grows and when it grows, it grows over a cliff and an immense chunk of it will fall down, and when the people heard that they would say, Oh there's Thunderbird acting up.

jm Good lord. {laughs} So the glacier was calving as they say up in Alaska

jvp yeah it was And there are Whale rocks {kʷat'łayaxi < kʷat'ł = 'whale' + -yaxi 'rock'} all over, in every river in the …

jm They were Whales dropped?

jvp Yeah dropped by T-bird.

jm That is what the word means, it means a dropped Whale?

jvp Just a minute. It means 'Whale Rock'.

jm You just said it. It's under WISHKAH cause that is the connection

jvp OK OK And t'ist'ilal is the name of Thunderbird {pause} Yeah Blue Glacier is on the west side of Mt Olympus > 1:35:00 OK

    TOLEAK meaning "hole in the wall rock" But it is … {Quileute łiłok̲ʷayáxi = 'hole in the rock'}

jm Somewhere along the line I heard there was a Giant who lived there. Somebody from WSU did a test excavation there. And was told by an elder while he was digging at Toleak that was the name of the Giant

jvp um   There were 2 Giants and there are stories about them in that area, but I can't remember them {shuffling papers} I'll check on them for you Anyway, the whole t'ist'ilal = Thunderbird thing has to do with all that. OK We've done Solduc. Where have we gotten to? Spokane?

jm We are at the end!

jvp We finished it?

jm Yeah

jvp Yelm Toleak

jm Last place is Goodman Creek?

jvp Yeah

jm Again, somewhere I was told it was some kind of dividing line?

jvp OK Goodman Creek Oh Oh And Toleak Point is there.

jm That's where Toleak?

jvp In that area. I don't, I never heard of a Giant named Toleak.

jm He may have said who told him. Again that is one of the things I inherited from Doc Daugherty.

jvp OK that is under Goodman Creek. OK

jm Here is 'hole in the wall' again. > 1:40:00 Verne Ray got it as a whaling base.

jvp I am not very comfortable with his …

jm ethnographic …

jvp No Well, the places always had to be something, rather than

jm just a place

jvp it may have had

jm you're right hunting, they are all {assigned tasks}

jvp yeah, they are all something, rather than just a name for an area

jm And he does not say where he got it, who his sources were

jvp No but he did say he said he had the pleasure of riding up all the rivers with informed
     Quileutes, who pointed out locations, and probably one of them was Big Bill. Or maybe even
     Little Bill

jm right {pause}

jvp Oh I forget we were looking at 'hole in the rock place'

jm He has it too

jvp OK Toleak Point łiłok̓ʷayáxi Is that what he had written there? Let me put

jm It is not exactly Toleak

jvp Sounds like its been corrupted to Toleak OK That is his. Can I write OK Rock actually…
     Good Going That's yours.

jm That's yours.

jvp Do I get to keep that Yippy

jm It does not have little dots on the top to tell it's archived. And do you know who's on the
     cover? {Ron Hilbert Coy}

jvp That is yours Just a minute, there's one that has writing in it. OK Where are we? Yup,
     that's yours.

jm This {Quileute Dictionary} one does not have writing in it.

jvp No OK Where are we?

jm This page   > 1:46:23

NL/SL = Dawn Bates, Thom Hess, Vi Hilbert 1994 *Lushootseed Dictionary*. Seattle:
     University of Washington Press.
Virginia Beavert & Sharon Hargus 2009 *Ichishkiin Sinwit ~ Yakama / Yakima ~ Sahaptin
     Dictionary*. Seattle: University of Washington Press.
B04: = William Bright, ed. 2004 *Native Placenames of the United States*. Norman: University
     of Oklahoma Press.

<u>Original</u>

TRANSLATION OF GEOGRAPHIC NAMES OF INDIAN ORIGIN
By
Alfred J Smith
and
William E Penn

(8,835 words)

Tacoma, Washington
January 6, 1939

{WPA state & federal writers projects, Seattle & Tacoma}

Alfred J. Smith,
Tacoma, Washington,
December 29, 1938. _8,835_ words

Ql = Quileute
NL = Northern Lushootseed
SL = Southern Lushootseed

Subject: **Translation of Indian names for geographical places in Washington**

ARCH-A-WAT, a corruption of the Quillayute Indian words "he cha wa" (hā chå wå) meaning "good beach".

> Archawat is an Indian village on the coast, 2 miles, south of Cape Flattery, in northwestern Clallam County. *speaker* ~~informant~~, *William E Penn.*

BAABOK, from "ba e da" (bā ā dåk), the name of a Makah Indian tribe. (Meaning unknown). This tribe of Makah Indians are located in northwestern Clallam County. ~~informant~~, *William Penn.* {Ql = ? + –ok^w = locative}

BOGACHIEL, a corruption of the Quillayute Indian words "be qua tchiel" (bō qwå tchēē el) meaning "gets riley after a rain"

> Bogachiel Peak, at the head of the Bagachiel River, about 8 miles northwest of Mount Olympus, in south central Clallam County.

> Bogachiel River, a large stream of the western Olympics, uniting with the Soleduok to form the Quillayute River, near Mora, in southwestern Clallam County. ~~informant~~, *William Penn*

CALAWAH, from the Quillayute Indian words or name "ca la wa" (kå lå wå), meaning "middle fork". {"one in the middle"}

> Calawah River. A stream which rises in the Olympics, flows west and joins the Bogachiel about 6 miles above the mouth of the latter, in southwestern Clallam County.

> Calawah River, North Fork. A northern tributary of the Calawah, joining the main stream near Forks, in southwestern Clallam County. ~~informant~~, *William Penn.*

CAPE JOHNSON, formerly was called by the Quillayute Indians, "tå qwå åt" meaning "Big curve in the bay (Several other points carry this name).

> Cape Johnson. A cape 4 miles north of the Quillayute River, in southwestern Clallam County. ~~informant~~, *William Penn.*

CAMAS, (see La Camas). {Ql = k^{w}ala }

CEBALOP, a corruption of the Puyallup Indian words "ci bal Ap" (chēē båll ŭp), Meaning "shadow monster". Indian name for village formerly occupying present site of Old Tacoma. Source, *Mythology of Southern Puget Sound*, Ballard; p117, U of W Press.

CHIBAHDEHL ~ KASHUKUDDIB. A corruption of the Quillayute Indian words "chi chi a qwl" (chēē chēē å qŭil) also meaning "standing rocks". The Makah Indians call these rocks "kla't 'la Itc kos" (klå tlå klĭtch kōs), which also means "standing rocks". ~~informant~~, William Penn. [2]

> Chibahdehl Rocks. Rocky inlets near the beach, 5 miles east of Cape Flattery, in northwestern Clallam County.

CLALLAM, meaning unknown.

CLOQUALLAM, a corruption of the Quillayute Indian words "klu kwe li" (klōō kwā lēē) the name of a Quillayute Indian secret society, and the Chehalis word "ob" or "uum", meaning "the people of that place". The words "kwe li" (kwā lēē) means "a dangerous being charged with magic".

The "klu kwe li" (klōō kwā lēē) dance was performed by members of this secret society, composed mainly of warriors, the purpose of which was to gain magic powers (superhuman) in war expeditions. It, therefore, pertains somewhat to the eastern Indian's War Dance.

A Quillayute Indian legend relates: "A long time ago, a party of Quillayute Indians visited the tribe of Chehalis Indians living on a branch of the Chehalis River, heading in the Olympics. Here a great "patshatl"(meaning "giving away" feast) was given by the hosts, and in return the visiting Quillayutes gave, or introduced, the klu kwe li dance.

From that time the Chehalis Indians referred to this tribe as the "Klu kwe li ub" (klōō kwā lēē ŭm) which means in substance "the people living at the place of the Klu kwe li".

> Cloquallam. A village on Cloquallam River, 12 miles southwest of Shelton, in south central Mason County.

> Cloquallam River. A tributary of the Chehalis River, from the north, near Elma, in southeastern Grays Harbor County. ~~informant~~, *William Penn.*

COMAX, CUMTUX, (See Kumtux) {Comox ?}

COPALIS, a corruption of the Quinault Indian name of Chief John "Chi pe lis, (Chēē pā lĭs), for whom it was named.

> Copalis. A village near the mouth of the Copalis River, in west central (Gray's Harbor County.

> Copalis Creek. A small stream entering the Pacific Ocean, from the northeast, in west central Gray's Harbor County.

> Copalis Crossing. A station on the NP Ry {Northern Pacific Railway}, 12 miles northwest of Hoquiam, in west central Grays Harbor County.

> Copalis Rock. A small rock island near the shore, about 7 miles south of Moclips, in west central Grays Harbor County.

Copalis Head. A headland on the seacoast, about 7 miles south of Moclips, in west central Grays Harbor County. ~~informant~~, *William Penn.* [3]

COWLITZ, a corruption of the Salish Indian words "tå wå litch" which means "capturing the Medicine Spirit." Lewis and Clark called it "Coweliske". Dr Tolmie, 1835, wrote it "Ta wallitch". {Tah is 'spirit' in Chinookan}

Cowlitz Bay. A bay in north central San Juan County.

Cowlitz Chimneys. The divide between Kotsuck and Fryingpan Creeks, east of Mount Rainier; elevation 7,607 feet.

Cowlitz Cleaver. A cleaver or divide between the heads of Cowlitz and Nisqually Glaciers, on the southeastern slopes of Mount Rainier.

Cowlitz County. A county in southwestern Washington.

Cowlitz Divide. The divide between upper Muddy Fork of Cowlitz River and Ohannapecosh River, in Pierce and Lewis Counties.

Cowlitz Glacier. A large glacier, about 5 miles long, on the southeastern slopes of Mount Rainier.

Cowlitz Junction. A junction on the C.M. & St.P. RR., 8 miles north of Morton, in central Lewis County. {Chicago, Milwaukee & St Paul Railroad}

Cowlitz Park. A park northeast of the lower end of Cowlitz Glacier.

Cowlitz Pass. A pass on the Cascade Divide, about 20 miles southeast of Mount Rainier; elevation, 5,191 feet.

Cowlitz River, flows in a westerly and southerly direction through the southwestern part of Washington.

Cowlitz Rocks. Peaks on the divide between Cowlitz and Paradise Glaciers, on the southeast slopes of Mount Rainier. ~~informant~~, *Henry Sicade* (prominent Puyallup Indian).

COWITCHE, or COWICHE, comes from the Salish Indian words "Kow itch" meaning "get hunchback".

During the long winter evenings, about the campfires, the old-time Indian story-tellers would lie outstretched in the center of a group of youngsters, all eager to hear the stories of long ago. Each youngster was required to say at intervals, "Haboo, kowitch" meaning "all attention, get hunchback!"

Cowiche. a post office about 12 miles northwest of North Yakima, in north central Yakima County.

Cowiche Creek, Middle Fork, A middle headwater of Cowiche Creek, northwest of Tampico, in north central Yakima County.

Cowiche Creek, North Fork. A northern headwater of Cowiche Creek, near Cowiche, in north central Yakima County. [4]

Cowiche Creek, South Fork. A southern headwater of Cowiche Creek, northwest of Tampico, in north central Yakima County.

Cowiche Mountain. A divide between Cowiche and Atanum creeks, west of Yakima, in north central Yakima County; maximum elevation, 4,300 feet. informant, *Henry Sicade* (Deceased), prominent Puyallup Indian author.

CUITIN, a corruption of the Chinook jargon word "kŭ ĭ tăn" meaning "horse".

Cuitin Creek. A small eastern headwater of Diamond Fork, east of Cispus Pass, in west central Yakima County. Source, *Gill's Chinook Dictionary*.

CULTUS, a corruption of the Chinook, jargon word "kŭl tŭs" meaning "worthless", "bad"; "purposeless". {1 of 3 CJ words for "bad"}

Cultus Bay. A bay at the southern end of Whidbey Island, between Scatchet Head and Possession Point, at the south end of Island County. Source, *Gill's Chinook Dictionary*.

DESTRUCTION ISLAND, was formerly called by the Indians "hōb tō lå bĭish". The word of Salish origin, either Quinault or Lower Chehalis. The Quinault Indians called it "Ta tchist qᵘ" (Tå tchist qh). Meaning Unknown. informant, *William Penn*.

DTOKOAH, a corruption of the Makah and Quillayute words "'ta qua" (dtå quå) meaning unknown - just a place name. {Dickey #2}

Dtokoah Point. A point on the coast, about 8 miles east of Cape Flattery, in northwestern Clallam County. informant, *William Penn*.

DICKODOCHTEDER, a corruption of the Quillayute Indian name "de tho datct doh" (dā tó dótcht dōh, applied to a branch of the Quillayutes living on that stream. It means "people who live in the first branch of the Quillayute River.

Dickodochteder River. A stream in western Clallam County, rising in lake Dicky, and emptying into the Quillayute near the mouth of the latter; sometimes called Dickey River.

Dickodochteder River, East Fork. The principal eastern tributary of the main river of that name, southeastern Clallam County.

Dickodochteder River, West Fork. The principal western tributary of the main river of that name, in southwestern Clallam County. informant, *William Penn*.

DUCKABUSH, from the Indian (Twana) name "Duckabush", applied to the chief of the mythical Salmon People … supposed to have a crooked mouth. {Southern Lushootseed = daxʷ 'place' + yabus 'crooked jawed salmon' B04: 137} [5]

The river was so named by the Indians 'because of the frequency that duckabush, or crooked-mouthed salmon were caught there. ~~informant~~, *Laqh-kla-dub (Robert Lewis)*,[48] one of the oldest living Skokomish-Skagit Indians, Born about 1821-1825.

Another translation persists that the name is derived from the Twana Indian words "do hi a boos" meaning "reddish face". A reddish escarpment on the mountainside near the village is said to bespeak the origin of the name. (This personally has not been confirmed). {Ql = ałk^{w}ak}

> Duckabush. A town on Hood Canal, near the mouth of Duckabush River, in southeastern Jefferson County.

> Duckabush River. A river heading in the eastern Olympics and emptying into Hood Canal, near Duckabush, in southeastern Jefferson County.

DOSEWALLIPS, from the Clallam Indian name of a mythical Indian chief who was transformed by the Great Changer into a mountain, which the Indians now point out near the head of the Dosewallips River. (Re: The myth {sic}, "How T'coma got her name").

> Dosewallips River. A river heading in the eastern Olympics and emptying into Hood Canal at Brinnon, in eastern Jefferson County.

DUWAMISH, a corruption of the Salish Indian words "dux "duwa bc" (dŭx ů dūwå mĭsh) meaning "the people of that place (dux u duwa)" Meaning unknown. {SL = 'people inside' B04: 138}

> Duwamish Head. A headland at the south entrance to Elliott Bay, in northwestern King County.

> Duwamish River. A river entering Elliott Bay, from the southwest, in west central King County. Source, *The Indians of Puget Sound*, Haeberlin-Gunther, 1930, U of W Pub, pp 1.

ELWA, a corruption of the Quillayute Indian words or name "e ilth quatl" (ā īlth quåtł). An Indian place name. Meaning unknown. {Ql = iłx^{w}ak^w}

> Elwha, A town on the SPA & W Ry, 7 miles west of Port Angeles, in north central Clallam County; elevation 193 feet. {}

> Elwha River. A large stream draining the north central Olympics and entering the Straits of Juan de Fuca 7 miles west of Port Angeles. ~~informant~~, *William Penn.*

ENUMCLAW, an Indian brave of legendary lore, who was changed into thunder "for all time", by the Great Spirit. {Sahaptian inɨmłá 'he who makes noise' < inɨmn 'to neigh, bray, sing' + łá 'he who' B04: 145}

> Enumclaw, A town on the KP and CM & St P Railways, in south central King County; elevation 742 feet. ~~informant~~, *Henry Sicade*; prominent Puyallup Indian author. [6]

---

[48] Robert Lewis ~ *Laqh-kla-dub* was a Twana elder of great age, sometimes said to be 100.

HOH, a corruption of the Quinault Indian word "q^u" which means "that place" or "boundary". The Indian name for the river is "ch' la q^u" (chq lå qh) meaning," can speak chå lå (Quinault language) to that place". {Ql = hux^w}   {ča'la$\underline{x}$^{w}}

> Hoh. A post office 2 miles from the mouth of the Hoh River, in western Jefferson County.

> Hoh Head. A promontory 2½ miles north of the mouth of Hoh River, in west central Jefferson County. ~~informant~~, *William Penn.*

HOKO, a corruption of the Indian words "ho qwol th" (Hō kwō lth), being the name of a small tribe of Indians formerly living at that place. Makahs, Queets and Clallams use the same word. Meaning unknown. {'drift' Makah = hu:qu: }

> Hoko River, a large stream entering the Strait of Juan de Fuca, at Kydaku Point, about 4 miles west of Clallam Bay, in northwestern Clallam County. ~~informant~~, *William Penn.*

HOQUIAM, a corruption of the lower Quinault Indian name "ho qui a bits" or "ho qui ob" (hō kwēē ŭm), meaning "hungry for wood". This name is said to have been applied to those people who depended on driftwood for fuel. The suffix "um" meaning "people".

> Hoquiam. This city lies west of Aberdeen on Grays Harbor, in the southwestern part of Grays Harbor County. It has an area of about 8 square miles. Source of information has been lost.

> Hoquiam River. A river about 20 miles long, entering Grays Harbor from the north, in central Grays Harbor County.

> Hoquiam River, Middle Fork. A tributary entering the main stream 2 miles above the mouth of the latter, in southwestern Grays Harbor County.

> Hoquiam River, West Fork. A tributary of Middle Fork of Hoquiam River, uniting with the latter at Poison landing in southwestern Grays Harbor county.

HUMPTILIPS, a corruption of the Quinault or Lower Chehalis Indian words or name "hōb tō lå bĭish" meaning "hard to pole" people. The suffix "bish" meaning "the people of that place". {Lower Chehalis = ? + -apš 'stream' B04: 175}

> Humptulips. A town on Humptulips River 22 miles north of Hoquiam, in west central Grays Harbor County.

> Humptulips River. A river draining the south central Olympics and entering Grays Harbor, from the north, in western Grays Harbor County. This River has also the East Fork and West Fork joining near Humptulips post office, in central Grays Harbor County. [7]

KALALOCK, a corruption of the Quinault Indian words or name "k' E la ok" (kq â lā ók) meaning "a good place to land". In the old days, when the Indians traveled along the beach in their great ocean-going cedar canoes, this little sheltered beach was the only place to between the Hoh and the Queets rivers where the Indian canoes could safely land.

Kalalock Creek. A stream entering the sea, 5 miles north of the mouth of the Queets River, in southwestern Jefferson County. ~~informant~~, *William Penn.*

KASHUKUDDIB, same as Chibahdehl. Means "standing rocks".

Kashukuddib Point. A point on the coast, about ten miles east of Cape Flattery, in northwestern Clallam County. ~~informant~~, *William Penn.*

KLAHANEE, from the Chinook jargon, meaning "out-of-doors".

Klahanee Gardens are located near the foot of Mount Angeles, near Port Angeles, in north central Clallam County. Source, *Gill's Chinook Dictionary.*

KOILAH, a corruption of the Makah words "'o it la" (quō' ēēt lå). Meaning unknown. {Makah = q'ᵂitl'a 'rock slide' B04: 232}

Koitlah Point. A point on the coast, 5 miles east of Cape Flattery, in northwestern Clallam County. ~~informant~~, *William Penn.*

KULO KALA, probably a corruption of the Chinook Jargon words, "kula" (bird) and "kala" (goose). Also, "kăl a kăl åh ma" means "goose". {reduplication of Chinuk 'goose'}

Kulo Kala Point. A small headland half way between New Dingeness Bay and Washington Harbor, in northeastern Clallam County. Source, *Gill's Chinook Dictionary.*

KULTUS, from the Chinook Jargon word "kŭl tŭs", meaning "worthless," "bad," "purposeless".

Kultus Mountain. A mountain ridge about 1??) miles southeast of Sedro Woolley, in west central Skagit County; maximum elevation 4,089 feet. Source, *Gill's Chinook Dictionary.*

KLICKITAT, is the mythological progenitor of those tribes of Indians inhabiting the eastern slopes of the Cascade Mountains - also of the Squally (Nisqualli) people, an off-shoot of the Klickitats. Is said to mean "robber". Source, Klickitat is one of two sons who figure in the myth-legend of the "Origin of the Klickitats and Multnomahs". [8]

Klickitat. A town on the SP & S Rwy (Goldendale Branch), 14 miles northeast of Lyle, in west central Klickitat County; elevation 440 feet.

Klickitat County. This county lies in the south central part of the state, with Columbia River as its southern boundary. It has an area of 1,825 square miles. The county is mountainous in its western part, but the remainder of the section is made up of rolling plains and plateaus dissected by numerous valleys.

Klickitat Creek. A tributary of Klickitat River, from the east, in central Klickitat County.

Klickitat Creek. A small southern tributary of Cowlitz River, near Mayfield, in central Lewis County.

Klickitat Creek. A southern tributary of White River, heading near Chinook Pass, on the Cascade summit, in east central Pierce County.

Klickitat Glacier. A glacier on the southeastern slope of Mount Adams in southwestern Yakima County.

Klickitat River, West Fork. A western headwater of Klickitat River, northeast of Mount Adams, in southwestern Yakima County.

LACAMAS, from the Indian name of a small edible root or bulb (wild hyacinth) a native plant found in most parts of Washington state, and eastward to the Rocky Mountains. It formed a most important item of food in the Indian's fare. "La camas" was a name familiar to all tribes, although nearly every tribe had their own name for this plant. The Quillayutes called it "quå å la". {Ql = }

Lacamas Creek. A small eastern tributary of Muck Creek, at Roy, in west central Pierce County.

LaCamas Creek. A tributary of Cowlitz River from the northeast, near Vader, in southwestern Lewis County.

LaCamas Lake. A narrow lake, 2 miles long, on LaCamas Creek, one mile north of Camas, in southeastern Clark County. ~~informant~~, *William Penn.*

LA PUSH, named by a Frenchman who established a post office on the coast and named it La Push. "lå pĕsh" in the Chinook jargon meant "a pole"; especially a setting pole for a canoe. {French la bouche = 'the mouth'}

LaPush. An Indian village on the Quillayute Indian Reservation, at the mouth of Quillayute River, in southwestern Clallam County. ~~informant~~: William Penn. [9]

LILLIWAUP, from a Twana Indian word meaning "inlet". {Twana = sləláwap 'cove, inlet' s- nominalizer + láw 'enter' + -ap 'end' B04: 252}

Lilliwaup. A village on the west side of Hood Canal, in north central Mason County.

Lilliwaup Bay. A small bay on the west side of Hood Canal, opposite Dewatto, in north central Mason County.

Lilliwaup Creek. A small stream entering Hood Canal from the northwest, at Lilliwaup, in north central Mason County.

Lilliwaup Falls. A scenic falls on Lilliwaup Creek, ½ mile above its mouth, in north central Mason County.

MALACHITE, MALAKAT, MALAKUT, a corruption of the Indian words meaning "bait plenty". {1 of 3 Chinuk words for 'bad'}

Malachite Lake. A small lake on the West Fork of the Foss River, near Skykomish, in northeastern King County.

MESATCHEE, a corruption of the Chinook jargon word "mĕ såh chēē" meaning "wicked; bad; cruel; vicious".

>Mesatchee Creek. A southern tributary of the upper American River, near Bumping Lake, in northwestern Yakima County. Source: *Gill's Chinook Dictionary.*

MOCLIPS, a corruption of the Quinault Indian name "no mo 'klópc" (nō mō klópĭsh). Meaning unknown. {Quinault = nəw'muɬapš 'large stream' < nəw'- 'place' + -apš 'stream' B04: 292}

>Moclips. A town on the N. P. Rwy., and the sea coast, 28 miles northwest of Hoquiam, in west central Grays Harbor County. ~~informant~~, *William Penn.*

MUK KAW, a corruption of the Makah Indian tribal name "Makah", being spelled as pronounced.

>Mukkcaw Bay. A small bay on the west coast, 5 miles south of Cape Flattery, in western Clallam County. ~~informant~~, *William Penn.*

MUCKLESHOOT, a corruption of the name of a Salish Indian tribe. The word from which this tribal name is taken is "o kElcuɬ" (ó kŭ1 shōōel). Meaning unknown. { bəqəlšuɬ B04: 300?}

>Muckleshoot Indian Reservation. A reservation of 3,491 acres, all allotted, in King and Pierce Counties, along White River, southeast of Auburn. Source, *Indians of Puget Sound*, Haeberlin-Gunther, 1930, U of W Press, pp ?? [10]

IPSOOT, OR IPSUT, from the Chinook jargon "ĭp sōōt" meaning "to hide"; "keep secret"; concealed"; A liberal translation would be "hidden creek".

>Ipsut Creek. A small southern tributary of Carbon River, 4 miles below the end of Carbon Glacier, in east central Pierce County.

>Ipsut Pass. A pass at the head of Ipsut Creek, near Crater Lake, in east central Fierce County. Source, *Gill's Chinook Dictionary.*

NACHES, a corruption of the Indian name of a tribe, the "naxtcespam" meaning Naches River People. Note: Naxtce is pronounced "Nåh'tchēē". (Naxtce) {Sahaptin= naxič:s 'first water' B04: 307}

>Naches. A town on the NY & V Rwy (NP Rwy.) 14 miles northwest of North Yakima, in north central Yakima County.

>Nac hes Pass. A pass on the Cascade Divide, at the headwaters of the Middle Fork of Naches and Clearwater rivers; elevation 4,988 feet.

>Naches River. A large stream of northwestern Yakima County, joining Yakima River at Yakima.

>Naches River, Middle Fork. The middle headwaters of the Naches River, near the Cascade summit, on the Kittitas-Yakima County line.

Naches River, North Fork. A northern headwater of the Naches River, in southwestern Kittitas County.

Naches River, South Fork. A southern headwater of Naches River, in northwestern Yakim County. Source, Mythology of Southern Paget Sound; Ballard; pp 147, U of W Press.

NAHWATEL, a corruption of the Quinault Indian word "nåh wåtł" meaning "true". {Upper Chehalis = nawacál'ł 'big lake' < náw- 'big' + cál'ł 'lake' B04: 309}

Nahwatel Lake. A lake 1 mile long, 4 miles east of Matlook, in southwestern Mason County. ~~informant~~, *William Penn.*

NEAH, a corruption of the Indian name of a branch of the Makah Indians living at Neah Bay. The Indian name is "di ah" (dēē åh). Meaning unknown. {Makah chief's name}

Neah Bay. An Indian village, post office and store, on the shore about 7 miles east of Cape Flattery, in northeastern Clallam County. ~~informant~~, W*illiam Penn.*

NISQUALLY, a corruption of the Indian name of the "Squallay" tribe, and the French "nez qarrees". The Indian word "sqole" (squallay) is descriptive of the "waving motion of flowers and grasses" when stirred by a breeze. The French explorers from Canada found the local Indians had rather round faces and a flat nose. When the Indians were asked the name of their tribe, they replied, "Squal lay", whereupon the French exclaimed, "oh, [11] nez quarrees" which means "square nose". {SL = dx^{w}sq^{w}əliabš '' < dx^w 'of' + sq^{w}əli 'grassy' + abš 'people' B04: 329}

Nisqually. A station on the N. P. Rwy., 20 miles southwest of Tacoma, in southwestern Pierce County.

Nisqually Flats. The delta of the Nisqually River, at its mouth, in northeastern Thurston County.

Nisqually Glacier. A large primary glacier about 4 miles long, west of Paradise Park, on the southern slope of Mount Rainier. This glacier is the third largest on the mountain, and most accessible glacier in the United States.

Nisqually Head. A headland on Paget Sound, 2 miles west of the mouth of Nisqually River, in northeastern Thurston County.

Nisqually Indian Reservation.. A reservation of 4,717 acres, all allotted, in Pierce and Thurston Counties, along Nisqually River, near its mouth.

Nisqually Lake. A small lake about 4 miles northwest of Roy, in west central Pierce County.

Nisqually Reach. A section of Puget Sound, opposite the mouth of Nisqually River, between Anderson Island and the mainland, in Thurston and Pierce Counties.

Nisqually River. A river flowing southward, westward, and northwestward from the western slopes of the Cascades. It heads in several glaciers on the south side of Mount Rainier. It empties into Case Inlet, a part of Puget Sound, between Tacoma and Olympia. The approximate length is 81 miles. There are a number of creeks and rivers feeding it. The drainage area is 675 square miles. Source, *The Indians of Puget Sound*; Haeberlin-Gunther, 1950: 7 UW Press.

MOWICH, a corruption of the Chinook jargon word "Mŏw ĭch" meaning "a deer"; "venison"; and sometimes used in speaking of a strange or unknown animal, as "hu-loime mowich" meaning "a strange beast".

> Mowich River. A river heading on the west slopes of Mount Rainier and emptying into the Puyallup River, in e&st central Pierce County. Source, *Gill's Chinook Dictionary*. {Chinuk 'deer, venison' B04: 299}

OHANAPECOSH, from an Indian word or name, meaning "deep blue water". {Sahaptin = áwxanapaykaš 'standing at the edge' B04: 344}

> Ohanapecosh Glacier. A glacier about 2 miles long, south of Fryingpan Glacier, on the eastern slope of Mount Rainier.

> Ohanapecosh Park. A park at the head of Boulder Creek, east of Ohanapecosh Glacier, east of Mount Rainier.

> Ohanapecosh River. An upper tributary of the Cowlitz River, from the north, in northeastern Lewis County and southeastern Pierce. Source, Packwood Recreational Unit; US Forest Service. (Pamphlet). [12]

OLYMPUS, the mountain, was called by the Quillayute Indians "o ł sky" (ō el skī). Meaning unknown. ~~informant~~, *William Penn*.

ORTING, is of Puyallup Indian origin, meaning "a prairie in the woods".

> Orting. A town on the NP Rwy, 18 miles southeast of Tacoma, in central Pierce County; elevation 198 feet.

OTSO, is probably derived from the Puyallup Indian "ot sk". This was the largest type of saltwater canoe, employed for long trips and capable of carrying a large number of men. This type was used as 'War Canoes.' This point was adapted to landing these large canoes. {Nootkan = 'ə'utxs}

> Otso Point. A point at the north end of Anderson Island, in west central Pierce County. ~~informant~~, Jerry Meeker, a prominent Puyallup Indian.

OYHUT, a corruption of the Chinook jargon word "Oo e hŭt" or "weh hut" meaning "a road"; "path"; or "trail". {Chinuk 'portage'}

> Oyhut. a village on the west shore of North Bay, 5 miles north of Lone Tree, in southwestern Grays Harbor County. Source, *Gills Chinook Dictionary*.

OZETTE, a corruption of the Makah Indian name "o se łth " (ō sā el th) meaning "middle tribe". {Makah = 'use:'ił 'woman living apart from her husband' B04: 363}

> Ozette Indian Reservation. A small reservation on the Coast, near Ozette Lake, in west central Clallam County. It has an area of 640 acres, all unallotted.

Ozette Island. An island ½ mile long and ½ mile off shore, near Cape Alva, in western Clallam County; elevation 240 feet.

Ozette Lake. A lake 8 miles long, with maximum width of 2½ miles, about 2 miles from the ocean, in western Clallam County.

Ozette River. A stream about 4 miles long, outlet of Ozette Lake, near Cape Alva, in western Clallam County. ~~informant~~, *William Penn.*

PUYALLUP, a corruption of the Indian-words "spuya lupo bc" (spuya lupo mish) or "Spuya lupo people" or "generous people". "spuya" means "to pile up until it runs over" or "generous"; and "lupo" means "people". "mich" means "people". {SL = puy'álǝp 'crooked stream' B04: 400}

Puyallup River. An important river heading in the Puyallup Glacier, on the western slopes of Mount Rainier and flowing in a northwesterly course empties into Commencement Bay at Tacoma. [13]

Puyallup. A town located in north central Pierce County; elevation 49 feet. It has the distinction of being the only town of that name in the world.

Puyallup Glacier. A glacier about 3½ miles long, on the western slope of Mount Rainier.

Puyallup Indian Reservation. A reservation of 17,465 acres, all allotted, on the low lands at the mouth of the Puyallup River. ~~informant~~, *Indians of Puget Sound*, Haeberlin-Gunther, p9.

PYSHT, a corruption of the Clallam Indian word "p' he slth" (pkhā'sylth). Meaning unknown. {Klallam = pǝšc't 'against wind ~ current' B04: 401}

Pysht. A post office on the coast, 14 miles east of Clallam Bay, in northwestern Clallam. County.

Pysht River. A river entering the Strait of Juan de Fuca, near Pillar Point, in northwestern Clallam County.

Pysht River, East Fork. An eastern tributary of Pysht River in northwestern Clallam County. ~~informant~~, *William Penn.*

QUEETS, a corruption of the Indian name of the river by that name, which comes [from] the Queets origin myth. In the Quinault language, it is called "k' witz q^u" or "q^u itz q^u" (kw ā ts), meaning "out of the dirt of the skin". {Quinault = q'^{w}ícx̣^{w} 'dirt' B04: 403}

The myth relates that the Great Spirit, S'q'it^u (the Transformer) {c'ǝkati } was one day walking along the beach, traveling northward, when he came to the (Queets) river. He looked all around and found no people living there, so he sat down on the riverbank in meditation. As he sat there he rubbed his legs to restore circulation after crossing the river. Small rolls of dirt formed under his hand, which he threw into the water. From these, there came forth from the water a man and a woman. These he placed on the river as the ancestors of the present tribe, saying,

"From this time you shall remain on this river, and your name shall be K' witz q^u because from the dirt of the skin you were made" {c'əkati }

Queets Mount. A mountain 5½ miles southeast of Mount Olympus, in central Jefferson County.

Queets River. A river heading in the central Olympics, flowing southwest and entering the sea about 14 miles north of Cape Elizabeth, in southwestern Jefferson County. ~~informant~~, *William Penn.*

QUILCENE, a Salish Indian word meaning "salt water people". {Twana = q^{w}ə'lsíd B04: 404 NB: N > D}

Quilcene. A town on the NP Rwy, and on Hood Canal, in northeastern Jefferson County.

Quilcene Bay. A bay about 4 miles long, the northwest arm of Dabop Bay, in eastern Jefferson County.

QUILLAYUTE, the name of a tribe of Indians having a dialect or language different from all others. It is also the name of the main river flowing into the ocean, draining the territory occupied by the Quillayute tribe. Meaning of the name has been lost in antiquity. [14] {Ql *k^{w}oliy-* = chief of ancestral Wolves + *-ti-* = 'people there' + *-lo* possessive}

Quillayute Indian Reservation. A reservation of 857 acres, unallotted, at the mouth of Quillayute River, in southwestern Clallam County.

Quillayute Needle. A small needle, 1 wide off shore and 3 miles south of the mouth of the Quillayute River, in southwestern Clallam County; elevation 83 feet.

Quillayute River. The shortest navigable river in the United States, being 4 miles in length, and navigable its entire length. This large stream is formed by the confluence of the Sol Duck and Bogachiel rivers, entering the ocean at LaPush, in southwestern Clallam County. ~~informant~~, *William Penn.*

QUINAULT, a corruption of the Quinault Indian words forming the name of the tribe, "'wi mo 1th" (kwēē nī 1th), meaning unknown. {k^{w}ínayɫ '?' B04: 405}

Quinault. A post office on Quinault Lake, 42 miles north of Hoquiam, in north central Grays Harbor County.

Quinault Indian Reservation. A large reservation on the coast, west of Quinault Lake, in northwestern Grays Harbor County, with a total area of 225,545 acres.

Quinault Lake. A lake 4 miles long and 1½ miles wide, on the Quinault River, in north central Grays Harbor County.

Quinault River. A river draining the southwestern Olympics, and entering the Pacific Ocean in northwestern Grays Harbor County. ~~informant~~, *William Penn.*

SATSOP, A corruption of the Chehalis Indian word "tsa sup" (tså sup), meaning the "tyee salmon". {Upper Chehalis = sácapš 'made stream' < sá'a 'make, do' + capš 'stream' B04: 422}

> Satsop. A town on the N. P. Rwy, 6 miles east of Montesano, in southeastern Grays Harbor County; elevation 58 feet.

> Satsop River. A river heading in the south central Olympics, flowing south and entering Chehalis River, 6 miles east of Montesano, in southeastern Grays Harbor County.

> Satsop River, East Fork. An eastern tributary of Satsop River, uniting with West Fork about 6 miles above the mouth of main river, in eastern Grays Harbor County.

> Satsop River, West Fork. A western tributary, uniting with East Fork about 6 miles above the mouth of Satsop River, in eastern Grays Harbor County. ~~informant~~, *William Penn.*

SATULICH, A corruption of the tribal name of Indian Henry "Sotolick", the present name being applied to this point by PB Van Trump, one of the men who made the first successful ascent of the mountain.

> Satulich Point. A mountain point south of Henry's Hunting Ground, southwest of Mount Rainier, in southeastern Pierce County; elevation 5,574. Source: Hunt's History of Tacoma, Herbert Hunt. [15]

SAMIS, a corruption of the Quinault Indian words "Samms mish", "Samms" was a chief of the tribe living on that river. "samms mish" means "the people living on the Samis River" ("mish" or "amish" always meaning in Salishan dialect "the people of that place". {SL = -abš 'cluster of people', name if of a Quinault band, cf Sam's River}

> Samis River. A southeastern tributary of the Quests River, entering about 22 miles above the mouth of the latter, in southwestern Jefferson County. Note.__ This interpretation does not apply to any other geographical point which may bear a similar name. Interpreter, *William Penn.*

SELAH, a corruption of the Klickitat or Yakima {Yakama} Indian name of a tribe of Indians living near the present city of Yakima, the "Silapam" or "selah people". {Sahaptin = sila 'still, smooth water' B04: 430}

> Selah. A town on the NP Rwy, 3 miles north of Yakima, in north central Yakima County; elevation 1,108 feet.

> Selah Creek. An eastern tributary of Yakima River, at Pomona, in northeastern Yakima County.

> Selah Valley. A valley paralleling Yakima River, northeast of Wenas, in north central Yakima County. Source, *Mythology of Southern Puget Sound*; Ballard, p40.

SEQUALITCHEW, a corruption of the Salish Indian word "sqwalAts" (skwŭll ŭts). According to James Goudy,[49] Skagit Indian, "SqwallAts" means "the face is marked". Jack Stillman,[50] Snuqualmie Indian, says it means "fine rain". However, Squalluts was the name of the little mountain north of Riverton (site of the old stone quarry). It derived its name from the myth-story of the war of North-South Winds. In this myth the "old lady" was called "SkwallAts" because her "face was marked". {SL = sig^wáličču '?' B04: 431}

The British called the lake and creek, in the vicinity of old Fort Nisqually, "Sequalitz" the Indian name of these waters. Lake Sequalitchew is said (and on good authority) was so named by Indians because of a species of fish found in the lake, the face of which was marked with dark markings over a lighter background (as in some species of char, ie. the Dolly varden).

> Sequalitchew Creek. A small creek entering Puget Sound from the east, west of American Lake, in west central Pierce County. Derived its name from the lake which it drains.

> Sequalitchew Lake. A small lake southwest of American Lake, in west central Pierce County. See: *Mythology of Southern Puget Sound*; Ballard, p??; U of W Press. The name was officially given to by Wilkes' Expedition. [16]

SEQUIM, formerly called by the Clallam Indians, "ch qui d" (Tsh quēēd). Meaning unknown. {Klallam = sx^wchk^wi'in, sx^wčk^wiəŋ, sčq^wé'yéŋ B04: 432}

> Sequim. A town on the SPA & W Rwy, 19 miles southeast of Port Angeles, in northeastern Clallam County; elevation 209 feet. ~~informant~~, *William Penn.*

SHUWA, (shōō wå), name of an Indian village 4 miles north of Fork, in southwestern Clallam County. It is a corruption of the Quillayute Indian word name of a Quillayute Indian tribe living at that place, "shō wh quók". Meaning unknown. ~~informant~~, *William Penn.* {showak^w = home of Susie, once married to Chris Morganroth, a German born road engineer, whose heirs now include Chris V} {šo:waq^w = Chimakum village B04: 442}

SKOKOMISH, from the Quinault Indian name of this Twana tribe "quo quo lb dbish" (kwō kwól'mĭsh) which pertains to a lake with a mythical monster. Liberally translated, it would be "the people living near the lake with the monster"; "mish" in Salish, always referring to "the people of that place". (Note: Indian tribal names [on written records] were usually given a tribal group by neighboring tribes). {Twana = sq^wuq^wó'bəš 'river people' < q^wu' 'water' B04: 452}

> Skokomish Indian Reservation. A reservation of 7, 803 acres, all alloted, at the mouth of the Skokomish River, near Union, in central Mason County.

> Mount Skokomish. A peak 8 miles northwest of Lake Cushman, in northwestern Mason County.

---

[49] Arthur Ballard consulted James Goudy #23 Skagit Snohomish born about 1865 who helped rebury Leschi at Puyallup.

[50] Arthur Ballard consulted Jack Stillman, Tolt Snoqualmi born 1878, nephew of well informed Snoqualmie Charlie *siatxtəd.*

Skokomish River. A river heading in the southwestern Olympics and entering Hood Canal near Union, in northwestern Mason County.

Skokomish River, North Fork. A northern headwater of Skokomish River, in northwestern Mason County.

Skokomish River, South Fork. A south headwater of the Skokomish River, in northwestern Mason County. ~~informant~~, *William Penn.*

SKOOKUM, from the Chinook jargon "skōō kŭm" meaning "strong; brave; great; (originally a Chehalis word meaning a demon, a powerful spirit).

Skookum Creek. A tributary of Clark Fork, from the northeast, east of Usk, in south central Pend Oreille County.

Skookum Creek. An eastern tributary of South Fork of Nooksak River, northeast of Wickersham, in southwestern Whatcom County.

Skookum Inlet. A western inlet or tributary of Totten Inlet, in southeastern Mason County. Source, *Gill's Chinook Dictionary.* [17]

SKYKOMISH, a corruption of the Indian name "Skī xōbc" (Sky hō mĭsh). The Snohomish called them "squōqōmc" (Skō'kō'mĭsh). The Skykomish are also called "sq!e wabc" (skuk wǎ bĭsh), and "sq!e hob" (skukē wǎm); all are tribal names the meaning of which are unknown. {NL = sq'ix^{w}bəš 'upriver people' < s- nominalizer + q'ix^w 'upstream' + bəš 'cluster of people' B04: 453}

Skykomish. A town on the GN {Great Northern} Rwy, 22 miles west of the Cascade Tunnel, in northeastern King County; elevation 930 feet.

Skykomish River. This river is formed by the junction of the North and South forks, near Index, in southeastern Snonomish County. It combines with the Snoqualmie River near Monroe to form the Snohomish River. The river is about 30 miles long, and its drainage area covers the slope of the Cascade Range for 30 miles. Its largest tributary is the Sultan River. It is not navigable. Both forks of the river rise on the Cascade divide and drain a considerable area on the western slope. Important tributaries are Tye, Foss, Beckler, Miller, Wallace, and Sultan rivers.

Skykomish, South Fork. A river heading on the Cascade divide, flowing west and northwest and uniting with North Fork at Index, in King County, and Snohomish Counties. Source, *The Indians of Puget So*und; Haeberlin-Gunther; p9, U of W Press.

SKOOKUMCHUCK, from the Chinook jargon words "skookum chuck" meaning "a rapid". {Chinuk = 'strong water'}

Skookumchuck Creek. An intermittent stream entering Columbia River from the west, east of Ellensburg, in east central Kittitas County. Source, *Gill's Chinook Dictionary.*

SLUISKIN, the name of the Indian guide who accompanied Stevens and Van Trump on the first successful ascent of the Mount Rainier.

> Sluiskin Falls. A falls near the head of Paradise River, on the southeast slope of Mount Rainier, in southeastern Pierce County.

> Sluiskin Mountain. A mountain about 7 miles north of Mount Rainier, in east central Pierce County; elevation 7,015 feet. See: Account of Ascent of the Mountain by Stevens and Van Trump.

SNAHAPPISH, (pronounced as spelled). The name of a tribe of the Quinault Indians living "at that place". {Quinault band = ? B04: 454}

> Snahappish Creek. Named for tribe of Indians. A tributary of upper Clearwater River, from the north, in Western Jefferson County. informant, *William Penn.*

SNOQUALMIE, a corruption of the Indian tribal name "sdokwa lbix", liberally translated is (Snōkwȧlmie). {SL = sduk^{w}álbix < duk^{w}u 'change, transform ~ 'knife' B04: 454}

> Snoqualmie. A town on the NP Ry, (North Bend Branch), 3 miles northwest of North Bend, in central King County; elevation 434 feet.

> Snoqualmie Falls. Falls in the Snoqualmie River, below the junction of North, Middle, and South Forks, near the town of Snoqualmie, in central King County; vertical fall of river, 268 feet. [18]

> Snoqualmie Falls. A station on the CM & St P Ry, 12 miles north of Cedar Falls, in central King County; elevation 495 feet.

> Snoqualmie Lake. A lake 1 mile long, on the headwaters of Taylor creek, north of Snoqualmie Pass in northeastern King County; elevation, 3,225 feet.

> Snoqualmie Mountain. A peak 2½ miles north of Snoqualmie Pass, in east central King County; elevation, 6,270 feet.

> Snoqualmie National Forest. A forest located on the western slopes of the Cascade Range and extending well down the eastern slopes to Columbia National forest on the south; the Wenatchee National Forest on the east; and the Mount Baker National Forest on the north. It has an area of 1,521,690 acres. See (U. S. Forest Service (1935) MF-19 R. 6).

> Snoqualmie Pass. A pass on the Cascade divide, between headwaters of South Fork of Snoqualmie and Yakima Rivers; elevation 3,010 feet.

> Snoqualmie River. This river is located mostly in King County and flows in a northerly direction into Snohomish County, where it combines with the Skykomish to form the Snohomish River. It is made up of the South, Middle, and North forks, which unite near North Bend. It has a drainage area of about 475 square miles. The chief tributaries are Pratt and Tolt rivers.

> Snoqualmie River, Middle Fork. A river flowing southwest and uniting with the North Fork, near North Bend, in east central King County.

Snoqualmie River, North Fork. A river flowing southwest and uniting with Middle Fork, near North Bend, in central King County.

Snoqualmie River, South Fork. A river flowing west from Snoqualmie Bass and uniting with the main stream near North Bend, in east central King County.

Snoqualmie Tunnel. A tunnel 11,894 feet long, on the CM & St P Ry, at the summit of the Cascades, in King and Kittitas Counties; elevation, of Rockdale, near West portal, 2,520 feet. Source, *Indians of Puget Sound*; Haeberlin-Gunther; p7, U of W Press.

SOL DUC, SOLDUC, SOLEDUCK, corruptions of the Quillayute Indian name "sōls dAk qᵘᵘ" (sōls duck) meaning "clear, sparkling water". One of the tribes lived on the northern branch of the Quillayute River; the water of which was particularly clear and sparkling. In referring to the people of this village, they were called "so ls dAk qᵘᵘ" or the "people living at the place of the clear, sparkling water". In time this tribe came to be known by that name. {Ql = soliɬt'akʷ }

Sol Duc Falls. Falls in Soleduck River, 2 miles above Sol Duc Hot Springs, in central Clallam County.

Soleduc. A post office and hotel on the upper Soleduck River, about 7 miles due south of Lake Crescent, in central Clallam County. [19]

Soleduck River. A large stream, heading in the high mountains north of Mount Olympus, flowing northwest, west, and southwest, and uniting with the Bogachiel to form Quillayute River, in southwestern Clallam County.

Soleduck River, North Fork. A northern tributary of Soleduck River, about 8 miles below Sol Duc Hot Springs, in central Clallam County.

Soleduck River, South Fork. A southern tributary of Soleduck River, about 9 miles below Sol Duc Hot Springs, in central Clallam County. ~~informant~~, *William Penn*.

SPOKANE, from an Indian word meaning "Children of the Sun", or "Chief of the Sun". {= spoqín B04: 459}

Spokane. This is the County seat of Spokane County, and is located in the central part, on Spokane River; elevation 1,910 feet.

Spokane Bridge. A station on the CM & St P Ry, 18 miles east of Spokane, in east central Spokane County; elevation 2,114 feet.

Spokane County. This county is located in east central Washington, adjacent to Idaho. It contains 1,756 square miles. The topography of the county is generally rolling, with mountains along the eastern line.

Spokane, Fort. A village near the mouth of Spokane River, in north central Lincoln County; elevation 1,673 feet.

126

Spokane Indian Reservation. A large reservation, with a total area of 147,422 acres, located in southwestern Stevens County, near the confluence of Columbia and Spokane rivers.

Mount Spokane. A mountain northeast of Spokane, in northeastern Spokane County, near the state line; elevation 5,208 feet. (Formerly Carlton).

Spokane Rapid. A rapid in the Spokane River, ½ mile above the mouth of Spokane River, in Ferry and Stevens Counties.

Spokane River, A river traversing the northern part of Idaho and the northeastern part of Washington. It flows in a westerly direction in Washington and joins the Columbia at the common boundary of Ferry, Lincoln, and Stevens counties. As determined at Spokane the yearly run-off in acre feet is 6,640,000. There is a drop of about 1,083 feet from Couer d'Alene Lake to the mouth of the river. Source: *Geographic Dictionary of Washington*; Bulletin 17.

SQUAK, a corruption of the Salish Indian word "skwakw" (skwåk; "Raven" a mythical character, also the bird, raven. {SL = sq^{w}ásx^w B04: 459}

Squak Mountain. A mountain 2 miles south of Issaquah, in central King County; elevation 1,980 feet. Source, *Mythology of Southern Puget Sound*; Ballard; p98, U of W Press. [20]

SQUAXON, a corruption of the Salishian words "sqwå xciIdåbc" (squa hshudabish), which means "first to be changed". This reference is from the Salish origin-myth, in which the great Changer, at the time of the Great Change, changed certain things to conform to his plan of human occupation -- these people were said to be "first to be changed". {SL = sq^{w}áx̱səd B04: 461}

Squaxin Island. A small island in Puget Sound south of Hartstine Island, in southeastern Mason County.

Squaxin Pass. A channel at the south end of Squaxin island, in southeastern Mason County.

Squaxin Island Indian Reservation, A small reservation of 1,494 acres all allotted, on Squaxin Island, in Puget Sound, east of Shelton, in southeastern Mason County. Source, *Some Tales of Southern Puget Sound*, Ballard; p 72, U of W Press.

STEILACOOM, a corruption of the Salishian words "Stī lequem", meaning unknown. Smutas, an Indian of the Nisqually tribe, was called, "Chief Stilequem", after marrying a chief's daughter from the other Puget Sound tribe. It was for this Indian, Smutas, the city of Stellacoom was named, according to a tradition that persists in Steilacoom. {SL = č'tilq^{w}əbš < ? + bš 'cluster of people' B04: 461}

Steilaoooom. A town on Paget Sound and on the NP Ry, southwest of Tacoma, in west central Pierce County.

Fort Steilaooom. Was established (under the British flag) as an outpost of the Hudson's Bay Company at Nisqually. Following the treaty of 1846 it was garrisoned by a company of United States Artillery under Capt. Bennett H Hill, in 1849. This was the first U. S. Army Post, and these were the first US troops on Puget Sound. During its military days the post was twice an important war point − in 1855-57 during the Indian War, and in 1859 when war was impending with Great Britain over the San Juan island dispute. The Western State Hospital now occupies the former site of this fort.

Steilacoom Lake. A lake about 1½ miles long, 6 miles southwest of Tacoma, in west central Pierce County.

STUCK, a corruption of the Indian names formerly used by the natives, when referring to this stream. In former times, the waters of the White River flowed into Elliot Bay, at Seattle. At times, a dam of driftwood formed below the intake of the Stuck River, causing the waters to flow southward into the Puyallup River. This would continue until a flood removed the rubbish and permitted the waters to flow normally. The observant Indians noted this natural phenomenon and so named the stream, the names depending on whether it was applied during the time river was dry or otherwise. {SL = stəq 'log jam' B04: 463}

"StEq" (stuq), means "Closed". (See: Indians of Puget Sound, Haeberlin & Gunther p27.

"tså q!" (tsak), means "plowed through". [21]

Stuck River. A stream about 10 miles long, connecting the White River, near Auburn, with the Puyallup River, near Sumner, near the King-Pierce County line. Source, Mythology of Southern Puget Sound; Bollard; U of W Pub., 1929.

SUQUAMISH, a corruption of the Indian tribal name "Suk wa bc" (Suk wå bĭsh, or Suk wå mĭsh), meaning unknown. {SL = xʷsəq'ʷəb 'clear water' B04: 466}

Suquamish. Formerly a post office on Port Madison Bay, in northeastern Kitsap County. Source, *The Indians of Puget Sound*, Haeberlin & Gunther, UW Press.

SWADHUMS, a Puyallup Indian word, meaning "the Indians who inhabit the plains", (usually used in referring to the warlike Klickitats, from east of the Cascade Range). {SL = swadabš < s- nominalizer + wana = Sahapin 'water, river' + -bš = Wanapums B04: 467}

Swadhums Creek. A small creek at 24th Street, Puyallup.

TACOMA, or TAHOMA., a corruption of the Indian name for Mount Rainier. The name has its origin in the mythology of the Sahaptian and Salish Indian tribes living near the Great Landmark, and from there it spread throughout the state. {SL = təqʷúbə' 'snow capped peak' B04: 469}

"T'wx!" (tk -whēēk) "the little valley seen at a distance" or "T'wak", is explained this way. When Dosiwallips married and brought home his young bride from the land of the T'wheek, it was the custom of her new neighbors to name her after the land of her birth; thus her name became T'week, which would identify her as "the woman who came from the land of the T'week People. This name would remain with her until she had done something which would serve to identify her more certainly — Then her name would be changed.

Among the Salish Indians, the expression, "tacoma" is used constantly; it means, "hand me the water". Now, when T'week said to her boy, "ta co ma", that expression or command, coupled with the great event of her going away, served to furnish the necessary event to distinguish her, thus, her name became "T'coma". The name, in various forms, is used by all adjacent tribes.

The Clallams call the mountain "Ta co ma", "ta" meaning "the" an adjective of superlative degree; "co" means "water"; and "ma" means "frozen". Liberally translated, it would mean "the place from where comes good drinking water".

The Nisqually name was, "ta co bud" meaning "the place where the water comes from".

Snuqualmie called it "da qo bit", meaning "the great snow mountain".

Puyallups call it "T'qo bet", meaning "good drinking water", and the Upper Puyallups say "T' qo bud", meaning the same.

The Klickitats called the mountain "tack homa", pronounced like Yakima, [22] meaning "the mysterious mountain". Various thoughts were conveyed by this name, such as, "The great mountain, that gives thunder and lightning"; always referring to it as the home of the Spirits, (supernatural beings).

> Tacoma. The county seat of Pierce County, is located on the shores of Commencement Bay, a part of Puget Sound; elevation 21 feet; population (1930) 166,885. It has an area of 51½ square miles, and is well served with transcontinental railroads, as well as by transoceanic and coastwise steamship lines.

> Tacoma Pass. A pass on the Cascade Divide, between headwaters of Yakima and Green rivers, east of Lester, in King and Kittitas Counties; elevation, 3,500 feet.

> Tahoma Creek. A northern tributary of Nisqually River, southwest of Mount Rainier, in southeastern Pierce County.

> Tahoma Glacier. A large glacier, 4 miles long, on the southwest slope of Mount Rainier. Source, Henry Sicade, and the venerable people of the Red race.

TAHOLAH, named in honor of Chief Tahola, "Tå hō ō lå", of the Quinault tribe. {Quinault title = t'xʷúlə ~ taẋʷúlə' B04: 471}

> Taholah. An Indian town on the Quinault Reservation, at the mouth of the Quinault River, 9 miles north of the town of Moclips, in north-western Grays Harbor County. ~~informant~~, *William Penn* {chiefly title of Mason family line}

TWANO, and TAHUYA, a corruption of the Indian name "tᵘ wha dᵘ" (Tōō whå dōō), the name of a tribe of Indians whose village was at the present site of Twano State Park. Olympic

Peninsula Indians spoke of this tribe as "t^u wha d^u Ena tai" meaning "the village across the Seadakh (Hood Canal)". {Twana = tuwáduq 'people down below' < tu- 'from' + wǝd 'down, below' + -q 'voice, language' B04: 526}

> Tahuya Lake. A small lake 9 miles west of Charleston, in southwestern Kitsap County.

> Tahuya Creek. A tributary of Hood Canal, from the northeast, in northeastern Mason County. ~~informant~~, *William Penn.*

TEAWHIT, a corruption of the Quillayute-Indian name "tseal tla oq^u" (t sēal tlå ók) meaning "a creek going over a high bluff": liberally translated, a "waterfall".

> Tealwhit Head. A promontory about 4 miles south of the mouth of Quillayute River, in northwestern Jefferson County. ~~informant~~, *William E Penn.* {Ql = 'foot'; tiawit 'foot, leg' <? Kathlamet Chinookan tiáqo-it 'his feet ~ legs' B04: 484}

TOLEAK, a corruption and contraction of the Quillayute Indian name "t lō quē åh lquĭl q^u" (t lō kwē åh lquĭl ok) meaning "hole in the wall rock". [23] {Ql = łiłok'^{w}ayaxi = 'hole in the rock' łoloq'^{w}ayax̱iq^w < łolo:q'^{w}a 'tunnel, cave, hole + -yax̱i 'rock' + -q^w 'place' B04: 503}

> Toleak Point. A point about 9 miles south of the mouth of Quillayute River, in northwestern Jefferson County. ~~informant~~, *William E Penn.*

TSHLETSHY, a corruption of the Chehalis name "tAs lot chi" (tŭs lót shēē), meaning "pull up roots and all," a phrase from one of the Salish Legends, in which Chinook Wind was so strong that he "pulled up roots and all".

> Tshletshy Creek. A tributary of Upper Queets River, from the south, in central Jefferson County. ~~informant~~, *William Penn.*

TSA TSA DAKH, the Indian name meaning "tall, tall leaning rock". Name is of Makah origin. {Ql = tłatłakishx^{w}o'wis}

> These rocks, at the mouth of the Straits of Juan de Fuca, figure in the mythology of the Northwest Coast tribes. ~~informant~~, *William Penn.*

TENALQUELTH, or TENALQUOT, from the Indian name "tĕn ål quĕlth" (ten al quelth), meaning "the best yet". {? B04: 487}

> Tenalquot Prairie. A small prairie sometimes referred to in the early writings of Hudson's Bay Company. The town of McIntosh is now located on this prairie, situated about 4 miles east of Tenino. ~~informant~~, *WP Bonney*, sec. Washington Historical Society.

WAADAH, from the Makah Indian name "wå å dåh". Meaning unknown. {Makah = wa'ad'a 'echo island' ? B04: 536}

Waaddah Island, A narrow island, 3/4 mile long, opposite Neah Bay, about 7 miles east of Cape Flattery, in northwestern Clallam County. ~~informant~~: *William Penn.* {Ql = wa'da}

WAATCH, a corruption of the Makah Indian name "wå a tch", meaning unknown. Tribal name of branch of Makah Indians. {Makah = wa'ač' 'bundling up cedar to make a torch' B04: 536}

Waatch. An Indian village on a small bay, 5 miles south of Neah Bay, in northwestern Clallam County.

Waatch Point, A point on the shore, 3½ miles south of Cape Flattery, in northwestern Clallam County.

Waatch Slough. A tidal slough, heading near Neah Bay and flowing southwest to the ocean, near Waatch Point, in northwestern Clallam County. ~~informant~~, *William Penn.*

WAHKIAKUM, the name of an Indian Chief. {Kathlamet wáqayqam 'downriver' B04: 540}

Wahkiakum County. This county lies in the southwestern portion of the state and fronts the Columbia River. Source, Wash Geological Survey, Bulletin 17. [24]

WAPATO, the Indian name of a small edible tuberous root, (the Indian potato). This root formed one of the chief articles of food wherever they grew, and seems to have been known among all Salish and Sahaptian tribes by the one common name. {Chinuk = wápato 'arrowroot' < Upper Chinookan wa- 'nominalizer' + Kalapuyan -pdó' B04: 547}

Wapato. A town on the N. P. Ry, 12 miles southeast of Yakima, in central Yakima County; elevation, 855 feet.

Wapato Creek. A small stream flowing from Sumner to Commencement Bay, in north central Pierce County.

Wapato Lake. A lake ¼ mile long, surrounded by a metropolitan park, situated in the southern part of the city of Tacoma.

WAPOWETY, an Indian guide for the first attempted ascent of Mount Rainier, by Lieut Kautz, in 1857.

Wapowety Cleaver. A divide east of Kautz Glacier, on the south side of Mount Rainier, in southeastern Pierce County. Source, PB Van Trump, in *Mountain Magazine*; 1915; p 46; Also, *Mount Rainier*, by Meany, p 75.

WILLAMETTE, presumably from the Multnomah Indian word "wå ll å mĕt", meaning "running water" {Clackamas Chinookan village = wálamt B04: 567}

Willamette Creek. A small tributary of Cowlitz River, from the north, and Lewis, in east central Lewis County.

WISHKAH, a corruption of the Quinault Indian name "wUc kla" (wōōsh klå), meaning "stink river". {from the smell of a whale carcass blocking the river after it was dropped by

Thunderbird. Ql = > kʷat'łayaxi < kʷat'ł = 'whale' + -yaxi 'rock' ; Lower Chehalis = xʷəšqal' 'stinking water' < xʷəš- 'stinking' + qál' 'water' B04: 572}

Wishkah. Formerly a post office on Wishkah River, 9 miles north of Aberdeen, in central Grays Harbor County.

WISHKAH RIVER. A river about 25 miles long, entering the sea at the head of Grays Harbor, in central Grays Harbor County.

"Wishkah River, East Fork. An eastern branch, entering the main stream at Wishkah Post Office, in central Grays Harbor County. ~~informant~~, *William Penn.*

WOLLOCHET, said to have been derived from an Indian word meaning "squirting clams". {? B04: 573}

Wollochett. A town on Wollochet Bay, in Puget Sound, in northwestern Pierce County.

YELM, from the Salish word "chĕ'lm". This word is used to denote the "heat waves, or radiations" sometimes seen when looking across a flat surface, such as a road, or flat prairie. To the aboriginal Indian, this was the only visible manifestation of the Invisible Power (Great Spirit) which emanates from the sky. This [25] Unseen Power (an unconscious carry-over of the sun-worshiper's religion, infiltered from the south) constituted, according to their teachings, the male or fertilizing element which made Mother Earth productive. (? B04: 580}

Yelm. A town on the Northern Pacific Railroad, 14 miles northeast of Tenino, in east central Thurston County; elevation, 350 feet. Source, *WP Bonney*, Secretary, Washington State Historical Society.

GOODMAN CREEK, Many sportsmen mistake Goodman Greek for Jackson Creek. Jackson Creek is a smaller stream 2 ½ miles farther north. The Indian name for Goodman Creek is "tsā dĭs quålth qᵘ" given it by the Quillayute Indians. It means "mouth is narrow and overhanging with branches and brush". ~~informant~~, *William Penn.*

NOTE___: The following names of Geographic points, mainly in the northwestern part of the state, and of the Wakashan and Quillayute dialects, were translated by William E "Little Bill" Penn {born 1893}, formerly of Clearwater, Washington, recognized leading linguist and historian of his tribe.

His familiarity with the language of neighboring tribes – the Makahs on the north, and the Queets, Quinaults and Chehalis on the south and east, has made his assistance extremely valuable in this work. In each case he has indicated the tribe origin, of the words from which the present name was derived.

Office Copy

Alfred J. Smith,
Tacoma, Washington.
Tacoma Branch

Translation of Geographic Names. (Indian).

Form A

1.   ka' lap, A Quillayute Indian, 45 years of age (in 1938), legal name: Willliam Penn.

2.   These stories and translations were recorded during several interviews with Mr Penn, held during the week ending December 16, 1938, at which time Mr Penn assisted in translating the enclosed Geographical Names.

3.   The work was recorded at the United States Indian Service, 2002 east 28th Street, Tacoma, Washington.

4.   I was put in touch with Mr Penn through another member of the Indian Service, whose name was not learned.

5.   No one accompanied me on this trip, which was made for the sole purpose of translating Indian names.

6.   Have never visited home of ~~informant~~.

Form B

1.   Ka lap! (William Penn). Quillayute Indian. Until recently, was at home at Clearwater, Wash.; now at United States Indian Service, 2002 east 28th Street, Tacoma, Washington. Born about 1893.

2.   la. Dash chee tup (Esau Penn, {born 1872}), father of ~~informant~~, Quinalt-Quillayute.

 1b. To pish bi ik (Mary South) {born 1872}, mother of ~~Informant~~, Quillayute-Ozette.

 1c. Kla klatch buck id, "gets red easily", paternal grandfather, Quinalt.

 1d. Da a wocks, paternal grandmother of ~~informant~~, Quillayute.

 1e Kl kwy oks, maternal grandfather, Ozette.

 1f. See aah see tha, maternal grandmother, Quillayute.

 1g. Tsa sa ith tlkli a kla di, maternal great grandfather.

3.   Has been married. Now living in single status.

4.   No record.

5.   Educated to 6th grade in common public school.

6.   No record.

7.   No information.

8.   No record.

9.   ~~informant~~ is rather short of stature, but stocky and muscularly built. Is above the average Quillayute in looks. He is an accomplished story-teller; is conceded to be their highest authority on language and legendary history, also mythology.

10.   Much information gathered in addition to the translation of geographic names.

PREPARED BY WPA WRITERS PROJECT.

RH

134

Quileute Predicate Morphology

cfr V	rltnl		object	pronouns		modal	voice	aspect	subject
-i-	-l	*1S*	-ḵal	-tila	-sta	-(i)tḵaʔy	x̱at	-l	*1S* -li
prtc	*nvlv*					*desd*	-sid	*cnu*	*2S* -lich
-o-	-ts	*2S*	-ḵalawo	-tilawo	-swo	-(i)čhol	-tid		*3S* -x̱as +
loc	*drcd act*					*vol*	*rcpl*	-do	-x̱aks
-a-	-s	*3S*	ø	ø	-swa	-(i)stal		-sh	*1P* -lo
xtnc	*causal*					*cmd*	-tsil	*ncpv*	*2P* -ka
		1P	-ḵalo	-tila	-sto	-łḵa	-sil		*3P* -salayaʔas
		2P	ø	ø		*oblg*	-ḵa	-ʔ(V)	-salayaʔaks
		3P	ø	ø		-ḵʷa	*psv*	*prgv*	-li
						degree			-la
							-tsis	-y	-a
							-ts	*prgv*	*subordinating*
							-s		*interrogative*
							caus		*subjunctive*
									conditional

*Stem*s include the formal bases:
    hi- *particularizing*
    -a- *existential*
    -o- *partitive, locative*

cfr V = classifier vowel	*nvlv = involvement*	*desd =desiderative*	*rcpl = reciprocal*
rltnl = relational	*drcd act = directed activity*	*vol = volitional*	*psv = passive*
prtc = particularizing		*cmd = command*	*caus = causative*
loc = locative		*oblg = obligational*	
xtnc = existence		*degree*	

cnu = continuative
ncpv = inceptive
prgv = progressive

Both involvement and directed activity suffixes may express transitive actions, although the involvement suffix is generally intransitive. Stem semantics seem to condition the type of activity implied.

Note that the categorial labels for grammatical suffixes in the chart above do not imply traditional grammatical relations (necessarily. They are for convenience of classification only.

Arthur Ballard
(1876 - 1962)

As a child, Ballard had a native nanny, who taught him to speak southern Lushootseed. He was born 18 October 1876 on the family homestead near Slaughter, a town platted by his father Levi in 1886, named in honor of Lt William A Slaughter, who stood silhouetted by firelight when he and others were killed on 4 December 1855 during the Treaty War. Later the name was changed to Auburn, less sanguinary and more genteel to its growing population in rural King County.

Levi was born in 1858 in New Hampshire, and trained as an MD in Ohio. He was married twice. Children of the first marriage were Irving and William Rankin (who developed the Ballard neighborhood of Seattle), and of the second were Charles and Arthur. Another son (Edgar) and a daughter both died young. After living in Oregon, Levi moved to Kent, then homesteaded what became Auburn. As his son later noted, they had a favorite Indien, "The color line was strictly drawn and there was no common basis for friendliness. Certain families would attach themselves to certain white families. Old Nelson attached himself to our family".[51] Levi was a staunch Presbyterian, but his second wife was Methodist, so Arthur was strictly raised without dances or frolics. The Ballards were hard hit by the 1893 Panic, when the Auburn bank failed. Their home burned down in 1896.

Levi was very handy. For his family, he made all the brooms, tubs, buckets, handles, shoes, boots, and some of the furniture,[52] using only an ax, saw, and jack knife. As personal challenges, he made a bathtub for a neighbor and a farm wagon. Since money was scarce, his older boys hunted with bow and arrows until they could buy guns.

Mary, the second wife, had a supply of colorful quilts that the family traded to natives who cleared off their land. Otherwise, the standard price was $10 and a sack of flour per acre. Levi bought a flock of sheep in Steilacoom to keep the ground cover from growing back. Shearing them provided wool for knits and padding. Potatoes were a cash crop, sent by native canoe to Seattle, which took a few days. The usual rate was 50 cents for a hundred pounds, while churned butter cost 50 cents a pound.

The Ballard home was near the ancient thoroughfare where the Green and White Rivers converged to join the Duwamish flowing into Puget Sound. Many of these native people had been settled on the Muckleshoot reservation, established by the treaty of Medicine Creek but on land ceded at Point Elliott. Other reservations were delayed by lengthy congressional reviews in the aftermath of the war.

Education and reading were important to the family. The nearby university (UW) in Seattle was always an intended destination for the Ballard children. Arthur attended a local grammar school and went on to Whitworth College while it was still in Sumner (before moving to Tacoma, later to Spokane). He transferred and graduated in Latin from the University of Washington in 1899. His jobs included school teaching, postman, and Auburn city clerk, as well

---

[51] Interview with Arthur Condit Ballard, by Ella Brannan Wollery, Washington Pioneers, White River Historical Society, Auburn.

[52] Charles H Ballard, Pioneer Experiences of the Ballard Family on White River, King Co, Wash 1914-15. Washington Pioneers, White River Historical Society, Auburn.

as secretary of the Azurite Gold Company.[53] He and his wife had a daughter and two sons, who both became MDs.

Fearing ridicule by his white neighbors, Ballard hid his interest in native lore until he was taken to a lecture by JP Harrington, the first professional anthropologist at the University of Washington for a summer, who strongly encouraged this work. Inspired, Ballard took his first set of notes on 21 December 1911.[54] Later he worked closely with TT Waterman on a study of place names and oral literature.

He would walk from his home uphill onto the Muckleshoot plateau to visit elders. His most successful interviews were with blind John Xot ~ Hote, who married into the family of Jerry Meeker's mother. Through his interest and contacts, he guided most of the early anthropologists working from Seattle, including John Peabody Harrington, Thomas Waterman, Herman Haeberlin, Erna Gunther, Marian Smith, Melville Jacobs, and Leon Metcalf, who made sound recordings of several speakers and one of Ballard himself. In addition to collecting variants of the same story, in fine scholarly style, he was also careful to take down genealogical information on the family background of the storytellers and their own instructors.

Ballard lived alone after his wife Jane died in 1939, filling their huge house with artifacts and debris, probably as an obsessive-compulsive. Though he was always very concerned with native subjects, his grown family discouraged his work and, finally, suppressed his major book, *Listen My Nephew, Myth, Tradition, and History on Southern Puget Sound*, when he died while it was in press.

Only one collection of Ballard's work that can still be consulted, because Marian Smith[55] gave him $25 for these pages. An important source was Charlie Ashue, who in 1929 and 1931 expressed the anti-Eells and pro-Stanup sentiments frequent among the Puyallups. He insisted that $250,000 of native monies had been misappropriated to buy a dairy ranch and stock that later became his wife's property. Investigators could find nothing wrong. When the agent decided to get rid of Rev Peter Stanup, he had soldiers get him drunk as a trap and then "hired someone to push him into the water".

Ashue also provided details on the execution, in graveyard between Sumner and Puyallup, of a "bad" doctor by Old Kitsap "when he could hardly see". Old McKai (*nakco'ya*), a Tulalip married to a young Puyallup wife, was suspected of having killed two of Kitsap's daughters and the young man then being buried. Kitsap's wife guided his hand so he could shoot to kill. Old Kitsap went into hiding, but he was so old the authorities decided to treat him leniently. There was no jail, so his son-in-law (Joe Taylor) settled him in the schoolhouse where Charlie was a pupil (about 1873) and Rev Matthew Mann the teacher. Kitsap sat by the stove

---

[53] Virtually the only profitable gold mines in the North Cascades, the Azurite and Gold Hill were found on opposite sides of the same ridge near Hart's Pass. Charles Ballard staked the Azurite in 1916 and Hazard Ballard claimed Gold Hill in 1917. Just after Charles died, Hazard sold his mine in 1935 and became manager of the Azurite. See JoAnn Roe, *The North Cascadians* 1980: 49, 154.

[54] National Archives, RG 279, Indian Claims Commission, Docket 109, Duwamish, Ballard Testimony of 18 June 1952, Box 1168, Folder 7, page 33.

[55] Marian Wesley Smith, Microfilm Roll 4 (Reel A1739), British Columbia Archives, MSS 268:Box 8, Folder 4; Royal Anthropological Archives, MSS 2794.

and smoked his pipe. If he was thirsty, he would call out. The teacher would ask, "What does he want?" "Water" "All right, get him a drink".

The John Xot family is mentioned frequently. His father had been chief at the village on Clear Creek, which enters the Puyallup River from the south side perhaps a mile from Cushman school. Old Xot, this chief, was stabbed and killed by his wife's brother over a misunderstanding that began in jest.

John had a brief first marriage. Offers by his family had been rejected by that of the girl. Later the father and two daughters were seen digging clams on the beach at Buenna, north of Tacoma. Xot allies approached them in a sealing canoe (which was very quiet) and seized the two girls. John married the one he had desired, and gave generous gifts to her family. But this wife was not industrious and John had to find a polite way to divorce her. While they lived with her family, John gathered only green cottonwood for the fire until all the smoke made his mother-in-law scold him and he could leave with dignity.

John Xot himself provided "Notes on Village Sites and People". At Allen on North Bay were the skwa'ksdabc. Chiefs there were tca'auxc, ka'walac, and txA'pted. Ka'walac died after the white people came. Jim Goudy said this community was the "First to come back after the flood". At Quartermaster Harbor was *sdAgwa'luɫ*, derived from *udA'k^u* 'enclosed', sheltering ducks and other game in winter time. Their chief named *^{xwut}xwi'tkeb* is mentioned in Curtis' narrative of an expedition against the Cowichan people. He belonged to the sxwoba'bc, and died before white people came. His son *ko'yAlk^u*, also a chief, died before the War of the Treaties, and his grandson died about 1890. At Gig Harbor, dxwa'ulkoɫ was a village at the mouth of the bay. Another village was on the prairie back from there. At Wilatchet [Wollochet] Bay, the town was named *sxolo'tsiD* (mouth of *sxolo't*). At the head of Carr's Inlet were the *^{tux}sxo'tɬ'babc*. Their chief *wiɫa'tcalt^{xu}* died before the War of the Treaties.

At Long Branch Bay, the people were the *tksba'kebabc*. A chief there was to'lskid, who died after the war. He taught Michael Simmons's children the native language. They grew up to be interpreters. The beach had an abundance of clams and mussels, free from disease the year round. It was the oldest part of the Sound, *dok^webaɫ* couldn't change that place [Devil's Head]. McNeil's Island was named *suxo'xted* (steam house) [sweatlodge]. Its north side was full of clams. The island belonged to the Steilacoom people. At South Bay were located a branch of the *sxoba'bc* known as the *^{tux}tce'tsaɫabc* (people of the bark sliver).

As city clerk and booster of Auburn, Arthur Ballard was easy to find and engage. He lived as a neighbor of several native communities and came to know informed elders well. Aside from his articles, and the volumes of material in his court testimony, his book manuscript's suppression by his own family has meant that he is not as well known as he deserves to be because of his life-long dedication to "this vice" of scholarly study of traditional variations in dialects, folklore, and perception of nature.

ACB
Auburn's Collector of Indian Myths
By Charlotte D Widrig

STORIES of the Chinook Wind, the moon and the stars and the five mallard-duck brothers who brought the rain, and of the mythical origins of many natural Pacific Northwest landmarks are filed, indexed and cross-indexed in the home of Arthur C Ballard of Auburn, a field-research authority on Indian life.

Although he began his absorbing hobby in middle age, Ballard's childhood memories and family background greatly sharpen his personal interest and understanding of Indian affairs.

Ballard's parents were among the early pioneers of this region, migrating in 1857 from the New England states, because they considered the soil worn out, to the Pacific Coast where crops were reputedly prodigious. The family took a circuitous route to the opposite side of the continent, crossing the Isthmus of Panama on a little train which moved so slowly that the children hopped on and off, picking flowers that grew along the way.

After a seven-year sojourn in Oregon, the Ballards traveled on by covered wagon to Washington and permanently settled in 1866 where the city of Auburn now stands. William Rankin Ballard, one of the boys who picked the posies at Panama, later became captain of the steamer *Zephyr* and the Ballard District of Seattle bears his name today.

Not even a wagon road had been put through the White River Valley when the family took up a homestead beside a river which flowed through the area at that time. Indian villages of the Muckleshoots were not far away. Ballard's father built a home and went about farming his land, growing potatoes mainly.

Arthur was born on the property in 1876. As he was the last child of the family, his parents liked to have him nearby and his world of adventure when he was a young boy was limited. Besides, he had plenty of walking going to and from school.

The Indians always were friendly and helpful. Men were employed to harvest the crops and some of the women helped with housework and washing. One of the incidents Ballard remembers best is his mother's account of sickness and sorrow when diphtheria, the scourge of that era, struck the family. One of his older brothers died and the Indians living-nearby gathered beside the house to sing a mourning dirge of sympathy.

The pioneer mother in times of trouble would be worn and tired to the point of exhaustion. During another epidemic, Betsy Whatcom, the Indian woman who had mothered the King children after an early-day massacre, volunteered to come in and take over the care of the sick baby, Arthur Ballard, 2 years old. She forthwith stationed herself at his cradle, rocked it when he stirred and materially assisted in nursing him back to health.

As a young man Ballard attended Whitworth College in Sumner, one of several denominational colleges which were springing up in the Pacific Northwest. Later he attended the University of Washington, majoring in Latin. In 1901 he became a teacher at the Klickitat Academy at Goldendale, a Presbyterian institution.

This career did not last more than a few years, but Ballard's interest in education and civic affairs never has dwindled. The ground on which the Auburn Carnegie Library stands is one of his donations to the city.

Ballard's major hobby was born in 1911 when he overheard a chance remark to the effect that Indians in general were not understood. This remark piqued [2] his curiosity and started him on his research into a subject which was to become a lifetime pursuit. He learned the language of the nearby tribes and began to meet with a few of the old-timers and record their stories — stories of the origins of names, cosmic myths, ceremonials, tales of adventure and first-hand history of early days.

The deeper Ballard delved the more intrigued he became, until the subject overwhelmed his leisure and gradually became a romantic escape from the workaday world, a psychological effect not uncommon among those who "ride a hobbyhorse" and ride it hard.

"I've always been working against time," he explained, "with many a day lost on a wild-goose chase".

But all in all, Ballard feels that his achievement has justified the years of effort and large sums of money he has spent on this subject, for the source of such material has been lost inexorably with the passing of the older generation. The Indians had no written language and Ballard regrets that the young folk know but little of the old traditional … myths. Many of these stories he has compiled in an anthology, as yet unpublished, entitled "*Listen, My Nephew!*"

In the Indian myths and ceremonials which Ballard has studied so painstakingly, he finds the germs of science, drama, art, music and history. The Indian yearning to understand the forces of nature – life and death, summer and winter, fire and water, flood and drought, rain, snow, hall, and such – mixed them up with magic, superstition and psychology in attempts to explain and influence natural and supernatural powers.

Indian friends among Ballard's acquaintance have been responsible largely for the success of his studies. Many have co-operated further by reproducing ceremonial objects used in the dim past.

The two boards illustrated on this page belong to a complete half-size set of six known as "swowsh" boards, used in an imaginary journey to the under-world as practiced by the Duwamish, Skykomish and Snoqualmie Tribes. The medicine men would sing and put on a great act as the shaman went below, [3] crossed a mythical river on his way to the underworld and attempted to recover a wandering soul, stolen by the dead, and return it to the sick person on earth to whom it belonged.

The boards are of cedar, painted with ceremonial significance. The dots on them represent rain, symbolical of casting a fog so the dead couldn't catch them on their return journey. Other pictures represent mythical objects of magic to aid the shaman further.

When the boards were not in use they were kept hidden, for it was considered bad luck for anyone who disturbed them, even unawares. When they were in use people turned their faces aside and covered the faces of their children, for the magic was too powerful to be looked upon by ordinary human eye.

Of all the Indian legends, the one which appeals to me most is the Duwamish story of Quarry Hill, for this was the scene of many of my own childhood adventures. Often did we scramble, especially in the springtime, over the rocks and through the woods, lured on and on by flaming red-currant and dogwood blossoms that covered the hilltop. Little did we realize we were trespassing on the hallowed home of the Grandmother of the Chinook Wind! For, according to Ballard's story, that is where the Old Lady lived.

The myth is one of nature, a myth explaining summer and winter and, in a way, springtime and resurrection of life. It tells of a time when the North Wind claimed the valley with an icy breath until young and old perished in his relentless grip. But, the stalwart grandson of the Chinook Wind came to the rescue, battled on and on until he melted the snow in the mountains and poured the Duwamish River through the North Wind's frozen barrier. The proofs that are given for the reality of the myth are Quarry Hill, the Duwamish River and the outcropping of rock on the other side of the valley.

As an anticlimax to the story it may be noted that Quarry Hill, a familiar sight from Highway 99 southeast of the Duwamish Bridge, is being demolished slowly by rock-crushing operations. Contrasting the safe method used today, I recall the old crusher on the opposite side of the hill back in the years when I went to grade school. The long walk home was never dull, for plodding along between the river and the hill we always were alert to the cries of a blasting crew who shouted "FIRE!" three times before a fuse was touched off. Rocks at times would plummet clear across the field where we hid with pounding hearts pressed close against the nearest protecting stump we could find.

Shocked by the terrifying fright experienced, we could have believed easily the Indian's lament — "they're breaking up the Old Lady's bones!"

Sunday > Seattle Times 21 September 1952

Far R:
Ballard holds a natural spruce knot with Indian carved face and hair made from strands of cedar bark. This is a ceremonial representation of the "Spirit of the Earth".

Bottom middle:
"SWOWSH" BOARDS, which were used by the Indians in ceremonies representing visitation to the underworld to retrieve stolen souls.

| "SWOWSH" BOARDS, which were used by the Indians in ceremonies representing visitation to the underworld to retrieve stolen souls. | Ballard holds a natural spruce knot with Indian carved face and hair made from strands of cedar bark. |

Arthur Ballard, Son of Auburn founder,
Writes History of Indians to Be Published Soon

by Robert Johnson

Publication of a book soon by Arthur C Ballard, the son of one of Auburn's founding fathers, Dr Levi Ballard, is expected to be the capstone of a career in anthropology covering the major portion of Ballard's life.

To he published by Binfords & Mort of Portland, OR, the volume is titled: "*Listen My Nephew: Myth, Tradition and History on Southern Puget Sound*".

Ballard, who is 85 years old, has been studying and working in the field of anthropology for several decades. He has had numerous works and papers published, and most histories of Puget Sound Indians refer to him as a source.

The Ballard family has contributed much to the cultural life of Auburn. Arthur's father, Levi, donated sites for the Methodist and Presbyterian churches. Arthur Ballard and his wife, who died a number of years ago, donated the site for the present library.

Levi Ballard filed the first plat in Auburn, then known as Slaughter, February 23, 1886. Most of downtown Auburn lay within the confines of that plat. The older Ballard built the town's first store on the site of Manson's Drugs.

So Arthur Ballard, Levi's son, has been witness and participant in most of the history of his home town. He was born on the family homestead October 18, 1876, in the then Precinct of Slaughter in the Territory of Washington. The birthplace was within a stone's throw of his present residence behind the public library.

"What started me in anthropology," he explains, "was reading Prescott's works, and the mystery of the unknown that fascinated me. I was about 14 or 15 and those two volumes of Prescott's thrilled me".

Ballard matriculated in Auburn's only school which in its beginning had only seven students in 1867 and by 1888 had grown to 28 students. He remembers a town of board walks and wagon-rutted muddy streets, with a river running through what is now downtown Auburn.

He attended Whitworth College. He later entered the University of Washington, receiving a B.A. in 1899, having majored in Latin. There was no anthropology to speak of then.

He "had a fling" at teaching in public school and academy, employment in the postal service, and some eight years in the office of city clerk in Auburn. He served as secretary of private corporations until the infirmities of age forced his retirement.

Simultaneous with all this living, however, his consuming interest and pursuit of his life was the study of what he calls the "local history and the problems of the elder (Indian) race".

This led him to spend his spare time trekking to Muckleshoot, motoring to other reservations throughout Puget Sound, learning Indian languages so he could interview aged Indians about their vanished culture.

"Take a whole people," he says today, and there is still a note of excitement in his voice, "the Indians have a language, music, religion – any one of those subjects would be worthy of study. People told me they were a dying race, and not to fool with them.

"The Indians in their language have a grammar and a diction, and when they make speeches, they have a special form of address. Our Indians in this area were between the elaborate system of totemism of the north and the plains Indians. You can go into the different kinds of potlatch without end. Now there are fewer Indians, and more people studying them".

Since the Town of Slaughter in Ballard's youth was still a raw frontier, he had immediate and early contact with the area's Indians.

"Old Nelson", he recalls of one Indian, "he cleared the first acre for my father. He used to come to our home, then he took up with an old woman from Puyallup. Old Nelson one time was asleep in the front yard, and when he woke up the town was on fire".

His first experience with Indian language, however, was abortive.

"When I was 15 or 16", he recalls, "I wrote down a lot of Yakima words and was quite excited. I didn't know phonetics, though; so it didn't come to anything".

As years passed, however, he mastered the intricacies of the problem.

In the winter of 1911 and 1912, Ballard walked out to Muckleshoot to talk with Big John, but I didn't have an interpreter".

Another breakthrough into anthropology for Ballard came when John Hote, a Puyallup Indian who "knew it all," co-operated in five interviews before he died.

"That sort of broke the ice," Ballard remembers. "As opportunity offered, and I had the funds — I had to feed and pay my Indian ~~informants~~ – I had a walk up toward the Academy nearly every day".

When he was working as Auburn's city clerk, he was visited by the noted anthropologist, Thomas T Waterman.

"He was delighted when he saw what I had", Ballard explains. "A time or two we went to the reservation together. I remember one time he came in 1920 and I was tied up to that damned thing at City Hall and couldn't go with him. But we went up Green River together with a fellow who named places along the river for us.

"We got quite a bit of Indian mythology and the University of Washington published mine".

By that time he was using a system of notation adopted in 1916 by the American Anthropological Association for recording Indian sounds.

"I made over some keys in my old Woodstock typewriter so I could write them down," he explains.

Over the years Ballard has been prevailed upon for his store of unique historical data. In 1957 he testified on behalf of the Muckleshoot Indians before the Indian Claims Commission.

His original work in research among Puget Sound Indians has brought him the respect of such authorities as Waterman, and numerous other colleagues. Wherever researchers delve into the history of this area, they come across his works.

"He is a significant figure in the world of anthropology," says his publisher, Thomas Binford, "and we anticipate this book's being a distinguished contribution to that subject".

Ballard himself says of his latest book:

"Suffice it to say that narrations and remarks recorded from the lips of Indian ~~informants~~ during the years are useful source material of history even though revealing contradictory viewpoints among the narrators. Some events came to light only by chance while others still remain in obscurity — matters of both satisfaction and self-reproach to this writer.

"With so much that has been revealed and so much still remaining in shadow here is the essence of drama which will one day, so the writer believes, enlist the finest talent of stage and screen. Even now, after the flight of a hundred years, so the writer hopes, some incident hitherto unremarked may come to light to fill out the picture"   17 June 1962 *Auburn Globe News*

ACB

A C Ballard, Authority On Indians, Dies

Arthur C Ballard, 85, of Auburn, member of a King County pioneer family, died in a hospital Friday after a brief illness. He was an authority on Indian life in this area.

Funeral services will be at, 2 o'clock tomorrow [Monday] in the White River Presbyterian Church, Auburn. Burial will be in the Auburn {Mountain View} Cemetery under direction of the Price Funeral Chapel.

Mr Ballard was born in Auburn, the son of Dr Levi Ward Ballard, a pioneer physician, and [2nd] Mrs Ballard. The family went to Auburn from Oregon in the middle 1860's. One of Dr Ballard's other sons, Capt William Rankin Ballard, was the steamboat skipper for whom the Ballard District is named.

As a young man Mr Ballard attended the old Whitworth College when it was in Sumner and Tacoma. He was graduated in Latin from the University of Washington in 1899.

Mr Ballard taught briefly at the Annie Wright Seminary in Tacoma and at the Klickitat Academy in Goldendale.

Later he was a postal worker and during the 1920's served eight years as city clerk in Auburn. He also was secretary-treasurer of the Azurite Gold Co, a mining firm, primarily of family ownership [in Hartz Pass].

Mr Ballard was an authority on the Muckleshoot Indians, who lived near his childhood home. He had interviewed many aged Indians, about their vanished culture and served as a field research assistant in anthropology for the University of Washington.

Mr Ballard was widely known as a consultant on Indian life and had written on Indian tales and mythology. His latest work, "*Listen, My Nephew*", now being published is a history of Western Washington Indians told from their viewpoint.

Mr Ballard was a member of the Washington State and White River Historical societies and the University of Washington Alumni Association. His wife, Jane M, died in 1939.

Survivors are two sons, Dr Francis E Ballard and Dr Donald A Ballard, both physicians in Reseda, Calif; a daughter, Mrs Mary E McKee in Germany, six grandchildren, and a great-grandson.

Sunday > 13 May 1962 > *Seattle Times*

GEOGRAPHIC NAMES OF INDIAN ORIGIN

(KING AND PIERCE COUNTIES, WASHINGTON)

ARTHUR C BALLARD

Geographic Names of Indian Origin

Of the geographic names of Indian origin discussed in this paper by far the greater proportion will be found within the limits of the counties of King and Pierce where the writer has done considerable research in various aspects of aboriginals as life avocation for several hundreds, yes even thousands of place names of importance in the Indian tongue but a tiny fraction have survived in the English language and then in garbled form due to the limitations of our English orthography. Usually their history can be traced either through recorded field notes of the existing literature, always with caution. Caution is always to be observed since error travels faster than the truth. It is when called upon to set forth the hard facts that one becomes sharply conscious of his limitations. Oftentimes the actual meaning of the original term has remained unknown either because of oversight or because the aboriginal ~~informant~~ himself did not know the meaning even as we of the English speaking world lack acquaintance with the etymology of our own geographical name.

In some portions of the state, especially where more speakers of the aboriginal tongues are to be found extensive field research would contribute more fully to the results attained.

ARTHUR C BALLARD
Auburn, Washington,
May 9, 1959

SOME WASHINGTON GEOGRAPHIC NAMES OF INDIAN ORIGIN

MUCKLESHOOT (sbAxlcuł): One of a succession of swampy areas alternating with. wooded surroundings along the elevation between Green River and White River; about seven miles southeast of Auburn in King County. These prairies formerly abounded in edible roots and berries. These open places were occupied at certain seasons of the year by the aboriginal people who had their permanent dwellings in the Green River valley below and possibly from elsewhere.

Toward the close of the hostilities of 1855-56 a blockhouse was erected on Muckleshoot Prairie. It was occupied for some three years by the military and upon their departure fruit trees were planted, some of which remain to this day. Some years later a sub-agency was established and a reservation including this area was laid out bearing the name Muckleshoot and its residents, few at first but increasing in number by accessions from the valley became known as the Muckleshoqts, or Muckleshoot tribe. With minor exceptions these were the people denominated as Skopamish in the treaty preceeding of Point Elliott in 1855.

SKOPAMISH (t^{x}ske'pabc), "Green River People", now known as Muckleshoot. Unlike the streams of glacial origin, Green River, fed from springs and the run-off of frequent rainfalls, is subject to [fluctuating] increase and subsidence in its flow and the term might be interpreted to mean "variable". However, there is a more plausible interpretation. The primary meaning of the word "skop", or "skob" seems rather to be "shrink, draw in, attract". The use of this term is said to have arisen from the practice of people from east of the Cascades to spend a portion of the year trapping salmon in the milder climate of Green River. In time the Skopamish became a two-language people, speaking both the Duwamish [2] dialect of the Salish on the one hand and a Sahaptin dialect from east of the Cascades on the other.

LA TETE. This is the term used by Theodore Winthrop for Huckleberry Mountain on the ridge lying between White River and the Greenwater on the south and the upper waters of

Green River on the north. The name is a literal translation of the Indian word "head". On the former trail leading from near the mouth of the Greenwater to the summit there is said to be seen a stone in the semblance of a human head. According to tradition two malignant beings engaged in a struggle. In the outcome one was slain and the victor cut off the head of his slain enemy and threw the head to the north, at the same time throwing the entrails to the south. The head, turned to stone when the world was Changed, gave its name to the mountain and the mountain to the south of the Greenwater and White River is called in local parlance, "Guts Mountain". People fear to go there, while Huckleberry Mountain is the object of an annual pilgrimage in the fruiting season.

SUISE CREEK (sus). This stream, a tributary of Green River from the north, is the site of a Washington State salmon hatchery. In former times one, or possibly two, plank houses afforded permanent winter quarters for a segment of the Green River people, in mute witness of that fact an old and decaying cedar stump is to be seen a few rods from the highway near by. External evidence indicates that the tree whose timbers entered into the construction of the house, or houses, was felled about 1820. Green River, just above the mouth of Suise, was the conventional site of the aboriginal salmon weir.

NEWAUKUM CREEK. This is a tributary of Green River, emerging from a swamp on the upland to the south. A stream in Lewis [3] County bears the same name. Derivatives of the Indian name are employed to designate the mouth of the stream and the swamp which is its source, while the name of the stream itself as given me by an informant is "yE", or "yEsł", the identical name of Raging River, a tributary of the Snoqualmie. Since only one informant was consulted, this rendition awaits verification.

NACHES RIVER (naxt tces) (naxt tcis). In the Yakima tongue the literal meaning is "one water". This river is a tributary of the Yakima. The paternal ancestors of the Nelson brothers were from a tributary of that river. The people of that region were called "naxtce'spam".

TIETON. This the name of a tributary of the Yakima River. The original Indian name is part of a compound word denoting a group along the upper reaches of the Cowlitz River or tribe, on the west slope of the Cascades, speaking the Yakima language, the "Taitinapam". They were closely affiliated with the Naches people.

MASELLE (sᵊbcal). "Place of dark shadows in the water". This is a branch of the Nisqually river. The region is said to have been frequented by Leschi in his early years.

MOX LA POOSH. This jargon word and its English equivalent, "The Forks," were used alternatively to denote the Indian village situated at the confluence of Green River and White River near the present town of Auburn. It is also an approximation of the Indian term, "ila'qo", which means "between waters". The term "sqwa'lqo" denotes the forks of White River and Black River, which join to form the Duwamish, which term has a slightly different connotation from that of the former. [4]

STUCK RIVER (stAx): The name of a river and a village site of the same name in Pierce County.
Emerging from its confining hills a few miles southeast present day Auburn in King County, White River, a stream of glacial origin, formerly divided into two divergent channels.

In one channel, turning northward and bearing the same name, the river, after a few short miles, met with Green River, a stream of clear water fed from mountain springs surface waters. The two river currents, distinguishable for a time, finally merged, and continuing northward through the valley under the name of White River until united with Black River to form the Duwamish, leading to Elliott Bay and the Sound. (NB: now drained)

The Indian term (*aba'lxqo*) for White River is said to mean "mixed water". The leftward branch of upper White River, turning south, bearing the name of Stuck River through its course, and finally merged with the Puyallup a little beyond the present day community of Sumner.

Like many Indian words, the named employed to designate the river has several possible interpretations, such as ,"gouged", "furrowed", "dragged upon", "eroded". Perhaps the best rendition for our purpose is "furrowed", or "plowed out". Actually, the name of the river is based upon a myth. In the Ancient Time the valley north of Sumner was a big landlocked lake. Two whales, tired of their confinement therein made a dash for freedom and bored their way down to the sea, thus forming a channel for the river and bearing the name by which the river is known today. In the belief of the native people the course of the Puyallup River was changed at the same time. A certain slough, now called "river channel" in their tongue was believed to have been the former channel of the Puyallup. [5]

Until modern times there has been a salmon weir on Stuck River near its confluence with the Puyallup and the place is reputed to have been a village site bearing the same name as the river. Its people were the *stAxwabc* or, in the English orthography, the "Stukhwabsh". The name for the portage between Vashon and Maury Island during low tide was called by a term having the same root syllable as the word for the river and could be rendered "drag the canoe across". When the flood waters of a river are washing away its banks, the same root syllable is used in the verb picturing the process of erosion.

STUCK (stAq). This was a notable Indian village on lower White River northwest of present day town of Kent. The term signifies an obstruction and is the root syllable of a term designating a salmon weir. In referring to the village there was said to have been an immense jam of logs spanning the entire width of the stream and of such duration that trees were growing upon it. This afforded a convenient spot for snaring salmon and obligated the necessity of constructing a weir. It was from this log jam that the village took its name. These villagers were the *st$^\vartheta$qabc*, mentioned in the Pt Elliott treaty council proceedings as the StKamish. Another village, a short distance up stream from Stuck, whose name was based upon a myth was called "House of Flea. It was reputed to be "low class", while Stuck was "high class". The paternal [maternal!] ancestors of Chief Seattle were born in this latter village.

While the name of this village as such does not appear on any map and its identity is unknown to the present generation, it does seem advisable to treat it here in order to clear up confusion on the part of investigators by reason of its similarity to that of the river to the south. [6]

DUWAMISH. Strictly speaking the Indian language term of which Duwamish is attempted transliteration, and seems to mean, "people of the Duwamish River system" comprising the Cedar, Black and Duwamish rivers. In its broader sense, it has come to mean the inhabitants of a larger area affiliated with and speaking the same dialect as the more restricted group. A former spelling, "Duwampsh" more nearly accords with the Indian pronunciation. The Indian terms, "txudo" and "txudoabc" respectively might be denoted in English by "Twado" and "Twado-absh". According to one interpreter the name "Twado" denoted the dwelling place of a certain individual and signified, "enclosed, "sheltered, which term became applied to the entire region. I am satisfied his interpretation is not that of the original ~~informant~~. Another interpretation is "resounding", the sound of a Model T engine. This interpretation is not entirely convincing either, because the Duwamish is not a notably swift running stream. Whatever the interpretation, it is fairly certain that the term denoted the river, for a tributary stream within the present city of Renton, was called "txwadi'do", "Little Duwamish River". This term may have referred to the overflow from Lake Washington, which joined with Cedar River there to form Black River. The Indian term "kati'lbc", (Katilbsh) denotes a village at that location, whose inhabitants were named in the Point Elliott treaty as "Sktehlmish", (Katilbabsh).

SAMMAMISH. A river and a people, Sammamish Slough, or Squak Slough, as it was sometimes designated, was a sluggish crooked stream carrying the overflow from Lake Sammamish to Lake Washington, discharging near the northern tip of latter lake. In the Indian language the [7] term "*tsab*" is said to mean "crooked," thus identifying the stream by its just noticeable characteristics. The people living in that vicinity were called "tsababc, whence the English name Sammamish". However, there does not seem to have been a village site by that name. A village site a short distance to the north was called by a different name. Evidently this was the home village of the people called "ts'ababc". Like the term Duwamish, the name of the people, by a curious process of inversion, has come to name the river by which the people were identified. One should consult in the "Geographical Review" of April, 1922 where this topic was treated by Dr TT Waterman, upon which article the above summary is based.

SQUAK LAKE. This is the English, authentic in origin, for Lake Sammamish, as it is now called, which term we now know is a misnomer, without having definitely ascertained the truth. I suspect the name Issaquah for the town and tributary stream at the south end of the lake have the same derivation as "squak", which may indicate a part of the lake or the entire lake. The name in the Indian tongue is "skwax^{w}", and that of its people is "skwaxwabc". They were affiliated with the Snoqualmie. I have not learned the meaning of the Indian name. There is a tradition concerning the lake. "Tree trunks, to be seen standing upright below the surface of the water, date from the Ancient Time. Once, a party of Clallam warriors were on their wary to attack the people of Squak Lake, when the Great Change of the world took place. The canoes of the attacking party disappeared, but their spears remained, protruding above the water".   [8]

TOKUL CREEK. A stream, tributary to the Snoqualmie River from the north, just below the Falls. Due to vegetation through [which] it flows, or other causes, the water is dark, or even black, in appearance. The Indian term, "*t^{u}kwal*" expresses this attribute. There is a state salmon hatchery on Tokul Creek.

SNOQUALMIE. This word in the English language is used in modern times to denote a river and a people. It is to be doubted if there was any word in the Indian tongue specifically naming the Snoqualmie River as a whole. The origin and meaning of the term "Snoqualmie"' have been widely misunderstood and misconstrued, resulting in maze of contradictions. It is therefore desirable to unravel this tangle as far as one may. Following the 1916 plan of recording sounds in the native tongue within certain limitations, I would transcribe the word Snoqualmie as fellows "sdokwalbix^{w}". Since sounds of the mute consonants are often more strongly nazalized than usual, the word could be written somewhat differently as follows:

"sno'kwalmix^w", whence we get "Snoqualmie". Now, what is the meaning of this word? The root syllable, "dok^w" or "nok^w", appears in various words. One such word is "dok^{w}ibał", the name of the mythical being who changed the world, the Transformer of mythology. The term may also be used to denote a stranger, a foreigner, one who is "different". A person who is a little "queer" is said to "asdok^w". The final syllable of the word for "Snoqualmie" is a suffix denoting a people. The Snoqualmie, a proud, aggressive people who regarded themselves as high-class and privileged to work their will upon others, were wont to work their will upon their less aggressive neighbors by plundering and making sport of them. The latter, in turn, called their tormentors [9] "*sdokwalbix^w*", thus stigmatizing them as "strange, outlandish, fearsome".

While the Snoqualmie believed themselves to be related to Moon, child of the earth people and star people, I have never heard an Indian equivalent of the term "Moon people". Their term for moon is "łokwał". It will be noted that the word begins and ends with a surd "ł", similar to a sound frequently met with in the Gaelic languages. To the untrained ear this word, "łokwał" will be scarcely distinguishable from the first and second syllable of "sdokwalbi^w" and with the Snoqualmie mythology in mind, one falls into a trap.

SKYKOMISH (*sq'oxwabc*). A' river and a people. Literally the name Skykomish derives from a compound word denoting "people of the upper river", while the anglicized form is employed to designate the river itself. The Skykomish River is a companion branch of the Snohomish along with the Snoqualmie. However the Skykomish people speak the dialect of the Snohomish and regard themselves as Snohomish in the same way as the Sammamish regard themselves as part of the larger Duwamish group.

SUQUAMISH. The people of "tsu'keb", Port Madison (?). The extended Suquamish group claimed part of the mainland north of Seattle as their territory. Blake Island is said to have been Suquamish territory and is said to have been the birthplace of Chief Seattle, who might claim membership in the "tribe" through his maternal [paternal] ancestry.

SNOHOMISH (sdohobc). I do not know the meaning of the root syllable of that term. [10]

SQUAXIN. A village site at the tip of North Bay, not far from a neck of land separating that point fron Hood's Canal. The Squaxin people (*skwa'xcidabc*) were on of several coastal groups along the inlets westward from the present city of Tacoma. In the late 60's a small island was set apart for a reservation for the Squaxin people and was dubbed "Squaxin Island". The Island is poor in natural resources and without an adequate supply of water. The father of John Slocum, co-founder of the Shaker church, once lived on this island. The island contains scarcely a dozen inhabitants at this time. I do not know the meaning of the name.

PUYALLUP RIVER. The word is said to mean "shadow". I have not verified that definition. The two main branches of the river have names of their own, one of which is said to mean "open", because of stones of volcanic origin to be found there. The name of the other branch is said to be an alternative name for Mt. Rainier.

STITATTLE CREEK. A stream tributary to the upper Skagit River. While this name is of Indian origin, it is not the name formerly used by the Indians for that stream. How it came into use was as follows; so it was told me: Years ago Indians from Fisher Creek in Canada used to come to fight the Indian people here. The trail followed by them lay along the course of that stream. When miners and prospector halted on their way to the "diggings", they asked the name of that creek. "Stitattle, bad people there, the Indians replied, and "Stitattle" became the name of the creek. In the Indian language that term is used to denote a mythical "wild people, bad people". [11]

TOLT (toltx^w). A river and a town. The Tolt River is a tributary of the Snoqualmie, a few miles below the Falls. Its people were called "*to'ltxwabc*" (Toltkhwabsh), a part of the larger Snoqualmie community. According to mythology the Tolt River was created by five wolf brothers, turned human. They created the river from elk's tallow and called it by that name. Later the name of the river was changed to Tolt. I have not learned its meaning. The modern village of Tolt is now known by the name of Carnation.

TACOMA (d^{ɂ}qobid). Mountain (Rainier) and city. The English language name of the mountain is a softened form of the Puget Sound Indian term. Various interpretations of the word have been put forth, most of them fanciful. The one thing that seems certain is that the middle syllable, "qo" is the Indian term for fresh water. An Indian ~~informant~~ has suggested "master of storms" as the meaning of the name, the first syllable,"ta" signifying "master". It has been said that the name *d^{ɂ}qobid* signifies any snow-capped mountain. The mountain bears another appelation which is the same as that for the south fork of the Puyallup River.

According to mythology, the mountain was a malignant being who devoured all who came within reach until her power was broken by the Transformer, personified in the myth as Coyote. There are other myth tales in which the mountain figures.

The present city of Tacoma received its name from those had read the account of Theodore Winthrop in his "Canoe and Saddle".

SEATTLE. A city and a chief ("siyał"). Somewhere a about the foot of present day Yesler Way in Seattle was the starting point of an Indian trail leading over the hill to Lake Washington, the "big lake". The starting point of the trail was called "dzidzala'lic" said to mean "over the hill". Employees of Yesler, both white and Indian began to take up residence there. Whereas the aboriginal people formerly made temporary camps on the beach to gather shellfish, return to their winter homes on the lake or the river, became a winter residence as well. One big "smoke house", owned by "Old Mose", was situated near Yesler's mill. Another, to the south, beyond a swamp, was owned by Seattle Curley. At a later date Seattle and others built domiciles on open ground in the quarter locally known as Belltown and lived there until after the death of Yesler when he removed across the bay. Whether Seattle had a domicile near Yesler's mill before treaty days and the time of hostilities, I have not ascertained. The father and grandfather of Seattle were born at "tcutupaltx^w") but his maternal [paternal] ancestry was Suquamish.

SNOHOMISH (sdohobc). A tribe, a river and a town. The two main villages of the Snohomish were on the river not far from the coast. One village was said to be high class and the other low class. I have not ascertained the meaning of the original term. [12] x2 >

LA TETE. This term, which is borrowed from the French and used in the Chinook jargon, meaning "head", is employed by Theodore Winthrop in his volume, "Canoe and Saddle", to designate a ridge between Green River and the Greenwater, a tributary of White River. The Indian term is "sxa'yus". Thither the Skopamish customarily repaired in season to gather the huckleberry, which grew in profusion there. On the ascent from the Greenwater to the summit of the ridge, there used to be seen beside the trail a stone of such contour as to suggest a human head. This accords with a myth tale which relates that two malignant creatures engaged in combat. One was slain and the victor severed the head of his victim and threw it to the north and thus gave the name to Huckleberry Mountain. The entrails he threw to the south where they became "Guts Mountain", a place which one approaches with trepidation.

WENATCHEE ("we-na-tcha"). A river and a city named for the river. The name in the Indian tongue is said to mean "boiling up", alluding to the turbulence of the stream.

CONCONULLY. A stream that gave its name to a town. Conconully was formerly the county seat of Okanogan county. The name was said to mean "Salmon River", and was called by that name for a time. There has been a different {lewd} interpretation in late years, however.

SHILSHOLE. A watercourse and an Indian group in the vicinity. According to Waterman, the Indian name meant "drawing a thread through a bead". This expression indicated the narrow portion of the watercourse extending inland from the broad entrance from the Sound, Salmon Bay. Of late years the term "Shilshole" has come to be identified with Salmon Bay itself.

ENUMCLAW. A town in southern King County traversed by the Nahches Pass highway and bordering the foothills of the cascade range. The word "Enumclaw" is a rendition of the Yakima term for thunder, which was personified as a bird with fiery eyes, the beating of whose wings gave rise to the phenomenon of thunder. The thunder being was believed to have his home in a recess of the mountains at a spot not far from where the railway emerges from the mountain gorges a few miles north of the city now bearing his name. I am not informed as to who chose this name for the town.

SKOKOMISH. One of three divisions of the Twana tribe, but now usually applied to the entire tribe, which speaks a dialect markedly different from the coastal groups to the east and north. Offhand the term would seem to mean "people of the fresh water". [13]

PIALCHIE. This was formerly the name of a community with railway stop and post office about two miles south of Kent in the White River valley. Mr John Thomas, one of the first pioneers of the valley, who also saw service during the Indian {Treaty} hostilities of 1855-56, named the place "Pialchie" for "Curly" Nelson, an Indian of note against whom he had once borne arms. The name was later changed to THOMAS in honor of Mr Thomas himself. The post office and railway stop have been discontinued, the mail service being carried on by rural free delivery free Kent, but the community still bears the name of Thomas.

OLALLIE. This is a community on the west shore of Vashon Island. The name is a jargon word meaning "berries". The name apparently was given because of the salt water huckleberry, or evergreen huckleberry, which is widespread in that region.

ALGONA. A community three miles south of Auburn, founded by CD Hillman, the real estate promoter. Algona, "Valley of Roses, was said to have been name for that of an Indian community "back east".

TUKWILA. This community has a history similar to that of Algona.   This also is supposed to have originated in some eastern Indian community.

215 Third St. N. E.
(P. O. Box 348)
Auburn, Wash.

Mr Robert Hitchman,
611 13th Ave. N
Seattle, Wash;

Dear Mr Hitchman:
The notes on geographic names of Indian origin in this part of the state are now complete as far as I can go without more research. Regrettably I have failed in some instances to learn the origin meaning of the terms but have included the Indian terms because of their geographical importance. Others I have omitted. Other data in the interest of truth have to be presented in a manner contrary to prevailing notions, so, on the whole, I believe the paper is worth while.
You are welcome to come and look it over and pick it up if you so desire.
Yours truly

AFTER 5 DAYS RETURN TO
Arthur C Ballard
P.O. Box 348
Auburn, Wash

Auburn, Washington,
215 Third St. N. E.
(P. O. Box 348)
May 7, 1959

Mr Robert Hitchman,
611 13th Avenue North,
Seattle, Wash.

Dear Mr Hitchman:
Pursuant to your suggestion of a few weeks ago, I have worked out a summary of geographical names of Indian origin chiefly in the counties of King and Pierce.
In spite of certain deficiencies I believe that it will add to a considered appraisal of the subject matter treated.
If you are coming out to Auburn in the near future, please advise me and 1 shall make it a point to be at home on the day you come.
Yours very truly,

215 Third at N. E.,
(P. O. Box 348)
Auburn, Wash,

June 12, 1959

Mr Robert Hitchman,
611 13th Avenue No
Seattle, Wash;

Dear Mr Hitchman:

Please accept my belated acknowledgement of the check from the Peter Binford Foundation for my paper on Geographic Names of Indian Origin.

Upon looking over the paper since some defects therein have come to my notice.

Upon reading the young lady's story of the Thomas community I realize that I did not spell the Indian word for that post office in the accepted manner, I omitted an s. It should have been spelled Pialschie instead of Pialchie. The l in that word or rather the ls combination is apparently an attempt on the part of Mr Thomas or someone else to represent the surd ł of the Indian, tongue, one of many sounds which our accepted orthography does not cover. It is the same sound as that occurring as the final consonant of the name of the noted indian chief whose lack Professor Meany attempted to remedy by the spelling "Sealth".

I note also that a second sketch of the name La Tete appears in the MSS. That is an inadvertence copied from a preliminary write-up and should be deleted. It is probably too late now to do anything about it but it should be deleted, if possible.

As for the historical effort, some additional field work should be done and it will be hard to refrain from obtruding some of my own conclusions or at least some explanatory comments, although my original purpose was to make the work anonymous. Anyway, it's my child and I am fostering it.

Best regards and thanks for the phonographic disks. Now my Indians are staying away when I want them.

Yours truly,

Arthur C. Ballard

154

Conclusions

1   These five lists illustrate the pleasures and pitfalls of studying place names over a century. Highly mobile and curious, George Gibbs set a high standard for a large region. He collected and mapped native names from the time he arrived in the Northwest, as well as on the westward trek. While serving on the international boundary survey, he began at the eastern edge of the Salish Sea – tracing names through Bellingham Bay, Birch Bay, a bit of the Gulf of Georgia, then up the Fraser River in Kwantan territory, via Nicometl, Sumas, Matsqui, Nooksack, Baker, Skagit, and across the Cascades into the Columbia, Sanpoil, Spokane, before venturing further east to the Flathead, Tobacco, and Kootenay Rivers. He named and plotted the successive camps of the survey, especially those of Henry Custer. In 1856, while serving during an aborted treaty in at Cosmopolis in Grays Harbor, he assembled place names for the north and south shores before moving up the Chehalis River then returning to the outer coast.

2   Eells provides an alphabetical list of names in Washington state, with a particularly strong showing for Hood Canal where he was based for decades. He defers to Gibbs, so had access to that work, and, as shown in his discussion of Twana as *Twa-dak^{hu}* recognized labialization, though not ejectives. Born and raised in eastern Washington, he was exposed to both Sahaptian and Salishan languages but never gained proficiency. Like so many others, he conversed and sermonized in Chinuk WaWa.
      Noteworthy in his discussions is accurate reference to the Wishkah River story of the rotting whale dropped by the Thunderbird. His discussion of Tacoma ~ Mt Rainier did not help the debate, easily resolved by consulting any Lushootseed dictionary. Gibbs says for Nisqually:

3   Thomas T Waterman focuses on Puget Sound, going north to south from Edmonds to Seattle, Alki, and Tacoma, then clockwise around Lake Washington into Lake Union. Academically trained in linguistics, with several recording firsts to his credit, his transcriptions are reliable and easily updated into current spelling conventions. His translations are more problematic since there was not available grammar to consult for morphemes and synonyms. As shown by the many ?? question marks diminishing speakers have had trouble puzzling these out.

4   AJ Smith also presents and alphabetical list, probably assembled by staff writers of the state guidebook. Wisely conferring with AC Ballard and relying on multilingual Bill Penn this list is heavy on Washington Coast, aside from a few Yakama and Chinuk WaWa names. He occasionally uses a raised ^{u}, but probably was copying from another source.

5   AC Ballard concentrates on names in King & Pierce Counties, around Seattle & Tacoma, with an incongruous reach to Wenatchee and Conconully across the Cascades. Though he started his linguistic work with a short list of Yakama words, he quickly switched to southern Lushootseed ~ Tx^{w}əlshootseed, interviewed Big Jim, and began to amass extensive information that benefited tribes during land claims and in revitalization efforts.

Conclusions

Improving on the substantial work by ES Meany, Hitchman added information from Ballard as well as consulted published and manuscript sources, but these names are still printed in English using its meager alphabet. Only the combined linguistic efforts resulting in 2004 Bright points the way to a reliable future of scholarly and popular appreciation.

In all, across the Americas, toponyms ~ place names are descriptive, positional, activity related, or referential to cultural historial epics ~ events, such as myth age characters turned to stone. Using linguistic grammatical components, many are constructed to evoke a vivid visual image of that place. Descriptions involve physical appearance, associated vegetation and foods, characteristics of resident species, seasonal activities, analogy to anatomy, fancied resemblances, color aspects, and, rarely, accompanying sounds. Positional concerns are up / down river, offshore / inshore, sunrise / sunset, waterward / landward, big / little, and similar orientations.

With a century of these place name lists to studt, accompanied by useful maps that have dropped away but may still be found, interest in toponymy ~ toponomastics, the study of place names, leads us ahead to onomastics, from the Greek ὀνομαστικός (*onomastikós*) = 'of ~ belonging to naming' < ὄνομα (*ónoma*) = 'name' for the Northwest and beyond.

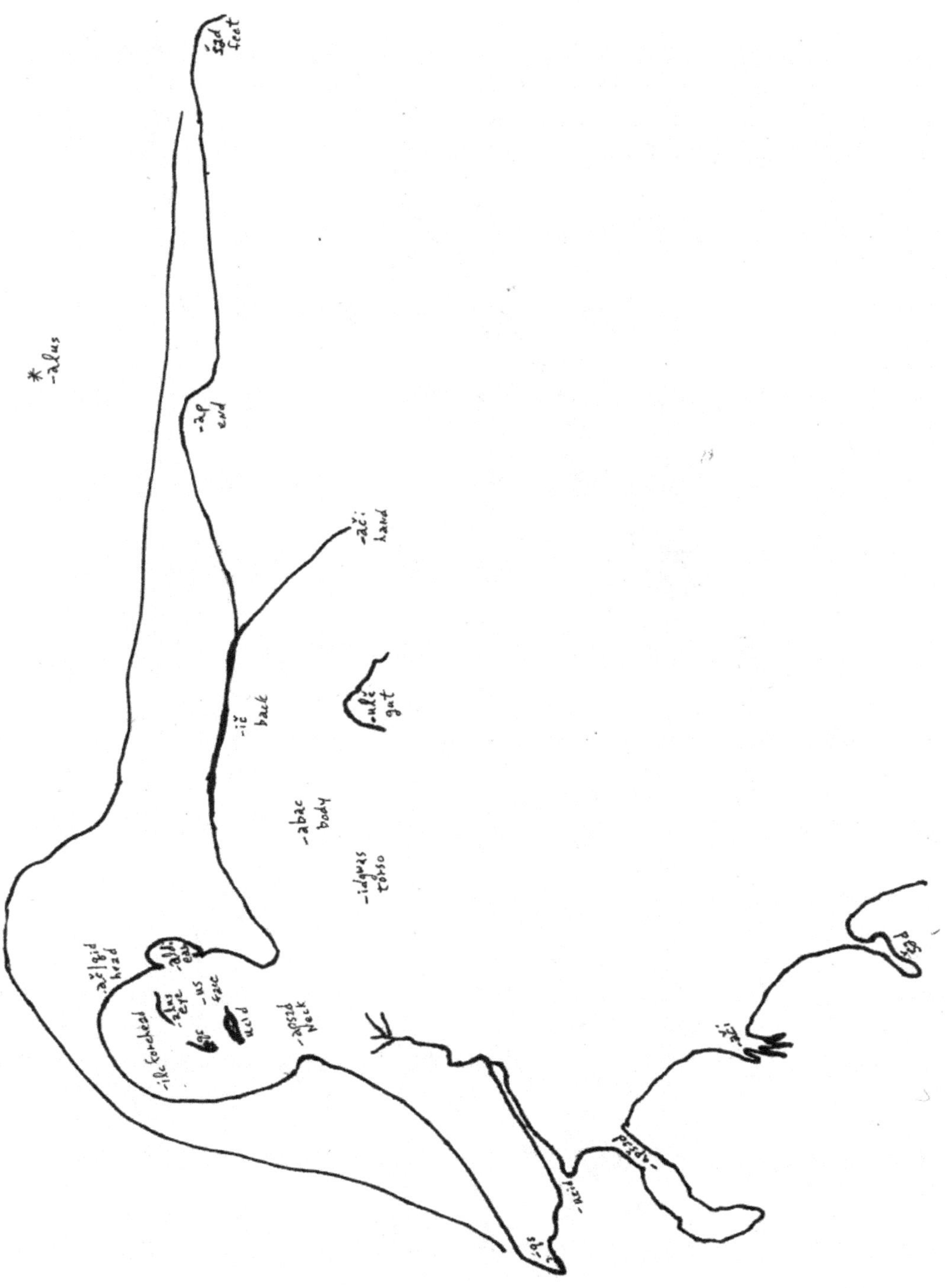

embodied lexicals landscape

Lushootseed Alphabet

For Lushootseed Sounds, the rule is one sound = one letter. Glottalized ejectives (marked ')
means the gate in the back of the throat is closed tight then opened with an explosive sound.
Labialized (marked ^{W}) means the lips are rounded to produce a breathy quality. "Same" means it
sounds much like that English sound.

a	same, like father		p	same, p like post
b	same, replaces m of other Salish languages		ṗ	glottalized p
c	ts like cats		q	like k but with back of the tongue raised against the back roof of the mouth
ċ	glottalized ts		q̇	glottalized q
č	c wedge, ch like church, chair		qʷ	labialized q
č̓	glottalized ch		q̇ʷ	glottalized and labialized q
d	same, replaces n of other Salish languages		s	same
dᶻ	ds like rods		š	sh like sure, shore, shut
ə	schwa, like a in sofa, u in but		t	same
g	same, like get, go		ṫ	glottalized t
gʷ	labialized g		u	same, sometimes o, Lushootseed speakers regarded both sounds as the same
h	same, like hit		w	same
i	ee like seed		ẇ	glottalized w
j	dj, sqajet (Skagit)		x̌	same as x
k	same, k like kin		x	ch like German ich, Scottish loch, said deep in the throat
k̓	glottalized k		xʷ	labialized, wh like where
kʷ	labialized k, qu like queen, quick		x̌ʷ	glottalized and labialized
k̓ʷ	glottalized and labialized k		y	same, like yell, you
			ẏ	glottalized y
l	same, like look			
l̓	glottalized l			
m	now replaced by b, rare use in archaic, baby, and Ravenese words		ʔ '	glottal stop, throat gate closed, like pause in uh'oh
n	now replaced by d, rare use in archaic, baby, and Ravenese words		ł	barred l, said out of the sides of the mouth with the tip of the tongue behind the upper front teeth
ṅ	glottalized n		ƛ̓	glottalized barred lambda, tl like night-light, said deep in the throat with tongue flattened against the front roof of the mouth
o	same, written as u in Lushootseed alphabet			

Locatives
Lushootseed
čad = where?

Locatives are parts of speech to specify place-based geographical locations, both lexical suffixes *–ali* = "place where something is typically located" (BHH: 28): *hud-ali* = fire + place, stove, and lexical prefixes *dxʷ–* = toward, *tul–* = from, *liɬ–* = by what route, *'iɬ–* = in comparison to, *lə–* = waterward. Some lexicals apply to both anatomy and georgraphy, such as *–ádiʔ* = ear ~ side (see list p144). Whole words specify placement, reference, and orientation: *'al* = be located at ~ by some specific point in time ~ space, location with reference to something named, to water = sea *xʷəlč* ~ river *stuləkʷ* ~ lake *x̲áču*; shoreline ~ *s'ílgʷiɬ*; and land ~ *swátixʷtəd*.

Whole words express both the location of a speaker (be ~ is there) and the flow of the water itself from that person's sensory perspective, as detailed in Hess 1976 *Dictionary of Puget Salish*, 1979 A Comparison of Marine and Riverine Orientation Vocabulary in Two Coast Salish Languages) and Bates, Hess, Hilbert 1994 *Lushootseed Dictionary*:

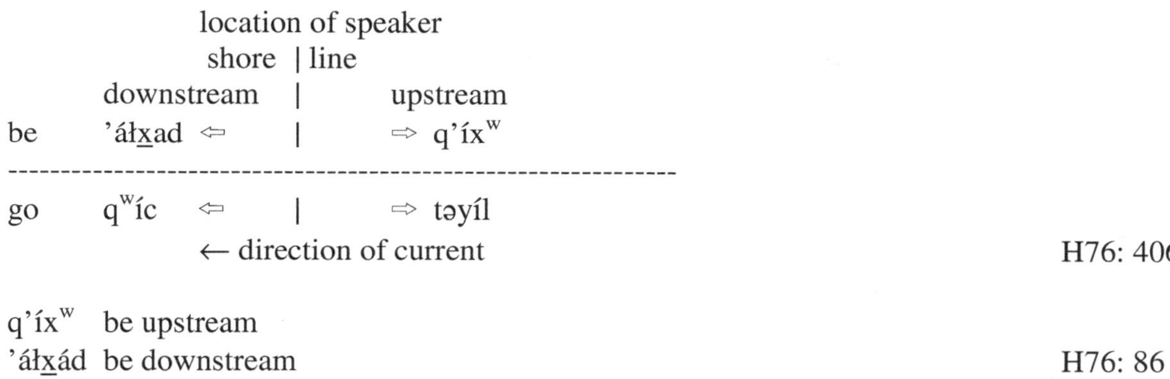

H76: 406

q'íxʷ be upstream
'áɬx̲ád be downstream

H76: 86

Movement among these places and perspectives is specified:

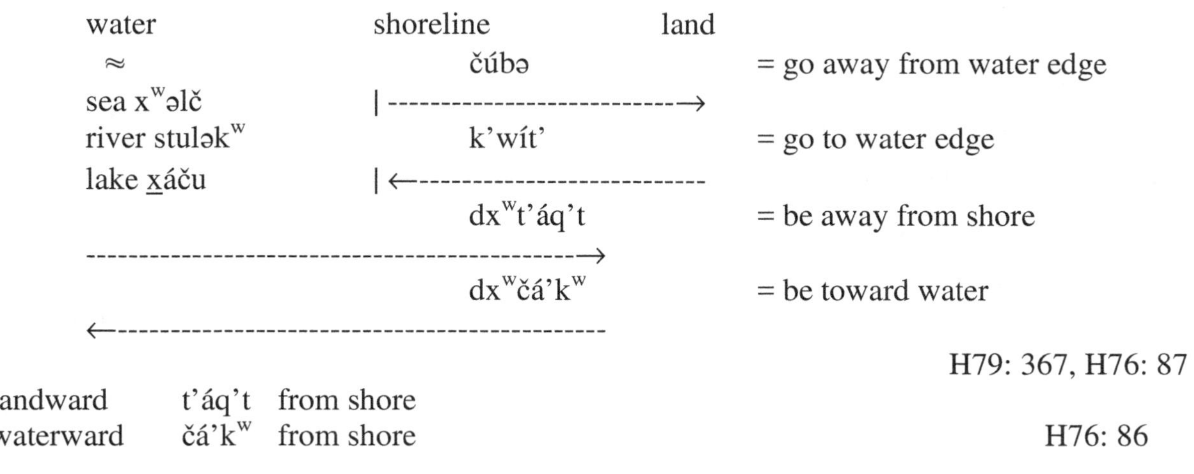

H79: 367, H76: 87

landward t'áq't from shore
waterward čá'kʷ from shore

H76: 86

Living spaces have their own specific terminology:

At Home

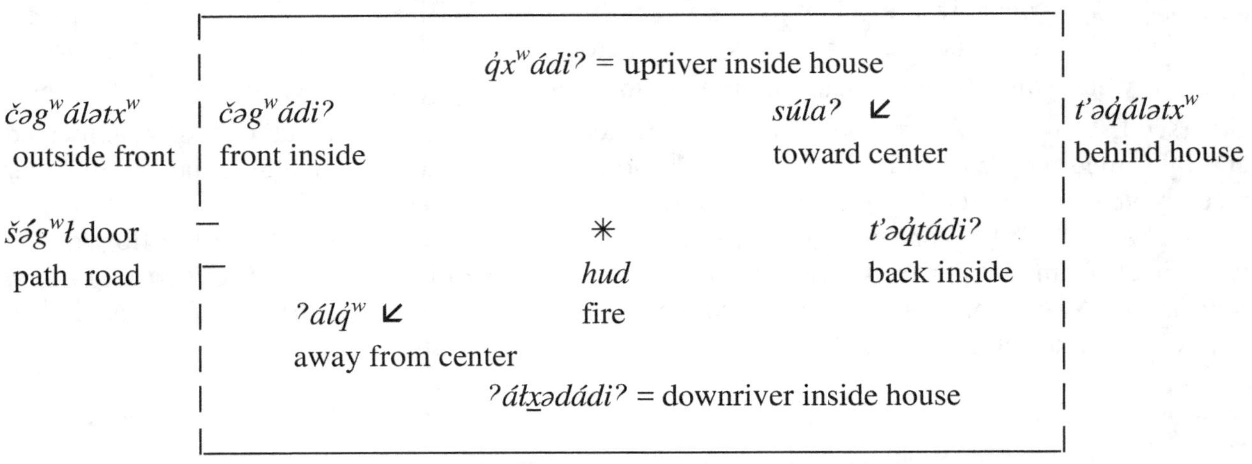

$\dot{q}x^w\acute{a}l\partial tx^w$ outdoors upstream side

$\dot{q}x^w\acute{a}di^\gamma$ = upriver inside house

$\check{c}\partial g^w\acute{a}l\partial tx^w$ outside front | $\check{c}\partial g^w\acute{a}di^\gamma$ front inside

$s\acute{u}la^\gamma$ toward center

$t'\partial\dot{q}\acute{a}l\partial tx^w$ behind house

$\check{s}\acute{\partial}g^w\acute{l}$ door path road

$t'\partial\dot{q}t\acute{a}di^\gamma$ back inside

hud fire

$^\gamma\acute{a}l\dot{q}^w$ away from center

$^\gamma\acute{a}\underline{t}x\partial d\acute{a}di^\gamma$ = downriver inside house

$^\gamma\acute{a}\underline{t}x\partial d\acute{a}l\partial tx^w$ outdoors downstream side

$^\gamma\acute{a}\underline{t}x\partial d\acute{a}l\partial tx^w$ = outdoors downstream side

$\dot{q}x^w\acute{a}l\partial tx^w$ = outdoors upstream side

$\check{c}\partial g^w\acute{a}l\partial tx^w \sim \check{c}\partial g^w\acute{a}di^\gamma$ = in front of house < –$\acute{a}di^\gamma$ = ear ~ side

$t'\partial\dot{q}\acute{a}l\partial tx^w$ = behind the house

$^\gamma\acute{a}l\dot{q}^w$ = away from center

$s\acute{u}la^\gamma$ = toward @ center

hud = fire

$t'\partial\dot{q}t\acute{a}di^\gamma$ = back of house

$^\gamma\acute{a}\underline{t}x\partial d\acute{a}di^\gamma$ = downriver side of house

$\dot{q}x^w\acute{a}di^\gamma$ = upriver side of house

$\check{c}\partial g^w\acute{a}di^\gamma$ = front of house

$\check{s}\acute{\partial}g^w\acute{l}$ = door, path,

H79: 374

Lushootseed Suffixes for Body & Landscape

anatomy	lexical	word	also
back	-ič	s'ilidčəd	
body	-abac	c'uq^wəb ~ bayac	
butt	-ap	cəq	
chest		s'ilidəg^wəs	
ear	-adi	q'^wəladi'	
eye	-alus	qəlub	star
eyebrows		cubəd	
face	-us	s'acus	
finger	-qsači'	šdəxalqsači	
forehead	-ilc	pəq^wus	
hair	-alqid	sq'əd^zu	
hand	-ači'	čaləš	
head	-ač ~ -qəd	axayus	top
heart		sc'ali' ~ yədwas	
knee		xqp'ucid	
leg	-šəd ~ šad	jəšjəšəd	
mouth	-ucid	qədx^w	language
neck	-apsəd	cqapsəd	isthmus
nose	-qs	bəqsəd	point
rib	-g^was		
shoulder	-axad	t'alək^w	
stomach	-ulč	k'^wyəx^w	
thigh	-alap	s'alap	
throat	-apsəd	q'iyuq'	
toe	-q(s)šad	šdəxalqsači'	
tooth	-dis	d^zədis	
tongue	-alap	łalap	

topographic suffixes

-abš	people cluster
-ac	plant
-aču	water
-ali	place of
-altx^w	house of
-aq^w	water
-bix^w	people bunch
-idg^was	innards
-ils	rocks

Nuxalk ~ Bella Coola voweless words
Speaker: Mr Andy Schooner, age 75

bad	sx	wound	sq'
white	c'x̱ʷ	animal fat	sc'q
fat	x̱s	that's my fat over there	sc'qc tx
seal fat	sxs	stone	t'xt
strong	tł	sand	sqc'
dry	ł'ł	salt	st's
wet	łq	black	sk'x
crabapple	p'x	thick	płt
rough	kʷs	NE wind	sps
big	łk'ʷ	crooked	qʷt
tight	q's	get there	c'kt
loud	c's	I get there	c'ktc
undo it!	sk'ʷtx̱	true	c'xł
tear	cq'	birthmark ~ freckle stp	stp
tear it!	cq'tx̱	a berry (unid.)	p'x̱ʷłt
see	k'x	rib	ck'łp
open your eyes	k'xx̱	to taste	q'pst
they see you	k'xct	taste it!	q'psttx̱
pull	qs		
pull it off!	qstx̱		
jump	sq'ʷ		
jump!	sq'ʷx̱		
go to shore	tq'		
go to shore!	ł'ptx̱		
cut w scissors	ł'p		
cut it!	ł'ptx̱		

Note: ł plain lateral fricative; 1' glottal lateral affricate; k, k' are very palatal; q, q' rather front (in comparison to other Salish languages). Notice that the words are vowel- and sonantless. About a dozen more words of this type were recorded after the tape was made, and there undoubtedly are still more.

Bibliography

Anastasio, Angelo

1972 The Southern Plateau ~ An Ecological Analysis of Intergroup Relations. *Northwest Anthropological Research Notes ~ NARN* 6 (2): 109-229.

Angulo, Gui de

1995 *The Old Coyote of Big Sur ~ The life of Jaime de Angulo.* Berkeley: Stonegarden Press.

Ballard, Arthur

1927 Some Tales of the Southern Puget Sound Salish. *University of Washington Publications in Anthropology* 2 (3): 57-81.

1929 Mythology of Southern Puget Sound. *University of Washington Publications in Anthropology* 3 (2): 31-150.

1935 Southern Puget Sound Salish Kinship Terms. *American Anthropologist* 37 (1): 111-116.

1950 Calendric Terms of the Southern Puget Sound Salish. *Southwestern Journal of Anthropology* 6 (1): 79-99.

1951 Deposition on Oral Examination of Arthur Condict Ballard. November 26, 27, 28. Testimony before the Indian Claims Commission of the United States, Docket 98. Carolyn Taylor, court reporter. 2 volumes.

1957 The Salmon-Weir on Green River in Western Washington. *Davidson Journal of Anthropology* 3: 37-53.

1999 *Mythology of Southern Puget Sound.* Kenneth (Greg) Watson, ed. North Bend, WA: Snoqualmie Valley Historical Museum.

Barnett, Homer

1955 *The Coast Salish of British Columbia.* Studies in Anthropology 4. Eugene: University of Oregon Press.

1957 *Indian Shakers ~ A Messianic Cult of the Pacific Northwest.* Carbondale: Southern Illinois University Press.

Bates, Dawn, Thom Hess, Vi Hilbert

1994 *Lushootseed Dictionary.* Seattle: University of Washington Press.

Beavert, Virginia, and Sharon Hargus

2009 *Ichishkiin Senwit ~ Yakama/Yakima Sahaptin Dictionary.* Seattle: University of Washington Press.

Boldt, George

1975 Finding of Fact #5, Order of 18 April 1975. C70-9213 US v WA

Boreson, Keo

1998 Rock Art. Handbook of North American Indians. *Plateau.* Deward Walker, ed. Volume 12: 611-19. Smithsonian Institution.

Boyd, Robert

1996 *People of the Dalles ~ The Indians of Wascopam Mission.* Lincoln: University of Nebraska Press.

1999 *The Coming of the Spirit of Pestilence: Introduced Infectious Diseases and Population Decline among Northwest Coast Indians, 1774-1874.* Seattle: University of Washington Press.

Boyd, Robert, ed.

1999 *Indians, Fire, and the Land in the Pacific Northwest.* Corvallis: Oregon State University Press.

Bright, William, ed.

2004 *Native Placenames of the United States.* Norman: University of Oklahoma Press.

Brunton, Bill

1968 Ceremonial Integration in the Plateau of Northwestern North America. *Northwest Anthropological Research Notes ~ NARN* 2 (1): 1-28.

Carlson, Keith Thor

2001 *A Sto:lō and Coast Salish Historical Atlas.* Vancouver: University of British Columbia Press.

Carpenter, Cecilia Svinth, Maria Victoria Pascualy, and Trisha Hunter

2008 *Nisqually Indian Tribe.* Charleston: Acadia Publishing, Images of America.

Chafe, Wallace

1962 Estimates Regarding the Present Speakers of North American Indian Languages. *International Journal of American Linguistics* 28 (3): 162-171.

1965 Corrected Estimates. *International Journal of American Linguistics* 31 (4): 345-346

Collins, June

1974 *Valley of the Spirits*: The Upper Skagit Indians of Western Washington. Seattle: University of Washington Press.

Costello, James

1895 *The Siwash ~ Their Life, Tales, & Legends of Puget Sound & Pacific Northwest.* Seattle: Calvert Co.

Danaan, Llyn De

2013 *Katie Gale ~ A Coast Salish Woman's Life on Oyster Bay.* Lincoln: University of Nebraska Press, Bison Books.

Desmond, Gerald

1952 Gambling Among the Yakima. *The Catholic University OF America Anthropological Series* # 14. Washington, DC: The Catholic University OF America Press.

Deur, Douglas, and Nancy Turner, eds.

2005 *Keeping It Living ~ Traditions of Plant Use and Cultivation on the Northwest Coast of North America.* Seattle: University of Washington Press.

Dyen, Isidore and David Aberle

1974 *Lexical Reconstruction*: The Case of the Proto-Athapaskan Kinship System. London: Cambridge University Press.

Eells, Rev Myron

1892 Aboriginal Geographical Names in the State of Washington. *American Anthropologist* V: 27-35.

Emmons, Della Gould

1965 *Leschi of the Nisquallies.* Minneapolis: TS Denison & Co.

Farrell, Brenda

1995 *Do You See What I Mean?* ~ Plains Indian Sign Talk and the Embodiment of Action. Austin: University of Texas Press.

Foster, Michael

1996 Language and the Culture History of North America. Handbook of North American Indians. Ives Goddard, ed. *Languages* 17: 64-110.

Fowler, Don D

2000 *A Laboratory for Anthropology. Science and Romanicism in the American Southwest, 1846-1930.* Albuquerque: University of New Mexico Press.

Galloway, Brent

2009 *Upriver Halkomelem Dictionary.* University of California Publications in Linguistics #141; I: 1-837, II: 838-1674.

Gibbs, George

1834 *The Judicial Chronicle.* Cambridge, MA: J Monroe & Co.
1846 *Memoir of the Administrations of Washington and John Adams*, edited from the papers of Oliver Wolcott, Secretary of the Treasury. NY: W Van Norden.

1853 Indian Nomenclature of Localities in Washington and Oregon Territories [West of the Cascades]. 14pp. ms # 714. [SI 248] DC: National Anthropological Archives.

1853 California Languages. Henry Schoolcraft federal report in five volumes, Volume III.

1854 *Pacific Railroad Reports*: Reconnaissance of the Country Lying upon Shoalwater Bay and Puget Sound 1:465-473 (1 March); Geology of the Central Portion of Washington Territory 1: 473-486 (1 May).

1855 *Indian Tribes of Washington Territory*. Reports of Explorations and Surveys to Ascertain the Most Practical and Economic Route for a Railroad from the Mississippi River to the Pacific Ocean. Senate Executive Document 78. pp. 400-449 in volume I. 33rd Congress, 2nd Session.

1856 Tribes of Western Washington and Northwestern Oregon. Full Manuscript. Madison: Wisconsin Historical Society.

1858 Vocabularies, Washington Territory. Manuscript No. 227, National Anthropological Archives, Smithsonian Institution, Washington, D.C.

1862 *Grammar and Dictionary of the Yakima Language* by Fr Pandosy. NY: Cramoisy Press.

1863a Instructions for Research Relative to the Ethnology and Philology of America. Smithsonian Miscellaneous Collections VII: 1-51.

1863b *A Dictionary of the Chinook Jargon, or Trade Language of Oregon*. NY: Cramoisy Press. DC: Smithsonian Miscellaneous Collections VII (10).

1863c Alphabetical Vocabularies of the Clallam and Lummi. NY: Cramoisy Press.

1863d Alphabetical Vocabulary of the Chinook Language. NY: Cramoisy Press.

1873e Physical Geography of the North-Western Boundary of the US. *Journal of the American Geographical Society of New York* 3, Part 1: 134-157; 4, Part 2: 298-415.

1877a Tribes of Western Washington and Northwestern Oregon. Washington, DC: Department of the Interior, *United States Geographical and Geological Survey of the Rocky Mountain Region*, Part II: 157-241. {½ ethnography}

1877b Dictionary of the Niskwally. {Appendix to ½ ethnography}. Smithsonian Annual Reports for 1866, 1870 *Contributions to North American Ethnology* 1: 285-361.

Goddard, Ives

1975 Algonquian, Wiyot, and Yurok: Proving A Distant Genetic Relationship. *Linguistics and Anthropology*: In Honor of CF Voegelin: 249-262. M Dale Kinkade, Kenneth Hale, and Oswald Werner, eds. Lisse: The Peter de Ridder Press.

Griffin, Trenholme

1990 *Ah Mo. Indian Legends from the Northwest*. Blaine: Hancock House.

1993 *More Ah Mo. Indian Legends from the Northwest*. Blaine: Hancock House.

Gunther, Erna

1925 Klallam Folk Tales. *University of Washington Publications in Anthropology* 1 (4), 113-170.

1927 Klallam Ethnography. *University of Washington Publications in Anthropology* 1 (5), 171-310.

1928 A Further Analysis of the First Salmon Ceremony. *University of Washington Publications in Anthropology* 2 (5), 129-173.

ms.   Culture Element Distributions: Puget Sound (Duwamish, Skokomish, Klallam, Makah). Berkeley: Bancroft Library.

1949 The Shaker Religion of the Northwest, *Indians of the Urban Northwest*: 37-76. Marian Smith, ed.

1973 *Ethnobotany of Western Washington*. The Knowledge and Use of Indigenous Plants by Native Americans. Seattle: University of Washington Press. [1945]

Haeberlin, Herman

1916-17 Puget Salish, 42 Notebooks. DC: National Anthropological Archives. # 2965.

1918 "SbEtEtda'q, A Shamanic Performance of the Coast Salish".   *American Anthropologist* 20 (3), 249-257.

1924 Mythology of Puget Sound. *Journal of American Folklore* 37 (143-144), 371-438.

Haeberlin, Herman, and Erna Gunther

1930 The Indians of Puget Sound. *University of Washington Publications in Anthropology* 4 (1), 1-84.

Haas, Mary

1969 *The Prehistory of Languages*. The Hague: Mouton.

Harmon, Alexandra

1995 Different Kind of Indians. Negotiating the Meanings of "Indian" and "Tribe" in the Puget Sound Region, 1820s-1970s. University of Washington: History Ph.D. I - 1-365, II - 366-741.

1999 *Indians in the Making* ~ Ethnic Relations and Indian Identities around Puget Sound. American Crossroads Series. Berkeley: University of California Press.

Hess, Thom

1971   Prefix Constituent With /x^w/. pp. 43-69 in *Studies in Northwest Indian Languages*. James Hoard and Thom Hess, eds. Sacramento Anthropological Society, Paper 11.

1976 *Dictionary of Puget Salish*. Seattle: University of Washington Press.

1977 Lushootseed Dialects. *Anthropological Linguistics* 19 (9): 403-419.

1979   A Comparison of Marine and Riverine Orientation Vocabulary in Two Coast Salish Languages. *Anthropological Linguistics* 21 (8): 363-378.

Hilbert, Vi taq^{w}šəblu

1983 Poking Fun in Lushootseed. *Proceedings of the 18th International Conference on Salish and Neighboring Languages*. Seattle.

Hilbert, Vi, Jay Miller, and Zalmai Zahir

2001 *Puget Sound Geography*. sda'da g^{w}əł dibəł ləšucid 'acaciłtalbix^w. A Draft Study of the Thomas Talbot Waterman Place Name Manuscript and Other Sources, Edited with Additional Material. Seattle: Lushootseed Press.

Hockett, Charles

1966 What Algonquian is Really Like. *International Journal of American Linguistics* 32 (1): 59-73.

Howell ~ Braveheart, Philip Hugh

1922-26 *The American Indian Newspaper.*

1927-47 *The American Indian Yearbook.*

1948 *Dictionary of Indian Geographical Names* ~ The Origin and Meaning of Indian Names. Seattle: The American Indian Historical Society.

Hymes, Dell

1990 Mythology. Handbook of North American Indians. *Northwest Coast* 7: 593-601.

Judson, Katharine Berry

1910 *Myths and Legends of the Pacific Northwest.* Chicago: Star Publishing Co. AC McClurg. [reprint 1997, Bison Books]

Kinkade, M. Dale

1971 Roster of Linguists Studying North American Indian Languages. *International Journal of American Linguistics* 37 (2): 114-121, 38 (3): 201-202.

Kinkade, MD and JV Powell

1978 Language and the Prehistory of North America. *World Archaeology* 8 (l): 83-100.

Kuipers, Aert

2002 *Salish Etymological Dictionary.* University of Montana, Occasional Papers in Linguistics 16.

Langdon, Margaret

1974 *Comparative Hokan-Coahuiltecan Studies*: A Survey and Appraisal. The Hague: Mouton.

Longenecker, Julia, Darby Stapp, and Angela Buck

2002 The Wanapum of Priest Rapids, Washington: 137-15. *Endangered Peoples of North America. Struggles to Survive and Thrive.* Tom Greaves, ed. Westport: Greenwood Press.

Lushootseed Press

1995 *Aunt Susie Sampson Peter*; The Wisdom of a Skagit Elder. Transcribed by Vi Hilbert. Translated by Vi Hilbert and Jay Miller. Recorded by Leon Metcalf. Seattle.

1995b *Gram Ruth Sehome Shelton*; The Wisdom of a Tulalip Elder. Transcribed by Vi Hilbert. Translated by Vi Hilbert and Jay Miller. Recorded by Leon Metcalf. Seattle.

1995c *Petius Isadore Tom*: The Wisdom of a Lummi Elder. Seattle.

1996 *Lady Louse Lived There.* Janet Yoder, ed. Complied by Vi Hilbert, Illustrated by Brad Burns. Seattle.

Lutz, John Sutton

2008   *Makuk ~ A New History of Aboriginal-White Relations.* Vancouver: University of British Columbia Press.

Mapes, Lynda

2009   *Breaking Ground ~* The Lower elwa Klallam Tribe and the Unearthing of Tse-whit-zen Village. Seattle: University of Washington Press.

Meeker, Ezra

1870   *Washington Territory West of the Cascade Mountains.* Olympia: Transcript Office.

1905   *Pioneer Reminiscences of Puget Sound, The Tragedy of Leschi.* Seattle: Lowman and Hanford. [1980]

1916   *Busy Life of Eighty-Five Years.* Ventures and Adventures. Seattle: by the author.

1921   *Seventy Years of Progress in Washington.* Seattle & Tacoma: Allstrum Printing Co.

1980   *The Tragedy of Leschi.* Everett: The Printers. [1905]

Miller, Jay

1975   Delaware Alternative Classifications. *Anthropological Linguistics* 17 (9): 434-444.

1985a   Salish Kinship: Why Decedence? *20th International Conference on Salish and Neighboring Languages*: 213-222. August 15-17. University of British Columbia, Vancouver.

1985b   Art and Souls: The Puget Sound Salish Journey to the Land of the Dead. *5th Conference of the National Native American Art Studies Association.* Ann Arbor and Detroit.

1985c   Free Translations of "Fly," pp. 33-41, "Moose," pp. 145-49, Verse Translation of "Boil and Hammer," Appendix 1, pp.169-78, Text Data, Appendix 2, Pp. 179-82, Bibliography, pp. 183-204, In *Haboo ~ Native American Stories From Puget Sound.* Translated and Edited By Vi Hilbert. University of Washington Press.

1988   *Shamanic Odyssey ~ The Lushootseed Salish Journey to the Land of the Dead, in terms of Death, Potency, and Cooperating Shamans in North America.* Menlo Park, CA: Ballena Press Anthropological Papers 32.

1990a   *Mourning Dove ~ A Salishan Autobiography.* Indian Lives Series. Lincoln: University of Nebraska Press. Paperback, 1994.

1990b   *Coyote Stories* by Mourning Dove. Introduction, Notes. Lincoln: Bison Books, University of Nebraska Press.

1992a   Native Healing in Puget Sound. Portrayal of Native American Health and Healing: 1-15. *Caduceus ~ A Museum Journal for the Health Sciences.*

1992b   A Kinship of Spirit ~ Society in the Americas in 1492: 305-337. *America in 1492.* New York: Alfred Knopf.

1992c   North Pacific Ethno-Astronomy: Tsimshian and Others: 193-206. *Earth and Sky: Visions of the Cosmos in Native American Folklore.* Claire Farrer and Ray Williamson, eds. Albuquerque: University of New Mexico Press.

1992d   Society in America in 1492.   America in 1492:   Selected Lectures From The Quincentenary Program, The Newberry Library. D'Arcy McNickle Center for the History of the American Indian. *Occasional Papers in Curriculum Series* 15:   151-169. Harvey Markowitz, ed.

1992e   Oral Literature. A Sourcebook. D'Arcy McNickle Center for the History of the American Indian, *Occasional Papers in Curriculum Series* # 13.

1997   Back to Basics: Chiefdoms in Puget Sound. *Ethnohistory* 44 (2): 375-387.

1998   Middle Columbia River Salishans. Smithsonian Handbook of North American Indians. *Plateau.* Deward Walker, ed. Volume 12: 253-270.

1999a   *Lushootseed Culture and the Shamanic Odyssey:* An Anchored Radiance. Lincoln: University of Nebraska Press.

1999b   Chehalis Area Traditions, a Summary of Thelma Adamson's 1927 Ethnographic Notes. *Northwest Anthropological Research Notes* 33 (1): 1-72.

2002   Dr Simon: A Snohomish Slave at Fort Nisqually and Puyallup.   *Northwest Anthropological Research Notes* 36 (2): 145-54.

2005   Dibble Cultivating Prairies to Beaches: The Real All Terrain Vehicle. *Journal of Northwest Anthropology (JONA)* 39 (1): 33-39.

2008a   Charlie Quintasket, Mourning Dove's Brother *JONA* 42 (1), 109-120, 2008 Spring.

2008b   Mourning Dove's Other Women *JONA* 42 (1), 121-129, 2008 Spring.

2012   *Honne, Spirit of the Chehalis.* Introduction. Lincoln: Bison Books Edition, University of Nebraska Press.

2014   An Overview of Northwest Coast Mythology. *Rescues, Rants, and Researches: A Re-View of Jay Miller's Writings on Northwest Indien Cultures.* Darby Stapp and Kara Powers, eds. *Journal of Northwest Anthropology* Memoir 9: 3-11.

Miller, Jay, and Vi Hilbert

1993   Caring for Control: A Pivot of Salishan Language and Culture. *American Indian Linguistics and Ethnography in Honor of Laurence C. Thompson.* University of Montana, Occasional Papers in Linguistics 10: 237-239.

1996   Lushootseed Animal People: Mediation and Transformation from Myth to History: 138-156. *Monsters, Tricksters, and Sacred Cows: Animal Tales and American Identities.* A. James Arnold, ed. New World Studies. Charlottesville: University of Virginia Press.

2004   "That Salish Feeling…" *Studies in Salish Linguistics in Honor of M Dale Kinkade.* Donna B. Gerdts And Lisa Matthewson, eds. University of Montana, Occasional Papers in Linguistics # 17: 197-210. (Vi Hilbert first author)

Mithun, Marianne

2006 *The Languages of Native North America.* Cambridge Language Surveys. NY: Cambridge Univesity Press .

Munsell, David

1968 The Ryegrass Coulee Site (KT88). Approved 29 November 1967. UW: Anthropology MA thesis.

Nelson, Charles M

1969 The Sunset Creek Site (45 KT 28) and Its Place in Plateau Prehistory. Washington State University, Laboratory of Anthropology, *Report of Investigations* 47.

1973 Prehistoric Culture Change in the Intermontane Plateau of Western North America: 371-90 in *Explanations of Culture Change*: *Models in Prehistory.* Colin Renfrew, ed. London: Gerald Duckworth.

Nestor, Sandy

2001 *Our Native American Legacy* ~ Northwest Towns with Indian Names: Washington, Oregon, Idaho, Alaska. Caldwell, Id: Caxton Press.

Norton, Helen H

1979 The Association between Anthropogenic Prairies and Important Food Plans in Western Washington. *NARN* 13 (20), 434-449. *Northwest Anthropological Research Notes.*

1980 Evidence for Bracken Fern as a food for Aboriginal Peoples of Western Washington. *Economic Botany* 33 (4), 384-396.

1985 Women and Resources of the Northwest Coast: Documentation from the 18th and Early 19th Century. University of Washington, Anthropology, PhD Dissertation.

1990   Fort Nisqually: A Little Known Historical Treasure, Index for 1833-1849, *Seattle Genealogical Society Bulletin* 39 (3, Spring), 103-118.

1990a Fort Nisqually: A Little Known Historical Treasure: Part Two, *Seattle Genealogical Society Bulletin* 39 (4, Summer), 161-177.

1990b Fort Nisqually Index, Part Two, Index for 1849-1859, *Seattle Genealogical Society Bulletin* 39 (5, Autumn): 7-14.

1990/1   Fort Nisqually Index, Part Three – Settlers' Accounts of 1841-1879, *Seattle Genealogical Society Bulletin* 39 (3, Winter), 59-67.

1991   Index IV: Fort Nisqually Servants' Accounts 1836-1867, *Seattle Genealogical Society Bulletin* 39 (3, Spring), 111-115.

1991   Fort Nisqua*lly Index 5: Women and the Frontier – 1840-1872,* Seattle Genealogical Society Bulletin 39 (5, Autumn): 5-10;

Ms Huntington Microfilm, misfilmed inventory. (Norton 1990-91).

Phillips, Walter Shelley

1902 *Indian Fairy Tales*: Folklore ~ Legends ~ Myths; Totem Tales as Told by the Indians; Gathered in the Pacific Northwest, With a Glossary of Words, Customs and History of the Indians; Fully Illustrated by the Author. Chicago: Star Publishing Co.

Powell, Jay V

2008 *Quileute Dictionary*. La Push: Quileute Tribal Press > 1976 NARN).

2017 *Our Land ~ Quileute Territory*. La Push: Kwashkwas Jay Squawks.

Ray, Verne

1932 The Sanpoil and Nespelem ~ Salishan Peoples of Northeastern Washington. *University of Washington Publications in Anthropology* 5: 1-237.

1933 Sanpoil Folktales. *Journal of American Folklore* 46: 129-87.

1936 Native Villages and Groupings of the Columbia Basin. *Pacific Northwest Quarterly* 27: 99-152.

1939 *Cultural Relations in the Plateau of Northwestern America*. LA: Southwest Museum.

1960 The Columbia Indian Confederacy: A League of Central Plateau Tribes: 177-89. *Culture in History: Essays in Honor of Paul Radin*. Stanley Diamond, ed. Columbia University Press.

Reichard, Gladys

1951 *Navaho Grammar*. New York: JJ Augustin. AES-PXXI (21).

Reece, Gary Fuller

1989 *Origins of Pierce County Place Names*. Tacoma: R&M Press.

Reid, Robie

1942 How One Slave Became Free, An Episode of the Old Days in Victoria. *British Columbia Historical Quarterly* 6(4), 251-256.

Richardson, Allan, and Brent Galloway

2011 *Nooksack Place Names* ~ Geography, Culture, and Language. Vancouver: UBC Press.

Rigsby, Bruce, and Michael Finley

2009 Priest Rapids: Places, People, and Names. *JONA* 43 (1): 57-86. Spring.

Roberts, Natalie Leberg

1975 A History of the Swinomish Tribal Community. Seattle: University of Washington PhD Dissertation (Anthropology).

Romney, Kimball

1957 The Genetic Model and The Uto-Aztecan Time Perspective. *Davidson Journal of Anthropology* 3: 35-41.

Ruby, Robert, and John Brown

1965 *Half-Sun on the Columbia*: *A Biography of Chief Moses*. Norman: University of Oklahoma Press.

1989 *Dreamer-Prophets of the Columbia Plateau*: *Smohalla and Skolaskin*. Norman: University of Oklahoma Press.

Sapir, Edward

1916 Time Perspective in Aboriginal American Culture: A Study in Method. Ottawa: Canada Department of Mines, Geological Survey Memoir 90, Anthropology Series 13.

1929 Central and North American Languages. *Encyclopedia Britannica* 5: 138-141.

Scheuerman, Richard, and Michael Finley

2008 *Finding Chief Kamiakin ~ The Life and Legacy of a Northwest Patriot*. Pullman: WSU Press.

Seattle Times

1960 Fish? Psyche? Whence Came Pysht Name? *Sunday* 25 September: 5.

Sebeok, Thomas

1976 *Native Languages of the Americas*. New York: Plenum Press. Volume I.

Siebert, Frank

1967 The Original Home of the Proto-Algonquian Languages. **

Smith, Alfred, and William Penn   1938   Translation of Geographic Names of Indian Origin. Tacoma: WSHS, Hitchman Box 10.

Smith, Allan

2006 *Takhoma* ~ Ethnography of Mount Rainier National Park. Pullman: WSU Press.

Smith, Marian

1940a *The Puyallup-Nisqually*. Columbia University Contributions to Anthropology 32.

1940b The Puyallup of Washington. *Acculturation in Seven American Indian Tribes*, Chapter 1: 3-36. Ralph Linton, ed. NY: D. Appleton-Century Co.

1941 The Coast Salish of Puget Sound. *American Anthropologist* 43: 197-211.

1946 Petroglyph Complexes in the History of the Columbia-Fraser Region. *Southwestern Journal of Anthropology* 2 (3): 306-322.

Smith, Marian, ed.

1949 *Indians of the Urban Northwest*. Columbia University Contributions to Anthropology 36.

Stern, Theodore

1993 *Chiefs & Chief Traders*. Indian Relations at Fort Nez Perces, 1818-1855. Volume 1. Portland: Oregon Historical Society.

Suttles, Wayne, and Barbara Lane

1990 Southern Coast Salish, *Northwest Coast*. Suttles, Wayne, ed. Handbook of North American Indians. Volume 7: 485 - 502. DC: Smithsonian Press.

Suttles, Wayne, ed.

1990 *Northwest Coast*. Handbook of North American Indians #7. DC: Smithsonian Press.

Swanson, Earl, ed.

1970 *Languages and Cultures of Western North America*: Essays in Honor of Sven Liljeblad. Pocatello: The Idaho State University Press.

Swindell, Edward, jr.

1942 Report on Source, Nature, and Extent of the Fishing, Hunting, and Miscellaneous Related Rights of Certain Indian Tribes in Washington and Oregon, Together with Affidavits Showing Location of a Number of Usual and Accustomed Fishing Grounds and Stations. Los Angeles: US Department of the Interior, Office of Indian Affairs, Division of Forestry and Grazing. July.

Teit, James

1928 The Middle Columbia Salish. *University of Washington Publications in Anthropology* 2 (4): 83-128.

Thompson, Laurence C. and M. Terry

1972 Language Universals, Nasals, and the Northwest Coast. *Studies in Linguistics in Honor of George Trager*. Estellie Smith, ed. The Hague: Mouton.

Thrush, Coll

2007 *Native Seattle ~ Histories from the Crossing-Over Place*. Seattle: University of Washington Press.

Underhill, Ruth

1959 *Beaverbird* ~ A story of Indians on the coast of Washington, before the coming of the whites. Illustrated by Robert Gartland. NY: Coward-McCann, Inc.

Waterman, Thomas Talbot, and Geraldine Coffin

1920 Types of Canoes on Puget Sound. *Indian Notes and Monographs*, Museum of the American Indian, Heye Foundation, New York.

Waterman, Thomas, and Ruth Greiner

1921 Indian Houses of Puget Sound. New York: Museum of the American Indian, Heye Foundation, *Indian Notes and Monographs*, Miscellaneous Series 5.

Waterman, Thomas, and Collaborators

1921 Native Houses of Western North America. New York: Museum of the American Indian, Heye Foundation, *Indian Notes and Monographs*, Miscellaneous Series 11.

Waterman, Thomas

1920 The Whaling Equipment of the Makah Indians. *University of Washington Publications in Anthropology* 1 (2).

1922 The Geographical Names Used by the Indians of the Pacific Coast. *The Geographical Review* 12 (2): 175-194.

1924 The Shake Religion of Puget Sound. *Smithsonian Report* for 1922: 499-507.

1930 The Paraphernalia of the Duwamish 'Spirit-Canoe' Ceremony. New York: Museum of the American Indian, Heye Foundation, *Indian Notes* 7 (2): 129-148, 295-312, 535-561.

1973 Notes on the Ethnology of the Indians of Puget Sound. New York: Museum of the American Indian, Heye Foundation, *Indian Notes and Monographs*, Miscellaneous Series 59.

2001 See Hilbert, Miller, and Zahir.

White River Historical Society, Auburn

Arthur Condit Ballard Interview.

Charles H Ballard, Pioneer Experiences of the Ballard Family on White River.

Wickersham, Judge James 1898 Nisqually Mythology. *Overland Monthly*, 2nd Series, 32: 345-351.

WPA 1941 *Washington ~ A Guide to the Evergreen State*. American Guide Series. Portland: Binfords & Mort. [revised 1950]

Please help wipe out

Typo-gnomes

ACCULTURATING AMELIA ~ Round Valley 1937 California
ALASKA EDGE ISLAND ~ Siberian Yupiks of St Lawrence Island
ALL SOULS ~ Conjuring, Divining, Redeeming, Reviving Native Vitalities
ALLIED MOUNDS ~ Touching the Earth, Modeling the World, Reaching the Sky
ANIMAL PEOPLE ADVENTURES ~ Native North American Tribal Stories
AT BAY ~ Cultures Converging through Southwest Washington
BALLARD BULWARK ~
CHACO ECHOES ~ Pervasive Keresan Priesthoods
CHACOKIA ~ Chaco, Cahokia, Cities & Ceremonies ~ Bundles & Blood Lines Centuries Ago
CREEK MVSKOKI TALWA TOWNS ~ Speck, Swanton, Hewitt, Opler, Howard   > 10
CHEHALIS CHANGER ~
CHINOOK CONCERNS ~ Emma Millett Luscier, Isabella Bertrand, Verne Ray
CIRCLING FOUR CORNERS ~ Re-Viewing Native American Indiens
CROSSING ~ LINES: An Educational Memoir of Native North America
DEL-AWARE ~ Lenape Legacies
DELAWARE INTEGRITY ~ Rituals, Removals, Reforms by Lenape Indiens
DISCLAIMING TREATIES I ~ Puget Tribes 1927 Testimonies
DISCLAIMING TREATIES II ~ Puget Tribes 1927 Testimonies
ELDERS' DIALOG ~ Ed Davis & Vi Hilbert Discuss Native Puget Sound Language, Culture, & Heritage
EVERGREEN ETHNOGRAPHIES ~ Hoh, Chehalis, Suquamish, and Snoqualmi of Western Washington   >20
FEDERAL FISH FILES ~ Swindell 1942 Treaty Rights Report
GEORGE GIBBS NORTHWEST ARRAY ~ Full Reports, Place Names, Word List, Artifact Names, and Guide
GRASSROOTS JANET ~ Advancing Salish and Traditional Cultures
HERMAN HAEBERLIN REGAINED ~ Anthropology and Artifacts of Puget Sound 1916-17
HERSTORY NW ~ Women Upholding Native Traditions
INDIEN ~ ETHNOGRAPHY: Cultural Traditions of Native North America
INDIEN ~ ETHNOLOGY: Grounded, Gendered, Meaningful Cultural Traditions
LESCHI IN LOVE ~ A Novel of Native Puget Sound > x2
MARCO MUCK MASKS ~ Frank Cushing on Marshes and Mounds
MINTER BAY ~ Land, Lore, Loss, and Lucre in the South Salish Sea   > 30
NATIVE MET HOW ~ Improving Posterity
NATIVE PROPHECY NW ~ Dancing Hope
OLD LUKH ~ Native Puget Sound in Daily Life, Places, and Stories
OVER THE FALLS ~ Sdoqwalbixw Survivance Surrounding Seattle
PACIFIC PLATEAU PORTRAYALS ~ People Places Ponderings
RAY'S ARRAY ~ Raymond D Fogelson's Works
RIGHTING NATIVE PLACES ~ Adventures in Northwest Geography
SAHAPTINS STUDIES ~ Columbia River Plateau, Cora Du Bois, Homer Garner Barnett, Gerald Raymond Desmond
SALISH SYSTEMS ~ Kinship Networks of the Northwest
SDOQWALBIXW   > 40
SDOQWALBIXW SURVIVANCE
SM TSM'SYEEN ~ Real Tsimshians; Coast, Sgüüks, Gitxsan, Nisga'a
SOUND SALISH STRAITS ~ Central Salish Sea Cultures
UNSETTLING SEATTLE ~ Arresting Local Talent and Academic Illiteracy
WICHITA KINSHIP & CULTURE
WRITING WORDS IN WARY WORLDS ~ World Wide Improved Spellings of Native America Languages > 46

JONA Memoirs ($ varies)

RESCUES, RANTS, & RESEARCHES ~ A Re-View of Jay Miller's Writings on Northwest Indien Cultures ~ #9
TRIBAL TRIO of the Northwest Coast by Kenneth D Tollefson ~ #10
INTERWEAVING COAST SALISH CULTURAL SYSTEMS ~ Collected Works of Pamela Thorsen Amoss ~ #14

University of Nebraska Press

ANCESTRAL MOUNDS ~ Vitality and Volatility Crossing Native North America University of Nebraska Press 2015   > 50
HONNE ~ The Spirit of the Chehalis University of Nebraska Press 2015